D0408701

Kanban Made Simple

Kanban Made Simple

Demystifying and Applying Toyota's Legendary Manufacturing Process

John M. Gross
Kenneth R. McInnis

AMACOM
American Management Association
New York • Atlanta • Brussels • Buenos Aires • Chicago • London • Mexico City
San Francisco • Shanghai • Tokyo • Toronto • Washington, D.C.

Special discounts on bulk quantities of AMACOM books are available to corporations, professional associations, and other organizations. For details, contact Special Sales Department, AMACOM, a division of American Management Association 1601 Broadway, New York, NY 10019.
Tel.: 212-903-8316. Fax: 212-903-8083.
Web site: www.amacombooks.org

Library of Congress Cataloging-in-Publication Data

Gross, John M.
Kanban made simple : demystifying and applying Toyota's legendary manufacturing process / John M. Gross, Kenneth R. McInnis.
p. cm.
Includes bibliographical references and index.
ISBN 0-8144-0763-3
1. Just-in-time systems. 2. Production control. 3. Factory management. I. McInnis, Kenneth R. II. Title.

TS157.G74 2003
658.5—dc21 *2002154533*

Printing number

10 9 8 7 6 5 4 3 2

CONTENTS

Preface

We decided to write this book while traveling together on a business trip. Returning from a meeting with a supplier whom we wanted to place on kanban scheduling, we were discussing how resistant the supplier had been to the idea. Our discussion migrated to how most companies and individuals were resistant at first, but that they soon came on board once they understood the benefits of using kanban. We discussed how this resistance stemmed from lack of exposure and the lack of books about how actually to develop and implement kanban scheduling. Twenty miles later we were building what became the fourteen-page outline for this book.

The Best Way to Read this Book

To get the most out of this book, we recommend reading this book in three passes.

❑ On your first pass, flip through the entire book and look at all of the chapters, look at its organization, and look at the figures. Get acquainted with the style and flow.

❑ On the second pass, read the book chapter by chapter. At the start of each chapter, conduct another quick review of the chapter. During this review, flip through the chapter looking at the major topics and figures. Finish this review by reading the chapter summary.

❑ On the final pass, go back to the beginning of the chapter and read the entire chapter. During this final pass, look for the detail behind the topics in the chapter summary. Also, make notes and underline important information in the margins.

Although this process sounds like it might take forever and slow down your reading, the opposite is true. The three-pass process will not only improve comprehension, but also speed up your reading.

Acknowledgments

We wish to thank the following people for their support in making this book a reality: Sharon Lee developed the audit forms presented in Chapter 8; Loyd Bailie, Sharon Lee, Charles McInnis, and Ron Fardell read the drafts as sanity checks on our logic; Dean Kropp, of Washington University–St. Louis, provided ideas and support.

We wish to thank the companies that allowed us to document their kanban successes in the case studies. We would especially like to thank GDX Automotive for allowing us not only to document a case study, but also to take pictures to illustrate some of the kanban designs in Chapter 5. Their three-phased Lean implementation program, called Common Sense Manufacturing, is making dramatic strides in waste elimination.

We also would like to thank our wives, Karen Gross and Ruth McInnis, for their support during the writing and editing of the book. Their support allowed us to write the book and still maintain our hectic professional schedules.

Finally, we wish to thank you for taking the time to read this book. We hope it gives you the knowledge (and the courage) to implement kanban scheduling in your operation. We know from first-hand experience that the improvement in flow, the benefits of empowering the production operators, and inventory reductions will amaze you.

John M. Gross
Kenneth R. McInnis

Other Works by the Authors

John M. Gross, *Fundamentals of Preventive Maintenance,* AMACOM, 2002.

Kanban Made Simple

CHAPTER

1

INTRODUCTION TO KANBAN

Imagine a process where the operators schedule the line. Also, imagine this same process having visual indicators that allow you to instantly determine the schedule status of the process at a glance.

Does this sound like a fairytale? Or is this a process that has been converted to kanban scheduling?

A Short History of Kanban

The Japanese word *kanban,* which translates as "signboard," has become synonymous with demand scheduling.[1] Kanban traces its roots to the early days of the Toyota production system. In the late 1940s and early 1950s, Taiichi Onho developed kanbans to control production between processes and to implement Just in Time (JIT) manufacturing at Toyota manufacturing plants in Japan. These ideas did not gain worldwide acceptance until the global recession in the

1970s. By using kanbans, he minimized the work in process (or WIP) between processes and reduced the cost associated with holding inventory.[2]

Originally, Toyota used kanban to reduce costs and manage machine utilization. However, today Toyota continues to use the system not only to manage cost and flow, but also to identify impediments to flow and opportunities for continuous improvement. Interestingly, Mr. Onho modeled many of the control points after U.S. supermarkets—hence the term kanban supermarkets.

It should be noted that the idea of JIT manufacturing was originally conceived by Kiichero Toyoda, founder of the Toyota Motor Company, and son of Sakichi Toyoda, the founder of the Toyota Company, the parent company.* However, it was Mr. Onho who developed the strategy of kanban, which became one of the pillars of Toyota's successful implementation of JIT manufacturing.[3]

What Is Kanban

With kanban scheduling, the operators use visual signals to determine how much they run and when they stop or change over. The kanban rules also tell the operators what to do when they have problems and who to go to when these problems arise. Finally, a well-planned kanban has visual indicators that allow managers and supervisors to see the schedule status of the line at a glance.

We define kanban scheduling as demand scheduling. In processes controlled by kanbans, the operators produce products based on actual usage rather than forecasted usage. Therefore, for a scheduling process to be considered a true kanban, the production process it controls must:

- ❑ Only produce product to replace the product consumed by its customer(s)
- ❑ Only produce product based on signals sent by its customer(s)

* It is an interesting aside that the Toyota Company started the Toyota Motor Company with the money received from selling the rights to produce a weaving loom that had been designed by Sakichi Toyoda.[4]

The kanban schedule replaces the traditional weekly or daily production schedule most of us have become familiar with in manufacturing operations. This schedule is replaced with visual signals and predetermined decision rules that allow the production operators to schedule the line.

Think of kanban scheduling as an execution tool rather than a planning tool. The kanban, which can take many forms, directs the operation of the process on a day-to-day basis. Kanban scheduling does not replace material planning, but rather takes the material planning information and uses it to create the kanban. What kanban replaces is:

- The daily scheduling activities necessary to operate the production process
- The need for production planners and supervisors to continuously monitor schedule status to determine the next item to run and when to change over

It thus frees up the materials planners, schedulers, and supervisors to manage exceptions and improve the process. Finally, it also places control at the value-added level and empowers the operators to control the line.

We created this book to help the reader achieve this level of scheduling. To achieve this objective, we have proposed a set of steps to help the reader implement their own kanbans. The main body of the book will help the reader implement kanbans on lines that produce multiple part numbers that require changeovers between part numbers. The Appendixes will explain how to set up kanbans for several different types of dedicated work centers that do not change over nor produce multiple part numbers.

The book also addresses the concerns and fears that prevent organizations from implementing kanban scheduling. These fears arise because kanban forces many people to challenge their paradigms, or basic beliefs, about how production processes should be scheduled, or who should be scheduling and controlling production processes. As you progress through the planning process, think about the issues, concerns, and fears you have about converting to kanban scheduling. The book will help you to develop the structures and rules necessary to answer these issues, concerns, and fears.

Why Implement Kanban Scheduling

Besides the big-picture benefits spelled out above, what are the other benefits that justify the expenditure of time and resources to implement kanban scheduling? Figure 1-1 lists the benefits of kanban that lead to improved productivity and reduced capital cost.

As Figure 1-1 shows, the benefits of kanban scheduling extend well beyond the hard dollar savings associated with reducing inventory. Unfortunately, many kanban opponents fail to recognize these benefits, preferring instead to focus only on the economic order quantity (EOQ) versus the kanban quantity.

They fail to recognize that inventory generates hidden cost in overhead, rework, scrap, customer service activities, and material handling.[5] However, it is the inventory reductions coupled with these other factors that make kanban a necessity to remain competitive in today's business environment. Additionally, the benefits of kanban can become a driver for creating a culture of continuous

Figure 1-1. Benefits of kanban scheduling.

1. Reduces inventory
2. Improves flow
3. Prevents overproduction
4. Places control at the operations level (with the operator)
5. Creates visual scheduling and management of the process
6. Improves responsiveness to changes in demand
7. Minimizes risk of inventory obsolescence
8. Increases ability to manage the supply chain

process improvement; when the improvements are translated directly into lower inventory quantities, it allows people to see the benefits of taking action.

Reduces Inventory

When you calculate the kanban quantities based on current conditions (downtime, scrap, and changeover times), you should see a decrease in inventory levels. From our experience, inventories can be reduced by 25 percent to 75 percent. The exercise of calculating kanban quantities forces you to identify your real situation. It also forces you to examine the comfort levels and informal rules that allow inventory levels to build up over time. Additionally, since you will use realistic data, you have a measure of confidence that the calculated quantities will allow you to successfully continue supplying your customers.

From a financial side, the inventory reduction not only saves the carrying costs of the inventory but also the physical space occupied by the existing inventory. The freed-up space can then be used for new business opportunities or may eliminate the need for planned expansions or leasing of offsite warehouses.

Improves Flow

When properly implemented, kanban improves the flow of the operation. The improved flow results from not only reducing inventory space, but also the order created by designing the kanban material flow. The process of setting up control points, setting up flow lanes, hanging signs, and so on, provides directions for moving the material. The kanban process also gives the operators producing the parts guidance on what and when to produce. (They also know when not to produce.) The increased controls serves to tame the woolly beast called inventory.

Prevents Overproduction

In many production processes, control of production quantities can be haphazard. This lack of control can allow overproduction of parts, which is one of the seven wastes identified in the Toyota Production System (TPS). The kanban prevents overproduction by specifying the production container sizes and the maximum number of containers to be produced. This structure thus allows control without expensive or labor-intensive tracking systems.

The kanban uses visual signals that let operators know how many of each part to produce and what to produce next. These visual signals also tell operators (and their supervisors) when to stop and when to start production.

Places Control at the Operations Level (with the Operator)

Just as managers, supervisors, and materials planners can see the production schedule at a glance, so can the operators. Therefore, with proper rules and scheduling guidance, the operators can run the line. The kanban's design tells them what to run, how much to run, and what sequence to run. Additionally, the visual nature of the kanban tells everyone immediately when the process is in trouble, so that someone can step in to make course corrections.

Therefore, once again kanban reduces one of the seven wastes—not properly utilizing human resources. By creating a system that allows operators to control their production process, we proverbially harness their minds to help us succeed in the game of business.

This step can also lead to other opportunities for increased empowerment (and potential profitability). Additionally, by allowing the production operators to control the line, we free up managers and schedulers to move on to other activities, such as waste elimination and supply chain management.

By the way, control of the line by production operators does not happen for free. Before the operators can run the line with the kanban, they will need training and mentoring. You cannot throw them the "keys" and expect them to operate the line like experienced schedulers. However, if the kanban design sticks with the theme of keeping it simple, then training will not be a problem.

Creates Visual Scheduling and Management of the Process

With proper use of visual management techniques, the kanban system eliminates the need for a paper schedule. The visual kanban signals (containers, cards, floor markings, etc.) tell the operator the items to be produced and the production sequence. The use of scheduling signals (yellow) and danger signals (red) also tell the operators:

- ❑ What and how many to run
- ❑ When and who to call for help

These same visual indicators also tell managers and supervisors the schedule position of the process at a glance. This visual scheduling process thus allows managers, supervisors, and material planners to focus on production problems, future planning, and other continuous improvement activities rather than on the daily control of the production schedule.

Improves Responsiveness to Changes in Demand

The very nature of the kanban scheduling process sets up maximum and minimum inventory levels. These levels provide signals for when and when not to produce. These signals will stop production when demand decreases. Therefore, you avoid the issue of should you or shouldn't you build inventory when orders decrease since the system design tells you to stop.

Likewise, when orders begin to increase, the kanban inventory levels signal the restart of production. This addresses one of the main issues that make people build inventory during downturns— "What if I don't recognize when to turn the faucet back on?"

Minimizes Risk of Inventory Obsolescence

Just as the kanban stops overproduction, it prevents you from building inventory that can become obsolete. The kanban signals to start production based on demand (or sales) and not on forecast. Therefore, you only build what you need. So when conditions or models change, you only need to manage the material in the production pipeline, not a vast warehouse inventory. Kanban scheduling's visual nature also ensures that inventory does not get lost only to magically reappear in time for write-offs at the next physical inventory.

A subset of the obsolescence issue is freshness, which is an issue for many food items and some "nonconsumable goods."[6] The kanban structure controls the amount of inventory in the system and thus controls the material freshness. Rules for the kanban can specifically address the lifecycle of the goods and management of the materials age.

Kanban Implementation Process

How does one achieve all these fantastic benefits? First, you must make the commitment to make change and no longer accept the status quo. You must be willing to accept the uncomfortable feeling associated with implementing new ideas. You must be committed to making a plan and following through on this plan. If you can accept the above "musts," then the seven steps listed in Figure 1-2 are your roadmap to implementing kanban in your organization.

Figure 1-2. Seven steps to implementing kanban.

1. Conduct data collection
2. Calculate the kanban size
3. Design the kanban
4. Train everyone
5. Start the kanban
6. Audit and maintain the kanban
7. Improve the kanban

These steps allow you determine your current situation, what you want to achieve, and how you want to achieve it. Additionally, as we progress through the book, we will build these seven steps into a flow for continuous improvement.

Step 1: Conduct Data Collection

In this phase you will collect the data necessary to characterize your production process. The act of gathering data will allow you to make a decision based on facts instead of on desires or gut hunches. This data will allow you to calculate the kanban quantities (which is the next step). As you proceed through this step, be honest about the process's real capabilities so that you can calculate realistic kanban quantities that support customer demand.

The first step also represents a golden opportunity for conducting value stream mapping (VSM) for your entire plant and allows you to determine which production processes would be good candidates for implementing pilot kanban scheduling systems. Additionally, the plans for kanban can be considered in the larger scheme of implementing *lean manufacturing* during the VSM process.

Step 2: Calculate the Kanban Size

Once you know where you are, you can calculate the size of the kanban. Initially, you will calculate the kanban container size based on current conditions, not based on future plans or desires. However, step 7 will focus you on ways to reduce kanban quantities based on a realistic continuous improvement approach. The initial calculations will utilize the production requirements, the system scrap rate, the process productivity rate, planned downtime, and changeover times to calculate a replenishment interval. The replenishment interval (which will be explained in greater detail in Chapter 4) will establish your order quantities. The final kanban container quantities will also include a buffer for safety stock and to account for any process cure, drying, or normalization periods. These calculations will form the basis for the kanban design in the next step.

Chapter 4 will also address a quick method for setting kanban levels in mature processes or for those people who just want to jump in and swim.

Step 3: Design the Kanban

Once you have calculated the kanban quantities required to support production requirements based on current conditions, you're ready to develop a design for the kanban. The completed kanban design will answer the question of how you will implement the kanban. The design will consider:

- ❑ How will the material be controlled?
- ❑ What are the visual signals?
- ❑ What will be the rules for conducting the kanban?
- ❑ Who will handle the kanban transactions?
- ❑ Who will make the scheduling decisions?
- ❑ Who will resolve problems?
- ❑ What visual management items will be needed?
- ❑ What training will be required?
- ❑ What is the implementation schedule?

The end product of this step should be a plan for implementation of the kanban, including implementation actions, action assignments, and schedule milestones.

As you finish the design step, don't be afraid to commit to a start date. Don't be guilty of analyzing yourself into inaction. Pick a start date, build a plan to support this date, and monitor the plan for progress toward hitting this date.

Step 4: Train Everyone

Before starting to schedule with kanban, don't forget to train everyone on how the system will work and on their role in the process. Develop a simple presentation to explain the process and the visual signals. Also, review the rules during the training. Take the participants through what-if scenarios to help them understand their roles and the decision-making process. Conduct a dry run so that everyone knows how the kanban signals will be handled and what the signals mean. Keep the training focused on operating the kanban. Don't try to make everyone a kanban expert—just train them on their piece of the puzzle.

Step 5: Start the Kanban

Once you have a kanban design and training completed, you can start the kanban. Before you implement kanban scheduling, make sure you have all your visual management pieces in place. Having the signals set up, control points marked, and the rules completed and coordinated before you start will avoid confusion and make training much easier. As you deploy the kanban, anticipate problems that may impact success and take action to prevent or mitigate these problems. Finally, during the deployment stage, develop a scheduling transition plan—determine the exact point for the change and the amount of inventory required to make the change.

Step 6: Audit and Maintain the Kanban

After the kanban starts, you must begin the next step of the process—auditing the kanban. Auditing is the step that usually gets overlooked in most failed start-ups. So, when designing the kanban, identify who will audit the kanban. Typically, the auditor will be watching how the scheduling signals are handled and whether the customer stays supplied. When the auditor finds problems, then the problems need to be fixed immediately by the responsible party to maintain the integrity of the kanban design. Taking action prevents the kanban from being pronounced a failure by the operators.

The auditor will also look at future requirements to make sure the kanban quantities meet expected demand. If you don't adjust the kanban quantities to forecasted demand, then expect to continually intervene manually in the scheduling process (a sure way to kill the kanban).

Step 7: Improve the Kanban

Finally, after the kanban gets running, look at how to improve the kanban to reduce inventory quantities. Resist the urge to just start pulling containers. Look at how the system is running and identify any quantities that were oversized, and pull the necessary containers immediately. After this one-time adjustment, only reduce the quantities based on improvements made to the production process.

Chapter 9 suggests potential improvement areas that create opportunities to reduce quantities. Don't be fooled into the fallacy of just reducing the kanban quantities on a whim. Determine the amount that can be reduced by using the same calculations you used in sizing the kanban to calculate the new quantities.

It Takes a Team to Be Successful

Before we rush off to implement kanban, we need to address who does the implementation. The implementation of kanban will only work when you have the buy-in of the process stakeholders. Therefore, you need a cross-functional team to implement kanbans. This team, which needs to include operators, material handlers, supervisors, managers, and scheduler/material planners, will help you create kanbans that address operating conditions and logistics. They will also help create the buy-in needed to implement and operate the kanban since they become the voice of the stakeholders.

Although you may be able to design and set up the kanban without the help of the team, you cannot create the necessary buy-in by yourself. Additionally, each team member's input only improves the kanban design by ensuring that logistics items and team member concerns don't get overlooked.

Do You Need a Consultant?

Many people who are not familiar with kanban ask whether you need a consultant. The answer to this question is: it depends. To answer this question, complete this book and consider the following items when making this decision:

- ❑ Are the planned kanbans simple or complex?
- ❑ Do you have sufficient resources to manage the program?
- ❑ Do you have the necessary in-house expertise to lead a team in designing and implementing the initial kanbans?
- ❑ Are you implementing kanbans in one plant or multiple plants?
- ❑ Do you want to develop a cadre of implementers?

The answers to these questions will determine whether you need outside consultants. The only definite recommendation we have is that if you are planning to implement kanban in a large corporation with numerous sites, then use this book as a resource for your in-house teams, but hire a consultant initially to train the teams. However, as the in-house teams gain implementation experience you will have no need for outside support.

Choosing the Target Process or Department

In choosing a target process or department, follow these suggestions:

- ❑ Initially, start simple. Select a pilot area that will undergo full implementation. Complete all the phases and let your organization see the benefits before starting a second round of kanbans.
- ❑ Look across your organization and select a process that has a clear delineation between itself and the process it supplies.
- ❑ Because the kanban essentially replaces the traditional forecasted schedule, select a target area where a "customer-supplier" relationship is easy to identify and understand. The basic use of the kanban will be to meet the needs of the "customer."
- ❑ Consider a process with fairly steady demand. The steady de-

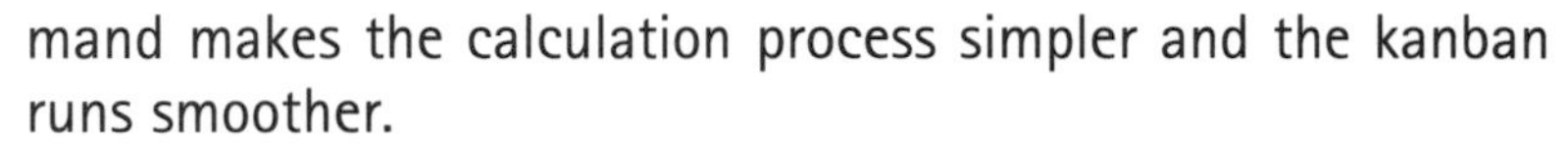

mand makes the calculation process simpler and the kanban runs smoother.

- ❑ Consider the readiness of the process operators to accept change and, more importantly, to participate in making kanban a success. Do not underestimate the power of resistance to change.
- ❑ Finally, go for a base hit or a double, not a homerun, when selecting the pilot site. The key in the pilot implementation is to make it successful and to create a learning experience for the organization. A successful implementation also gives the rest of the organization the confidence to overcome their fears of implementing kanban.

If your organization has conducted value stream mapping, then use the future state map to select the target site. The value stream maps (made famous by James P. Womack and Daniel T. Jones in their book *Lean Thinking*[7]) should ideally provide multiple targets to choose from if your plant is typical of most plants that start the process of lean manufacturing. Additionally, the value stream mapping process should help you with data collection.

We recommend against selecting a finished goods kanban as your first kanban project. Dealing with the external variables of the customer–supplier relationship can be tricky, so get some experience before implementing. Instead, select an internal process to learn the ropes. You should get good at kanban before you bring your external customer into the picture. (Remember that lean manufacturing is about serving the customer, so you don't want to endanger the paying ones!)

Keys to Successful Implementation of Kanban

Many organizations refuse/fail to implement kanbans due to their fears. They fear loss of control, they fear their employees lack ability, they fear running out of material, they fear. . . .

The answer to these fears is to develop plans that resolve these fears. Your response to these fears should be to put plans in place to prevent them from becoming reality so that the organization can reap the benefits of kanban scheduling.

Because we want you to be successful in implementing kanbans, we have identified several factors that greatly add to the chances of success. These ideas will be further discussed in later chapters, and their impact on success will become clear. We believe the following items lead to successful implementation:

- ❑ Size the kanban to current conditions
- ❑ Adapt container size to allow flow
- ❑ Make kanban signals visual
- ❑ Develop rules that provide decision points plus checks and balances
- ❑ Train the operators to run the kanban system
- ❑ Set up audit plans to keep assumptions current and maintain system discipline
- ❑ Develop a phased improvement plan to reduce the kanban quantities

Keep these ideas in mind as you read this book, and adopt these suggestions as you develop plans for addressing your process peculiarities.

Using the Workbook as a Guide

To assist in the implementation process, we have developed a CD-ROM *Workbook* (which is included with this book) that allows you and your team to progressively implement the steps. The workbook has forms that allow you to gather the information necessary to calculate quantities, design the kanban, develop an implementation plan, and develop a training plan.

Use the CD-ROM yourself or print out the forms for your team's use during the implementation team meetings.

What's in the Appendixes

To further increase your understanding of the kanban implementation process, we have included case studies and special topics in the Appendixes. The two case studies show implementation projects from different industries so that you can see the process in action. These case studies have been written as stand-alone works to allow use as a teaching aide and to fully illustrate the implementation process.

There are seven appendixes that deal with special topics, including:

Appendix A. MRP versus Kanban
Appendix B. Kanban Supermarkets
Appendix C. Two-bin Kanban Systems
Appendix D. Organizational Changes Required for Kanban
Appendix E. EOQ versus Kanban
Appendix F. Implementation in Large Plants
Appendix G. Intra-Cell Kanban

We broke these topics into separate appendixes because we felt that:

- they required more detail than was appropriate for inclusion in the main body of the book
- they would cause confusion if placed in the main body of the book

Summary

We define kanban scheduling as demand scheduling. Therefore, for a scheduling process to be considered a true kanban, the production process it controls must:

- ❑ Only produce product to replace the product consumed by its customer(s)
- ❑ Only produce product based on signals sent by its customer(s)

The kanban schedule replaces the traditional weekly or daily production schedule most of us have become familiar with in manufacturing operations. This schedule is replaced with visual signals and predetermined decision rules that allow the production operators to schedule the line.

To help in the implementation process we have proposed a seven-step process that will guide you through the implementation process. Keep these seven steps in mind as you progress through this book:

1. Conduct data collection
2. Calculate the kanban size
3. Design the kanban
4. Deploy the kanban
5. Train everyone
6. Audit and maintain the kanban
7. Improve the kanban

However, while these process steps will guide you through the implementation, the implementation of kanban does not happen in a vacuum—it requires a team approach.

The biggest obstacle to implementing kanban is you. The fear of losing control, running out of material, and the ability of the operators keep many companies from ever starting the journey. Don't become part of this group—recognize your own fears and put action plans in place to prevent these fears from being realized. Or, if your fear can't be prevented, then have a standard operating procedure in place to deal with the problem when it occurs.

To further improve your potential for successful implementation the chapter identified seven common characteristics of successful kanbans. The remainder of the book will expand upon these items and how they impact success.

To further aid you in the implementation process, we have developed a CD-ROM workbook. We have also included a series of appendixes covering special topics and illustrative case studies. These items will help reinforce and clarify the concepts in the main body of the book so that you can successfully implement kanban scheduling

Notes

1. Toyota Motor Corporation, *The Toyota Production System—Leaner Manufacturing for a Greener Planet*, p. 19.
2. Taiichi Onho, *Toyota Production System—Beyond Large-Scale Production* (Portland: Productivity Press, 1988), Chapter 1.
3. Onho, *Toyota Production System*, p. 123.
4. Onho, *Toyota Production System*, p. 89.
5. Michael L. George, *Lean Six Sigma: Combining Six Sigma with Lean Speed* (New York: McGraw-Hill, 2002), p. 38.
6. "Chasing the Make-To-Order Dream." White paper presented at the Logistics and e-Supply Chain Forum, 2001.
7. James P. Womack and Daniel T. Jones, *Lean Thinking* (New York: Simon & Schuster, 1996).

CHAPTER

2

FORMING YOUR KANBAN TEAM

A successful kanban will not happen without team implementation. Therefore, before you begin the process of developing and deploying kanban scheduling, get rid of any Lone Ranger ideas:

- ❑ Yes, you can calculate the size of the kanban by yourself.
- ❑ Yes, you can design a scheduling signal by yourself.
- ❑ Yes, you can design awesome visual management aids by yourself.
- ❑ No, you cannot make the implementation a success by yourself.

Success will require the use of a team to develop buy-in and to ensure all unique aspects of the operation get tied into the kanban design. To ensure this happens, bring the team together at the planning stage to participate in all the steps of the deployment process.

Do not expect to have the support and cooperation of the stakeholders, if you just tell them what they are going to do and how the kanban will work.

Additionally, as anyone with experience in working with cross-functional teams knows, the probability of developing a superior product goes up dramatically by seeking and using everyone's expertise. The team will identify the issues they currently face—some you know about and some you never dreamed of. They will also probably have a suggestion or a "why can't we" idea that will nullify these issues.

Finally, members of the team can help in explaining the design to their coworkers later in the deployment process. They will help the communication process and can reduce "flavor of the month" fears. The team members can also smooth over any start-up glitches by helping their coworkers deal with them as they occur.

This buy-in, however, does not come without a price. Gaining team participation and buy-in will require you (or the teamleader) to seek the team's opinion and to respect their ideas. The team will not provide their input freely or help sell a plan that they do not support. At best, if they feel railroaded, you may expect passive support or outright resistance.

How Should I Select the Team?

The team should be composed of all the stakeholders in the process. Set up the proverbial cross-functional team that includes all the disciplines that will operate, monitor, or support the kanban. Also include those people who have special data or just plain special interest.

Don't be afraid to include individuals not directly related to the operation. Remember that people who are not "close" to the daily operation sometimes propose unique out-of-the-box solutions because they do not possess the paradigms of the day-to-day operators and managers.

At a minimum, the team should include the following representatives:

- ❑ Production management/supervision
- ❑ Materials management
- ❑ Material handlers/warehouse associates
- ❑ Production operators

Try to keep the size of the team to between five and eight members. The team members must also have the authority to commit for their groups. If the team members are to coordinate the plan with their groups, then have their managers develop a coordination plan. Figure 2-1 pictorially shows the core members of the kanban team.

Other potential members to the team might include:

- ❑ Human relations
- ❑ Engineering and maintenance (if fixtures, signs, etc., are required)
- ❑ Sales and customer service
- ❑ Downstream customer(s)
- ❑ Trainees for future kanban projects

Make the selection of additional participants (or rather those people outside the traditional stakeholder groups) based on their ability to participate and bring information to the team.

One group that is sometimes left out is the customer. The customer can be a downstream process, a sister plant, or an external customer. Their presence can ensure that the design meets their needs. They can also tell you their requirements. This invitation can be a terrific opportunity to improve supply-chain management activities and possibly to move toward strategic alliances.

When inviting external customers, consider the invitation carefully in terms of the current relationship and how much they can contribute to the team. If the team decides to include the customers, make sure that the purchasing and customer service people are involved to make sure your company puts its best foot forward.

Figure 2-1. Core team members.

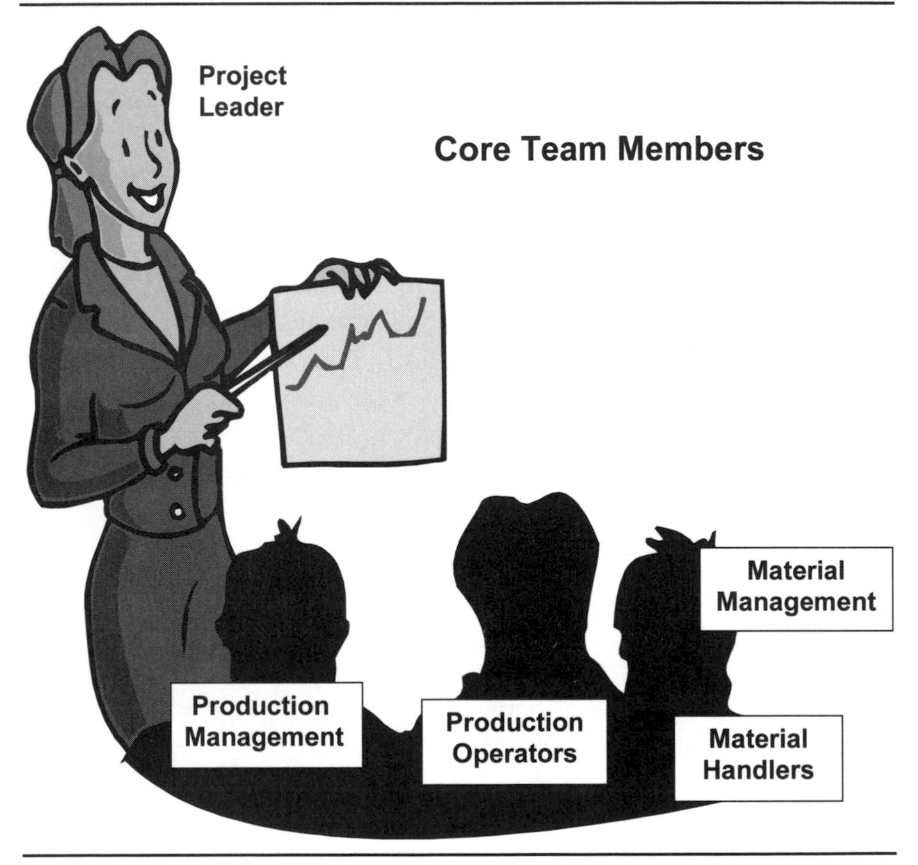

Also, consider future kanban plans and how this kanban system will parallel those plans. Assess the potential to get a leg up on training and the development of bench strength by developing future kanban team members. Figure 2-2 pictorially shows the potential additional members.

Appoint a Project Leader to Guide the Team

When creating the team, appoint a project leader to oversee the project. This person will be responsible for:

Figure 2-2. Other potential team members?

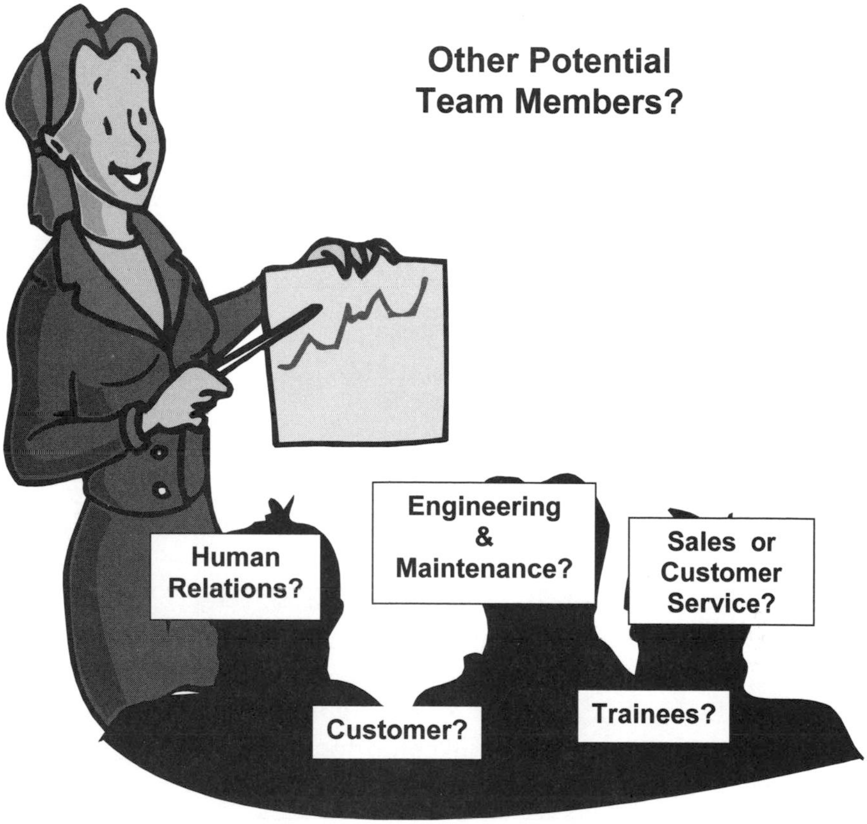

- ❑ Conducting the team meetings
- ❑ Overseeing the deployment of the kanban
- ❑ Making sure action plans are generated

The project leader should have the authority to make any final decisions if the team becomes deadlocked on an issue. Although project leaders should possess this authority, they should also possess sufficient facilitation skills to develop consensus and to guide team decisions rather than simply dictating decisions. Figure 2-3 shows pictorially the roles of the project leader.

When selecting the team leader, pick a stakeholder in the kan-

Figure 2-3. Role of the project leader.

- Conducts the team meetings
- Coordinates team logistics
- Ensures meeting minutes are taken and published
- Manages deployment of the kanban design
- Ensures proper management of project budget
- Resolves any team conflicts

ban—someone directly affected by the success of the kanban. Ideal candidates might be production manager/supervisors, materials managers, or warehouse managers. Also consider their ability to lead and communicate information, since kanban is dependent upon the transfer of information.

Set Up Team Rules and Develop Group Process

Once you have the team and the teamleader selected, then take the time to make them a team. Make sure they understand their charter, the timeline, and the expectations. Also, make sure the group understands the level (and limits) of their authority. Finally, the team should know whether any special conditions exist that might impact their final design, such as model changes, equipment moves, desire to not move equipment, or capacity issues.

The team should take the time to make introductions, to develop team rules, and to assign team roles. Some of the team rules might include:

- ❑ Courtesy to each other when speaking
- ❑ Everyone gets a chance to be heard
- ❑ No personal attacks
- ❑ The decision-making process
- ❑ Meeting rules (e.g., no late arrivals, attend or send substitute, agenda twenty-four hours in advance)
- ❑ Regularly scheduled meeting dates and times
- ❑ Regular meeting location

Create a list of the rules that apply to your organization or incorporate your own existing organizational rules that describe how the team will conduct their business and achieve their chartered outcome. The initial meeting should be led by the project leader, and the results should be documented for all to see.

In conjunction with the development of the team's operating rules, the team should also assign roles to facilitate the operation of the team. Some of the roles to consider include: note taker (or scribe), meeting arranger, and budget manager. The project leader should not play Mr. Nice Guy with the assignments, taking on all the team roles if no one volunteers. At a minimum, rotate the roles between group members to make it equitable.

Develop a Plan for Implementing the Kanban

Once you have selected the team and completed the essential elements for forming a team, it's time to make a plan. The team should develop a timeline and a budget for implementation.

Develop a Timeline

The timeline should include the time required for design and for implementation. The team should also consider the time required for creation of visual management items and fabrication/installation of any fixtures. Also, don't forget to include time for coordinating the plan and for training.

Team members should use their experience from prior projects to set the schedule. Don't let the team get hung up on the fact that they have never implemented a kanban system. Finally, the team needs to set a firm implementation date so that everyone can plan toward this date. Do not let this date float or you will never get the kanban started. Remember, if the start date becomes infeasible, change it.

We recommend shooting for one month as the implementation timeframe. One month allows:

- ❑ A week to form the team
- ❑ A week for group training and design
- ❑ Two weeks for implementation and operator training

If you extend beyond this timeframe without a concrete reason, kanban is likely to move to the back burner and become overshadowed by other activities. Needing more than one month may also signal that the team expects the implementation to be overly complicated. Figure 2-4 shows the suggested timeline for implementation.

Set a Team Budget

Once the team has a timeline for activities, the team needs to establish a budget to cover the costs of signs and minor hardware needed for the kanban. The project should make someone responsible for

Figure 2-4. Suggested timeline for implementation.

Action Plan: Kanban Implementation on Line A

Start Date: Today **Champion:** Joe Smith Plant Manager

Action Steps	Weeks	1	2	3	4
Create Team	1	■			
Appoint Project Leader					
Select Team Members					
Hold First Team Meeting					
Gather Initial Data					
Training and Design	1		■		
Implementation and Training	2			■	■
Startup	1/2				■

tracking the budget and the team should discuss the budget at each team meeting.

Establishing a budget empowers the team and gives them responsibility for implementation. Consider the budget as removing a potential roadblock to inaction.

To establish the budget amount, you can either let the team develop a detailed estimate to arrive at the amount, or the budget can be allocated as part of team chartering. Regardless of how the number is arrived at, the team must understand they are responsible for spending the money wisely and appropriately. They must understand that they cannot spend the allocated amount arbitrarily but that all purchases must be related to the implementation of the kanban.

If the team determines that they need something that exceeds their budget, then make them justify this expense like any other project. You should let the team know this groundrule up front. Also, let them know that the justification process will include identifying other options they considered and their backup plans.

Make Sure the Team Gets Training

For the team to be successful, they must get training in kanban techniques. The training should be formalized and should cover the following areas:

- The elements of kanban
- The process for creating a kanban
- Examples of successful kanbans

Also, consider creating simulations or scenarios to reinforce the concepts. A comprehensive and in-depth training program will last about a day.

Unless you have in-house expertise, consider this an area where a consultant will be needed. Consultants can bring a wealth of experience and should have a prepared "off-the-shelf" training presentation. Also, to develop an in-house capability, consider hiring the consultant to conduct a train-the-trainer session and purchasing the presentation charts as part of the contract.

The goal of the training is to provide the team with the knowledge (and confidence) to implement a kanban scheduling project. Also, consider integrating the kanban design into the training process. The implementation steps can be incrementally applied to your situation so that at the end of the training the team has a preliminary design. This design can then be finalized for implementation.

Provide the Team with Management Support

The last step of the group process comes from the top. As with any journey into uncharted territories, the team (and the whole organization) needs to know that kanban will be implemented. Every organization has its share of people who do not want to change and will do anything they can to prevent change from happening (either consciously or unconsciously).

Top management must set the stage for change. They must put those people who have placed roadblocks to implementation on the hook for developing a solution to their roadblocks. Management cannot let these people throw the proverbial hand grenade and run away. Also, management must let the team know that there will not be any public executions—only public celebrations.

If top management cannot support these behaviors, then they need to reconsider their readiness to implement kanban. Additionally, management should consider this failure as a wake-up call to assess their readiness to lead change.

Some of the activities that top management can perform to help in implementation are:

- ❑ Provide the resources promised/required promptly
- ❑ Issue a memo announcing the formulation of the team
- ❑ Request progress updates from both the team and process owner

- ❑ Discuss the team's progress at business or staff meetings
- ❑ Attend team meetings and team training
- ❑ Publicly congratulate the team upon completion of the project

In general, management should act in a manner that tells the organization that kanban is the new direction and that everyone had better point their wagons that way!

Using the Workbook

The CD-ROM *Workbook* contains the companion forms for this chapter (see Figure 2-5). Use these forms, listed below, to document the set-up of the team:

1. Team member list (name, phone numbers, position)
2. Group charter (timeline, expectations, level of authority, special conditions, and budget)
3. Team roles (name and role: scribe, meeting logistics, special roles)
4. Team rules (list by priority)

The completed forms should be viewed as a team charter. Depending upon your organizational culture, you may even want to

Figure 2-5. Forms from the companion workbook for documenting the formation of the team.

- Team member list
  - (name, phone numbers, position)
- Group charter
  - (timeline, expectations, level of authority, special conditions, and budget)
- Team roles
  - (name and role—scribe, meeting logistics, special roles)
- Team rules
  - (list by priority)

formalize this section by having each team member sign the forms to acknowledge their acceptance and support.

Summary

To successfully implement kanban scheduling, use a team. The team will ensure buy-in from the people that must operate the kanban while making sure that unique aspects of the process are considered.

This team needs to be cross-functional and contain representation from all the stakeholders. Definite team members include:

- ❑ Production management/supervision
- ❑ Materials management
- ❑ Material handlers/warehouse
- ❑ Operators (last but not least)

Other groups to consider for membership include human relations, engineering maintenance, sales/customer service, downstream customer(s), and trainees for future kanban projects.

Make the decision on what additional members to add based on their ability to contribute to the process. In the case of including external customers on the team, consider their potential contribution, the opportunity to enhance the supply chain, the potential to develop strategic alliances, and the current state of your relationship.

In conjunction with forming the team, appoint a project leader to oversee execution of the project. Make sure this person understands their mission and their level of authority.

Kick off the team by assigning roles and setting up team rules. The project leader is not the only person who should have team responsibilities.

Once the team members have established their roles and rules, they need to develop a schedule and a budget. Ideally, the implementation timeframe should not be greater than one month. When the team has completed the administrative task, it is time to begin the implementation process. The first step should be kanban training. This training should explain the concept and offer practical examples of successful implementation. If you are just starting out with kanban, then you may need a consultant to conduct this training.

Finally, top management represents the last brick in the team formulation process. Top management must demonstrate their support for the implementation. They must prevent resistance to change from creeping in and destroying the project. They should deal with those individuals who put up roadblocks by making these individuals responsible for developing and implementing solutions (which support the project timeframe). If top management cannot demonstrate their support, then reconsider kanban implementation.

CHAPTER 3

Conduct Data Collection

When thinking about kanban, many people get a cold shiver and fear that they will be changing over their production process every ten minutes with excessive scrap and downtime. They think this because they lack experience in kanban and they assume that kanban is an end unto itself. Kanban is an execution system that helps control the process schedule based on actual demand. Kanban is not a magic demon that makes you do dumb things against your will. If these fears do materialize, it is usually because the organization designed a system that was not based on the realities of their current operation.

Therefore, to avoid your own personal nightmare, start the kanban process by documenting your current state. Using the team, take a snapshot in time of your operating parameters, inventory, etc. Look at your organization as it is, not as you want it to be. When you have the data collected, summarize the data to understand the current state in preparation for calculating the kanban. We will use the data gathered in this chapter to calculate the size of the kanban in Chapter 4. Figure 3-1 graphically depicts this relationship.

Use this two-step process to ensure you have the necessary data for sizing the kanban in Chapter 4:

1. Gather data
2. Analyze the data

To further assist in the data collection process, we will present a data collection form and two examples to help explain the process.

Figure 3-1. The data collection process.

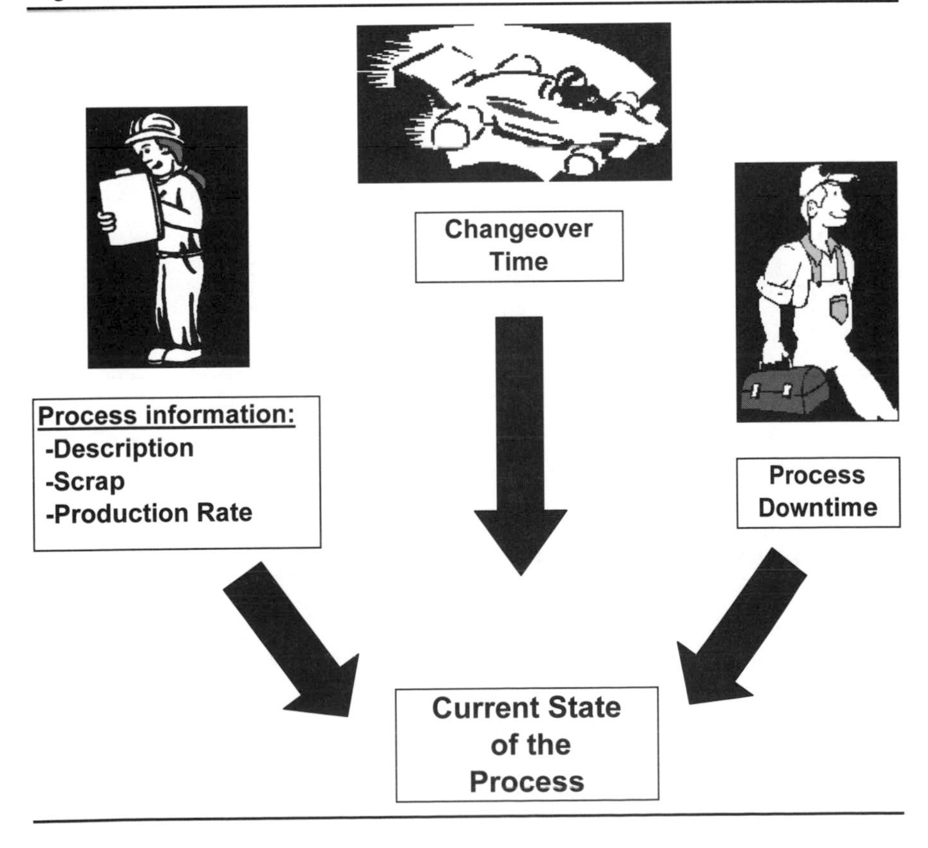

Gather Data

The process of developing the current status of kanban candidates begins with gathering the necessary data to help characterize the potential process. To adequately define the process you will need the following information:

- ❑ Number of parts produced by the process
- ❑ Changeover times
- ❑ Downtime
- ❑ Scrap levels

When collecting this data, be honest with yourselves. The data is intended to help you develop a usable design. If the data is inaccurate, then you will potentially doom the project to failure before it even starts. When starting the data collection process, use the following guidance to make sure the team collects the proper data:

- ❑ Be specific about the data required
- ❑ Assess the data to confirm that it matches the team's experience and knowledge of the process

If you discover that the data does not make sense, then review the data again and sort out the truth. Don't be afraid to collect new data!

Number of Parts Produced by the Target Process

Start the data collection process by identifying the parts to be produced by the target process. Begin by breaking the production down into individual part numbers. Do not combine part numbers just because they are part of a common family, the same size, the same configuration, or the same color. We will use these similarities later in Chapter 5 during the design process to address preferred operating sequences. At this point we need to understand the magnitude of the project, which we can only do by knowing all the part numbers.

Conversely, if a part is common at this stage, but it is transformed into different part numbers later, then it should be considered one part number. For example, a 4″×8″ plate that is produced by a stamping die in one process, but is turned into five unique pieces downstream through future processing, would be considered only one part number in the original stamping process.

Be descriptive when gathering data—look for both differentiation and commonality in the parts being produced. Take the time to sort through the data to determine these items; don't let a mound of data overwhelm you. During the data collection phase, keep asking questions until you arrive at a list that makes sense. Before beginning data collection by part number, you also need to determine what your production-scheduling interval will be. Essentially, do you produce to the monthly, weekly, or daily production requirements? The answer to this question will tell you the interval for the replenishment cycle. All your calculations must then be scaled to this interval, such as pieces per week, available time per week, etc.

Once you have selected a scheduling interval, then you need to determine the required parts for this interval. The required parts are the number of parts you use over the predetermined interval—per day, per week, or even per month. These quantities represent the parts consumed by the "customer" at regular intervals, which you must regularly replenish to keep the customer supplied. (We use "customer" to refer to both internal and external customers.)

In conjunction with identifying the products that will be produced by the kanban system, you must also determine the rates of production. Review each product's production rate for realism. If you receive a blanket rate answer, use the team's experience to ask: Does everything really run at the same rate? Also, make sure you use consistent units and measurement systems for the production rate and description. Once again, the wrong rates will skew your numbers when creating the kanban design.

Changeover Times

Changeover time is the time from the last good production piece of the previous production run to the first good piece in the new production run. Many people cheat when they report changeover time by reporting the time from the last good production piece of the previous production run to the time the line starts up on the new production run. They conveniently decide to omit the time it takes to debug the start-up and begin running continuously. This subtly can be very important if you are trying to optimize the run quantities.

Don't fall into this trap. The kanban quantities and calculated replenishment cycle must be based on the time the process runs at the planned production rate.

Just like the part's description, consider the different products produced by the process and verify the changeover time for each changeover. Avoid broad-brushing the times and underestimating or overestimating the total changeover time.

Downtime

Downtime, or rather unplanned downtime, is the total time the process is scheduled to be producing parts, but it isn't. Basically, how many hours is the process not producing product but was scheduled to do so. Examples of unplanned downtime include shutting down for breakdowns or for lack of raw material. Unplanned downtime should not be confused with planned downtime, such as time allocated for breaks, lunches, maintenance, or cleanup. Scheduling the line down because of no production requirements is also considered planned downtime.

Realistically, look at the process's downtime. Determine an average for the downtime using experience as well as historical data. However, when looking at the historical downtime, don't let recent process improvements be overshadowed by the data. (Once again—be honest and look at it as it is, not as you wish it were.)

Scrap Levels

Next, determine the system scrap rates for each product produced by the target process. System scrap is the process scrap rate plus the scrap rate of downstream processes. The system scrap rate will let you calculate the adjusted production requirements for each product. When calculating the adjusted production requirements you must account for the total amount needing to be produced. In Chapter 4 we will show you how to calculate the adjusted production requirements. If your plant tracks scrap by the process scrap *and* the downstream (or customer) scrap, then you will need to incorporate both numbers into the adjusted production requirement calculation.

To illustrate the impact of scrap on the adjusted production requirements let's look at the example in Figure 3-2. (Don't worry about the equations—we'll discuss them in detail in Chapter 4.) In this example, to produce 100 parts with a process scrap level of 8 percent and a downstream scrap of 2 percent, we would need to produce 119 parts. This number is slightly larger than the 111 parts we would need to produce if we had calculated the required parts as a combined scrap rate of 10 percent.

Figure 3-2. Example of calculating adjusted demand scrap when measuring scrap by process scrap and downstream scrap.

A plant produces a part in a process with 8% scrap and the downstream scrap for processes that use the part are 2%. To meet a daily production demand of 100 for this part, how many parts would need to be run?

Adjusted process demand = 100/(1–8%)
= 100/0.92
= 108.7 or 109

Total adjusted demand = 109/(1–2%)
= 109/0.98
= 118.5 or 119

Total adjusted demand for 10% = 100/(1–10%)
= 111.1

When looking at the scrap levels, check to see if your current schedule quantities already account for system scrap rates. If they do, then no further calculations will be required.

Document Your Findings

Once you have collected the data, compile it into a usable format to make decisions. Figure 3-3 contains a worksheet for recording the process information. You can use this form to record your data.

In Chapter 1 we alluded to value stream mapping as a product that would help in the selection of a target process. If your plant has not done value stream mapping, then this might be a golden opportunity to do so after you have collected all the above data. The value stream mapping process asks an organization to assess its current situation in the form of a "Current State" map. The organization then asks itself what it wants to become by developing its "Future State" map. When done properly with real data, the Future State map becomes a powerful roadmap to the future.

For the purposes of this book, we have not used value stream mapping to document the current production process, because value stream mapping asks the organization to look at and utilize all the Lean tools. Kanban is just one of those tools. We will assume that the organization has decided to implement kanban as part of its strategic plan (regardless of how the organization arrived at the plan).

Analyze the Data

Once you have the data consolidated, then it's time to take a look at the data. Analyze the data for:

- ❑ Consistency
- ❑ Accuracy
- ❑ Realism

Figure 3-3. Process Information Summary Sheet.

Schedule Interval: ____________________

Part Number	Part Name	Interval Production Requirement	Process Scrap Level	Downstream Scrap Level	System Scrap	Production Rate (for each unit)	Change-over Time	Comments

Fill-in either these two columns or the system scrap column

Total Change-over Time ________

By *consistency*, we mean:

- ❑ Are the units correct and are the numbers consistent with your expectations?
- ❑ Is everything recorded in the same measurement system, i.e., English or metric?
- ❑ Are the units mixed?
- ❑ Are the entries in the same dimensions—e.g., seconds versus minutes?

Nothing slows down the kanban design process like trying to decipher unit problems.

When considering *accuracy*, consider these items:

- ❑ Are these the true scrap numbers, changeover numbers, downtime numbers?
- ❑ Have we overinflated the numbers?
- ❑ Have we lumped all the parts into the same category by giving them all the same changeover time or scrap rate?

Also, look at the data for realism. Does the data really reflect how we run our process?

Make sure the numbers are consistent, accurate, and real. If you have misstated the numbers, it will become evident in the next phase when you calculate the kanban. You will see the errors when the calculated numbers tell you to increase inventory, or worse, when the errors tell you that you can cut your inventory in half. As the old computer saying goes: garbage in, garbage out!

Two Examples

Let's work through two examples to make sure everyone understands the data collection process and how to use the forms. The first example, shown in Figure 3-4, is a simple two-part number kanban for two plastic injection molded parts. Figure 3-5 shows the

Figure 3-4. Example 1: two-part number kanban.

Example 1: A plastic injection molding machine makes plastic rings for carnival games. Two different colors are produced—red (part A) and blue (part B). The machine makes 2 rings at a time with a mold cycle of 30 seconds. The process has a system scrap of 3%. The mold is not changed when switching between colors, but the raw material hopper must be cleaned out between colors. This color change takes 15 minutes.

The plastic molding pellets are delivered daily and the supplier has never missed a delivery. The rings must cool for 15 minutes. They are made to order for 5 different customers.

The company has steady weekly orders of 2,500 red rings and 4,000 blue rings. The company promises next-day delivery of any order.

The company produces the rings 1 shift per day, 5 days per week. The plant has two 10-minute breaks and a 30-minute lunch. Each day the shift has a 10-minute shift starter meeting and 5 minutes/day is allocated for the monthly kaizen meeting, 5s activities, and a safety meeting. The plant does not have a preventive maintenance program so they experience 1 hour of downtime each day for minor breakdowns and adjustments.

—Use this information to fill in the process information summary sheet.

summarized data. The second example, shown in Figure 3-6, is a process line that makes ten-part numbers—some that require changeovers and some that do not. Figure 3-7 shows the summarized data.

Take a close look at Figure 3-7 and perform the recommended analysis. Did you find the incorrect numbers? Did you see flags for follow-up? What about the mixed units? Figure 3-8 highlights the errors and flags in Figure 3-7. Figure 3-9 shows the corrected table. This example shows the necessity to carefully analyze your numbers to make sure you have the correct data to correctly calculate the kanban quantities.

(text continues on page 47)

Figure 3-5. Example 1: Process Information Summary Sheet.

Schedule Interval: Daily

Part Number	Part Name	Interval Production Requirement	Process Scrap Level	Downstream Scrap Level	System Scrap	Production Rate (for each unit)	Change-over Time	Comments
A	Red Carnival Ring	500			3%	15 seconds	15 minutes	
B	Blue Carnival Ring	800			3%	15 seconds	15 minutes	

Total Change-over Time 30 minutes

$\frac{2500}{5 \text{ Shifts/week}}$

$\frac{4000}{5 \text{ Shifts/week}}$

$\frac{30 \text{ seconds}}{2 \text{ rings per cycle}}$

Figure 3-6. Example 2: ten-part number kanban.

Example 2: A plastic extrusion process line extrudes 10 different profiles. Each profile is unique and is assigned a unique part number—3502 through 3512. The profiles are used in a downstream process where they are mold spliced to create environmental seals for the company's main consumer product—electronic component carrying cases. The extrusion process experiences 5% scrap and 2% scrap in the mold splicing process. All profiles have a changeover time of 35 minutes. The demand and speeds for each profile is as shown:

Part Number	Component Case Demand	Part Length (in mm)	Production Rate (ft/min)
3502	500	500	50
3503	750	588	50
3504	350	1200	50
3505	250	300	60
3506	500	300	60
3507	500	585	60
3508	1200	690	60
3509	1000	1250	45
3510	900	400	45
3511	100	400	45

The process line averages 95% uptime. The process line is scheduled 5 days per week for 1 shift. All PMs and 5s activities are handled while the operation is running or on overtime.

The plastic molding pellets are delivered daily, but the supplier misses about 15% of their deliveries. The extruded profiles require no further cure time once they are extruded and cooled in the production process.

Figure 3-7. Example 2: Process Information Summary Sheet.

Schedule Interval: Daily

Part Number	Part Name	Interval Production Requirement	Process Scrap Level	Downstream Scrap Level	System Scrap	Production Rate in seconds (for each unit)	Change-over Time	Comments
3502		500	5%	2%	NA	600.0	35	
3503		750	5%	2%	NA	705.6	35	
3504		350	5%	2%	NA	1440.0	35	
3505		250	5%	2%	NA	300.0	35	
3506		550	5%	2%	NA	300.0	35	
3507		500	5%	2%	NA	585.0	35	
3508		1220	5%	2%	NA	690.0	35	
3509		1000	5%	2%	NA	1666.7	35	
3510		900	5%	2%	NA	533.3	35	
3511		100	5%	2%	NA	533.3	35	
						Total Change-over Time	350 minutes	

Figure 3-8. Example 2: errors in the original data collection form.

Schedule Interval: Daily

Part Number	Part Name	Interval Production Requirement	Process Scrap Level	Downstream Scrap Level	System Scrap	Production Rate in seconds (for each unit)	Change-over Time	Comments
3502		500	5%	2%	NA	600.00	35	
3503		750	5%	2%	NA	705.60	35	
3504		350	5%	2%	NA	1440.00	35	
3505		250	5%	2%	NA	300.00	35	
3506		550	5%	2%	NA	300.00	35	
3507		500	5%	2%	NA	585.00	35	
3508		1220	5%	2%	NA	690.00	35	
3509		1000	5%	2%	NA	1666.67	35	
3510		900	5%	2%	NA	533.33	35	
3511		100	5%	2%	NA	533.33	35	

Total Change-over Time 350 minutes

Copied incorrectly; should be 500 and 1200.

Are scrap levels really the same for 10 different profiles?

The calculations have mixed units between Millimeters (the length) and Feet (the line speed - Feet/minute).

Same question as with the scrap: Do all the changeovers really take the same amount of time?

Figure 3-9. Example 2: corrected Process Information Summary Sheet.

Schedule Interval: Daily

Part Number	Part Name	Interval Production Requirement	Process Scrap Level	Downstream Scrap Level	System Scrap	Production Rate in seconds (for each unit)	Change-over Time	Comments
3502		500	3%	3%	NA	2.0	35	
3503		750	5%	2%	NA	2.3	15	
3504		350	6%	4%	NA	4.7	35	
3505		250	5%	2%	NA	1.0	20	
3506		500	5%	2%	NA	1.0	20	
3507		500	4%	2%	NA	1.9	35	
3508		1200	2%	1%	NA	2.3	35	
3509		1000	5%	2%	NA	5.5	30	
3510		900	3%	1%	NA	1.7	30	
3511		100	5%	2%	NA	1.7	35	

After further data collection, the team determined that the scrap and changeover times were not the same. They solved the dimension mismatch by converting feet to millimeters:

$$\textbf{Production rate} = \frac{\textbf{60 seconds/min}}{\textbf{(line speed x 304.8 Millimeters/foot)/ part length}}$$

Total Change-over Time 290 minutes

Using the Workbook

For individuals and groups that are using the CD-ROM *Workbook*, Chapter 3 on data collection contains a blank form for data collection. We have also included the two examples for reference purposes. Use the data collection form to collect the data for your kanban. In a meeting setting, you may want to make an overhead of the blank form and fill it in as you review the data.

Summary

The process of implementing kanban scheduling begins by collecting data on the target process. The data that needs to be collected includes number of parts to be produced by the process, changeover times, downtime, and scrap levels.

Use your team to collect this data. The team should follow the guidelines in the chapter to ensure you get the data needed to calculate the kanban's size.

Once you have collected the data, then use the data collection form to organize the data into a format for analysis. When you have the completed data sheet, then review the data to make sure the units are consistent, correct, and realistic. Look for errors in the data, such as tabulation errors, recording errors, and unit errors. Use the two examples provided at the end of the chapter to help illustrate the data summation and analysis process.

CHAPTER

4

SIZE THE KANBAN

In Chapter 3 you gathered data on your process in preparation for this point. In this chapter we will use the data from Chapter 3 to "size the kanban." Or, in layman's terms, you will determine how many containers of each product you will require to effectively operate the kanban (and keep your customer supplied). Figure 4-1 expands the model started in Figure 3-1 by adding this step.

Once you start kanban scheduling, these quantities become the maximum amount of inventory held. Therefore, when all these containers are full, then you stop production. This rule is one of the major tenets of kanban scheduling—you only produce when you have signals.

These quantities become the scheduling signals. To set up these signals, we will determine the emergency level (or red level), the schedule signal (or yellow level), and the normal level (or green level). In Chapter 5 you will develop a kanban design, which uses these signals to control the production schedule.

In this chapter we propose two methods for sizing internal kanbans. The first method calculates the container quantities based on

Figure 4-1. Calculating the kanban quantities.

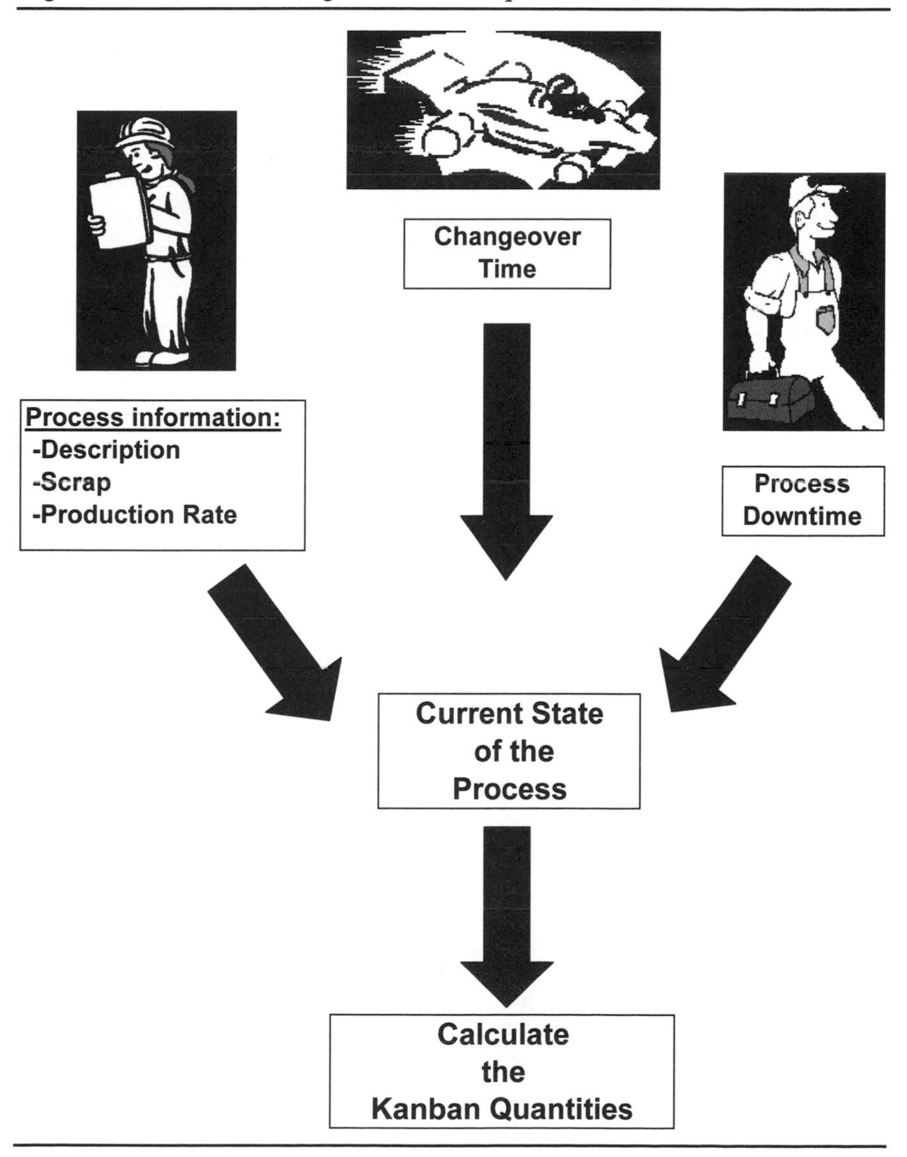

the data collected in Chapter 3. This method allows you to optimize and potentially reduce the quantities based on the characteristics of your process.

The second method uses your existing production schedule and makes the current production quantities the kanban quantities. This method allows for quicker implementation and less math, but does not offer the potential for reducing inventory levels.

We will discuss the benefits of each approach as we proceed through the chapter. However, our experience tells us that the first approach is better since it calculates the quantities based on the processes' capability. This method also typically leads to reduced inventory. We focus mainly on the calculation method, but also provide the information necessary to perform the second method. We will let you decide on which method to use for calculating your kanban quantities.

This chapter also addresses supplier kanbans. The primary issues with these kanbans will be safety stock and establishing the lead time for replenishment. As part of this activity we discuss kanbans with vendors who have already developed this type of scheduling system as well as kanbans with vendors who have no such experience. During the discussions about supplier kanbans, we show you a methodology for selecting the vendor parts that should be placed under kanban scheduling and how to address variability in order quantity. Additionally, Appendix H contains a case study that is based on a kanban in use at a plant with 3,000 different finished-goods part numbers, with batches as small as fifty units.

All of these initial kanban quantities should be based on your current condition instead of how you want the future to look. By using current data, you can start the kanban now, rather than waiting for your downtime, your scrap level, or your changeover times to be reduced.

Further, by using current data you reduce the risk of failure. Essentially when you size the kanban with wishful or projected future data, you open yourself up to raw material stock outs or production stoppages. Just like the case of overcompensating with buffers, sizing the kanban with future data creates an unreal production condition. Managers who make this mistake often wonder why every product is in the red level all the time.

Don't make the same mistake. Size the kanban with the current data, then set continuous improvement goals that will reduce the kanban quantities. Chapter 9 specifically addresses the various ways to reduce the kanban quantities. Best of all, these recommendations will be compatible with other Lean, or continuous improvement, activities you may already have underway.

Determining the Replenishment Cycle

In Chapter 3, we determined the scheduling interval and required production parts for the production process. We will refer to this cycle as the *replenishment interval*. It is the smallest batch size that your process can run and still keep the customer supplied. This interval essentially tells how long it takes to produce your adjusted production requirements. The replenishment interval is a function of the time available after considering your process parameter:

- ❑ Production rate
- ❑ Changeover times
- ❑ Downtime (both planned and unplanned)

The replenishment cycle will ultimately be determined by the time left over for changeovers after subtracting required production run time from available production time. Therefore, the length of this cycle will be a function of how long it takes to "bank" enough changeover time to make all the necessary changeovers.

These production requirements also need to account for your scrap. When the required parts include the scrap, then the term becomes your "adjusted requirements." These factors determine how many days, weeks, or months of inventory you keep on hand to supply the customer(s).

If this sounds confusing, then maybe some mathematical formulas will help. We'll start with calculating the adjusted production requirements. Adjusted production requirements are the quantity of a part that you must produce to cover the order quantity plus the system scrap. Mathematically, the equation for adjusted production requirements is shown in Figure 4-2.

Figure 4-2. Equation for adjusted production requirements using the system scrap.

$$\text{Adjusted Production Requirements} = \frac{\text{Average Production Order}}{(1 - \text{System Scrap})}$$

For those production processes that must also account for downstream scrap (such as for in-house customers), then this equation changes to the equation in Figure 4-3.

You will need to make this calculation for each item produced by the process. By summing the adjusted production requirement for each part you will determine the total production quantity.

Note that you may not need to make the adjusted production requirements calculation if your normally scheduled quantity accounts for scrap in your production process and downstream. In fact, if this is the case, then taking the production quantities and adjusting for scrap with the equations in Figures 4-2 or 4-3 will only incorrectly increase the amount you need to produce—i.e., by creating overproduction.

Once you know how much you have to produce, then you must

Figure 4-3. Equation for adjusted production requirements when scrap is tracked as process scrap and downstream scrap.

$$\textbf{Adjusted Production Requirements} = \frac{\textbf{Average Production Order}}{\textbf{(1 - Process Scrap) (1 - Downstream Scrap)}}$$

determine how long it will take and how much time you have to produce it (each day, week, or month). The answers to these two questions will allow you to determine the time available for changeovers.

To determine how long it takes to produce the adjusted production requirements, you need to determine the time required for production of each part. To determine the time required for production, multiply the adjusted production requirements by the cycle time per part and sum for all the parts produced by the process. Mathematically, the equation for available time is shown in Figure 4-4.

Figure 4-4. Equation for production time.

Time Required for Production = Sum (Adjusted Production Requirements × Cycle Time Per Part)

Now calculate the available production time to determine how much time you have available each day to produce parts. While this may seem ridiculous since you have twenty-four hours in a day, available time refers to the time left after considering breaks, lunches, end of shift cleanup, shift starter meetings, equipment warm-up, breakdowns, kaizen activities, safety activities, PM downtime, etc. It is the time left over to produce parts. Mathematically, the equation for available time is shown in Figure 4-5.

Typically, most production processes have from 410 to 430 minutes of available time per shift. Once calculated, available time usually becomes a production standard.

If you operate a continuous process, then the equation for available time simply considers planned downtime for preventative maintenance/cleaning activities and breakdowns. Mathematically, the equation changes to the equation shown in Figure 4-6.

Figure 4-5. Equation for available time.

Available Time = Total Time in a Shift − (Planned and Unplanned Downtime)

Figure 4-6. Equation for available time in a continuous process.

Available Time (Continuous Processes)	=	**Total Time in a Shift − (Time for Planned Maintenance, Cleaning, and Breakdowns)**

One source of confusion when calculating available time is how to allocate the time for events that do not occur every shift, such as safety meetings, kaizen activities, or preventative maintenance. To allocate time in the daily standard, simply determine the total time taken up by these events during a week or a month and divide by the shifts in a week or a month respectively. Once you have this number, simply subtract it from the total shift time. For example, if you allocate one hour per month for a safety meeting, one hour per week for kaizen and information meetings, and two hours per month for preventive maintenance (PM), total productive maintenance (TPM), and 5s cleaning, then the shift allocations would be calculated as shown in Figure 4-7.

The final result of all this calculating will be the total time available for production requirements and changeovers. To determine the total time available for changeovers, subtract the time required for production from the total available. The mathematical equation is shown in Figure 4-8. The example in Figures 4-9 and 4-10 should clarify these calculations.

Finally, you calculate the replenishment interval by determining the total time required for changeovers and dividing this number by the time available for changeovers. Mathematically, the equation is shown in Figure 4-11.

Taking our Figures 4-9 and 4-10 examples further, you can calculate the replenishment intervals for both production processes. Figures 4-12 and 4-13 show these calculations.

Once you have the replenishment interval and lead times established, you multiply these numbers by the adjusted production interval requirements to determine the maximum number of parts in the kanban.

Figure 4-7. Allocating improvement and meeting time for available time calculations.

$$\textbf{Shift Allocation} = \frac{\textbf{Total Time for Allocations}}{\textbf{Total Available Shifts in 1 Month}}$$

Where:

Total Time for Allocations = 60 minutes for monthly safety meeting
+ (4 × 60 minutes per week for Kaizen & information meetings)
+ 120 minutes per month for PM, TPM, & 5s cleaning

= 420 minutes

Total Time for Allocations = 3 shifts per day
× 20 production days per month

= 60 shifts

Finally:

$$\text{Shift Allocation} = \frac{420 \text{ minutes}}{60 \text{ shifts}}$$

= 7 minutes per shift

To determine the number of containers in the kanban, just divide the maximum kanban quantities by each part's container capacity. The container capacity will become the smallest unit of each part that you will produce. The total number of the containers then becomes the basis for determining the scheduling level and danger level.

Essentially, you will not receive a scheduling signal until the customer uses the replenishment interval quantity. (This quantity becomes the "green" level.) You then produce parts until you reach the part's maximum quantity. These assumptions should be tailored

Figure 4-8. Equation for time available for changeovers.

Time Available for Changeovers	=	Total Available Time − Time Required for Production

by the size of the kanban and specifics of your process. However, the fundamental rules of kanbans must be followed:

- ❑ Nothing is produced without a scheduling signal
- ❑ Production stops when no more signals exist

Implications of Scrap, Unplanned Downtime, and Changeover Times on Replenishment Intervals

If you remember, we started out this chapter by saying:

> Size your kanbans based on the current state of your production process.

This advice was based on our desire to help you avoid the agony of undersizing your kanban quantities, which can:

1. Cause you to continually operate at danger (or red) levels
2. Ultimately lead to your pronouncement of kanban as worthless and a waste of time

After seeing the calculation method, hopefully you see how scrap, unplanned downtime, and changeover times will drive the interval up or down. To illustrate this point, we varied scrap, downtime, and changeover time for the Figure 4.10 (or ten-part number) example. The graphs in Figures 4-14 to 4-17 show how the replenishment interval varies with the scrap, downtime, and changeover time changes.

Note that Figure 4-17 shows the benefits of an aggressive con-

Figure 4-9. Calculating the time available for changeovers for the two-part number example in Chapter 3.

Example 1: In chapter 3 we outlined the details of a process which produces injected molded plastic rings. Figure 3.5 summarizes the data for this example.
-Use this data to calculate the time available for changeovers

Schedule Interval: Daily

Part Number	Part Name	Interval Production Requirement	Adjusted Production Requirements	Time Required for Production (in minutes)	Buffer	Container Size	Replenishment Container Quantity	Buffer Container Quantity	Comments
A	Red Carnival Ring	500	515	129					
B	Blue Carnival Ring	800	825	200					

$\frac{500}{(1-.03)}$ → 515

$\frac{800}{(1-.03)}$ → 825

Available Time (using Equation 4.5):

Total Time in a Shift		480 Minutes
Planned Downtime	-	65 Minutes
Unplanned Downtime	-	60 Minutes
		355

Interval Run Time

Converting to Minutes :

A 515 Parts * 15 Seconds/part =7725 seconds = $\frac{7725}{60 \text{ secs/min}}$ = 129 minutes

B 825 Parts * 15 Seconds/part =12375 seconds = $\frac{12375}{60 \text{ secs/min}}$ = 207 minutes

Finally: **Total Time Available for Changeover = 355 - (129 + 207)**
= 19 minutes

Figure 4-10. Calculating the time available for changeovers for the ten-part number example in Chapter 3.

Example 2: In chapter 3 we outlined the particulars of a plastic extrusion process which extruded 10 different profiles. Figure 3.13 summarizes the data for this example.
-Use this data to calculate the time available for changeovers

Schedule Interval: Daily

Part Number	Part Name	Interval Production Requirement	Adjusted Production Requirements	Time Required for Production (in minutes)	Buffer	Container Size	Replenishment Container Quantity	Buffer Container Quantity	Comments
3502		500	531	17					
3503		750	806	31					
3504		350	388	31					
3505		250	269	4					
3506		500	537	9					
3507		500	531	17					
3508		1200	1237	47					
3509		1000	1074	98					
3510		900	932	27					
3511		100	107	3					
			Total	284					

$$\frac{100}{(1-.05)(1-.02)}$$

Where **Time Required for Production**
= Production Rate
x Adjusted Production Requirement

ex. Part 3502 = 1.97 seconds/part
x 531 parts
= 1046 seconds
= 1046/60
= 17 minutes

Available Time (using Equation 4.5):

Total Time in a Shift	480	Minutes
Planned Downtime	- 0	Minutes
Unplanned Downtime	- 72	Minutes
	408	

Total Time Available for Changeover:

Available Time	408
Time Required for Production	- 284
	124

Figure 4-11. Equation for replenishment interval.

$$\textbf{Replenishment Interval} = \frac{\textbf{Total Time } \textit{Required} \text{ for Changeovers}}{\text{Total Time } \textit{Available} \text{ for Changeovers}}$$

tinuous improvement program that drives all of these values down. Because of the impact of these improvements, we have dedicated Chapter 9 to discussing improvements.

Figure 4-12. Calculation of replenishment interval for the two-part number example.

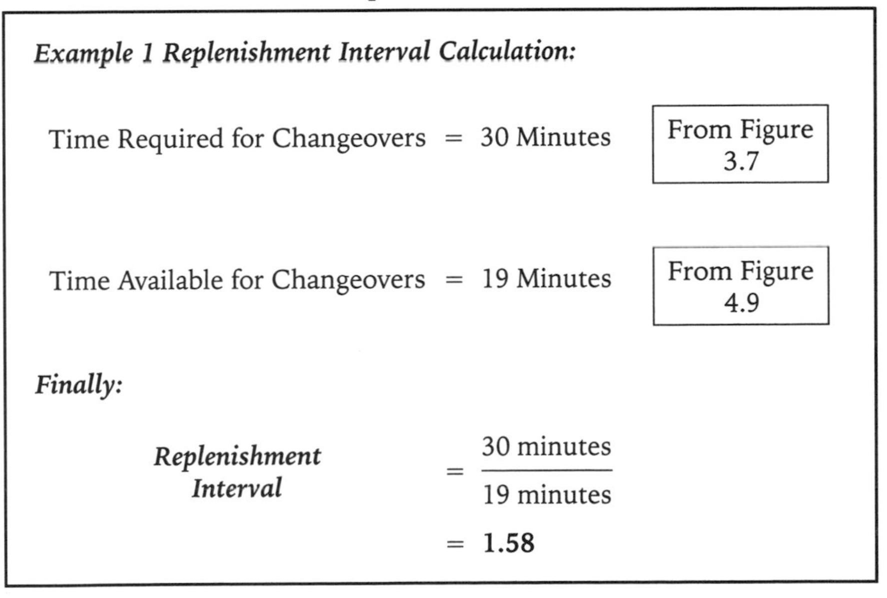

Calculating the Buffer

The last step in the process of sizing the kanban is to calculate your buffers. The buffers will provide you with the necessary lead time to produce the replenishment interval part quantities without stocking out your process or customer. The buffers also provide the necessary

Figure 4-13. Calculation of replenishment interval for the ten-part number example.

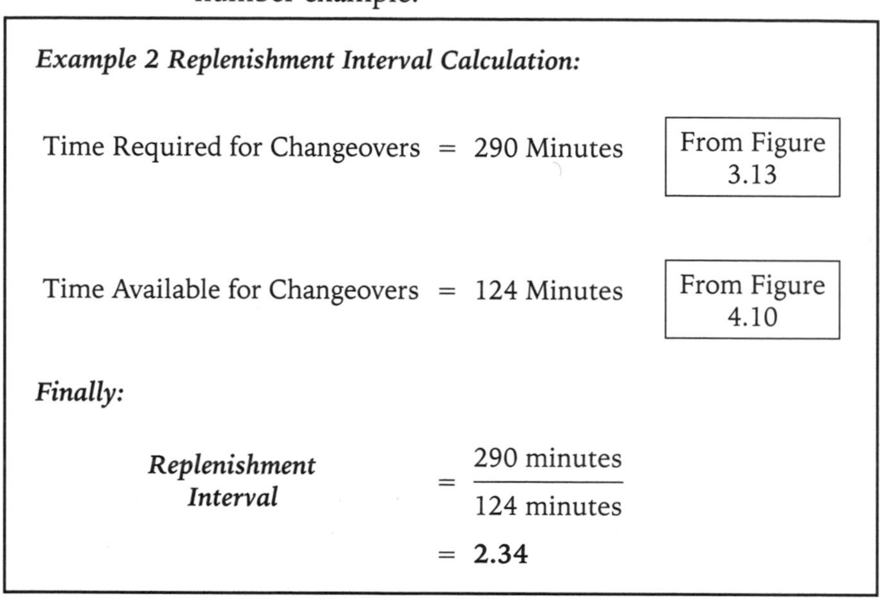

time required for process activities to occur. Buffer items that should be considered include:

- ❑ Customer delivery requirements (and your promised service)
- ❑ Internal lead times
- ❑ Supplier lead times
- ❑ Comfort level

Buffers should be considered in terms of how much inventory is needed to prevent the item from impacting the customer deliveries. The secret is to hold enough inventory to protect the customer without holding too much inventory.

Customer Delivery Requirements (and Your Promised Service)

The starting point for determining the buffer is the customer delivery requirements. Keeping the customer supplied should be the overriding driver in setting up the buffers. Therefore, the buffer must support the promised customer deliveries. So, when sizing the

Figure 4-14. Impact of scrap on replenishment intervals.

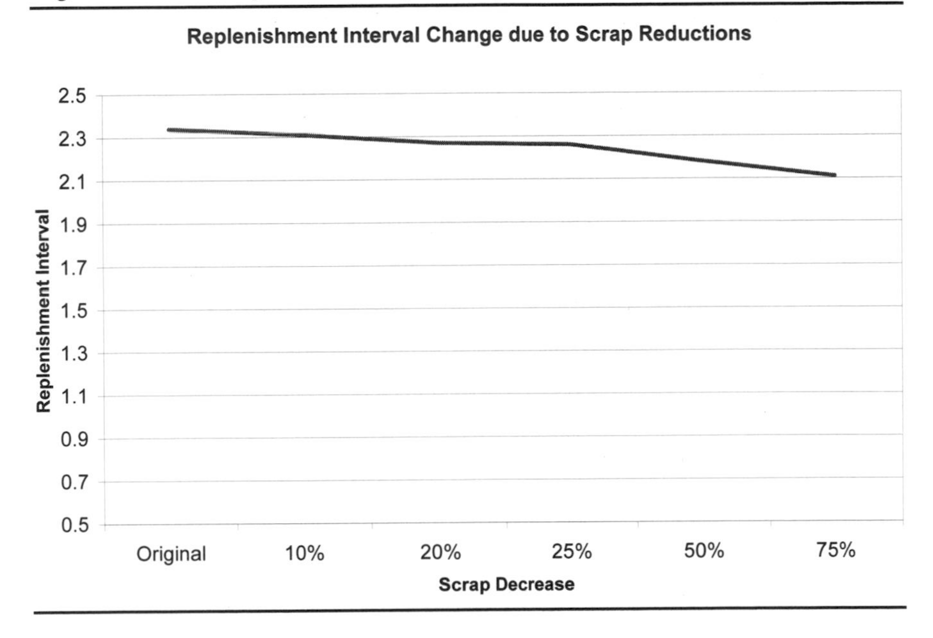

Figure 4-15. Impact of scrap unplanned downtime on replenishment intervals.

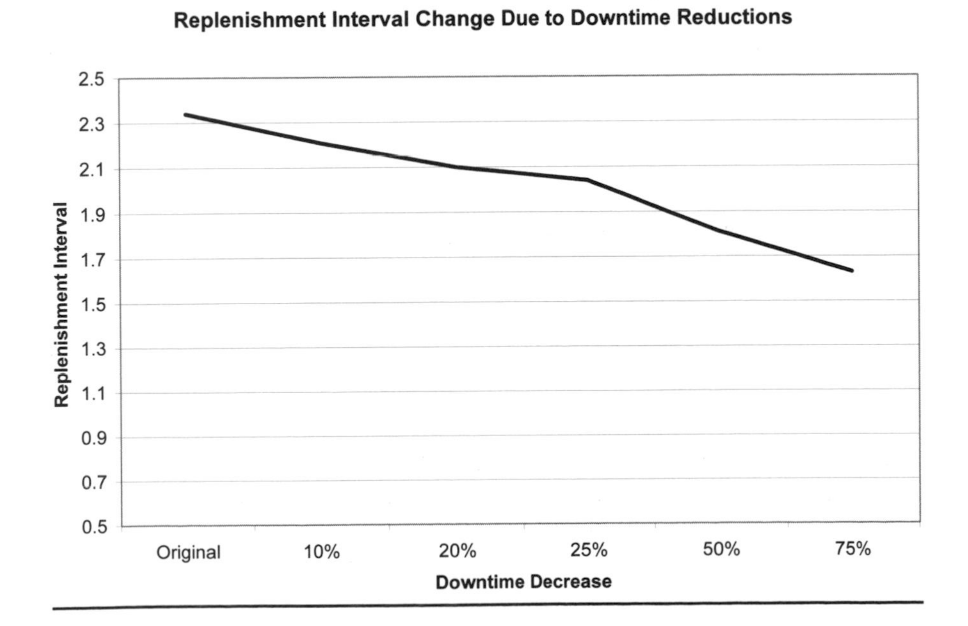

Figure 4-16. Impact of changeover times on replenishment intervals.

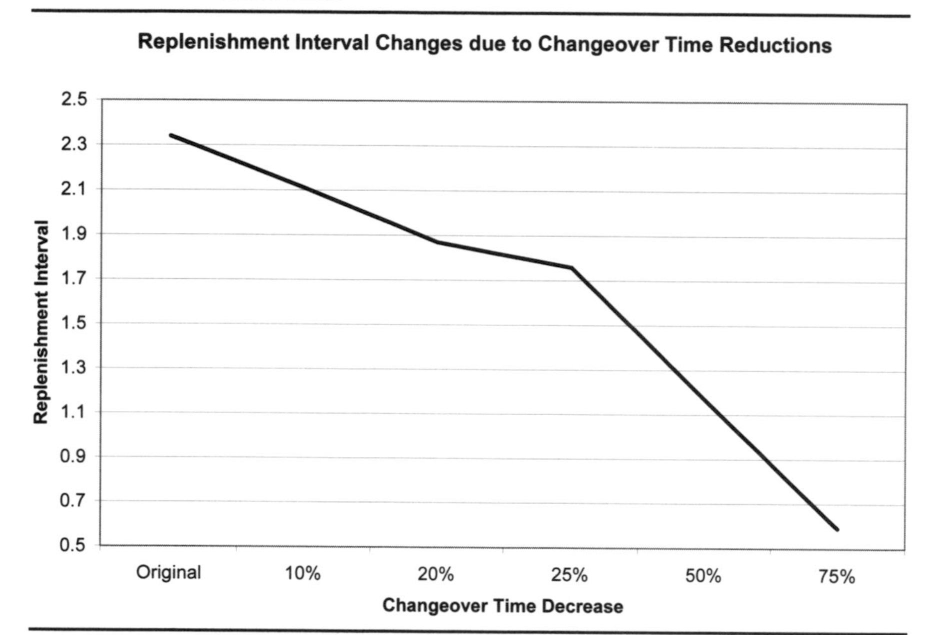

Figure 4-17. Impact of all three factors on replenishment intervals.

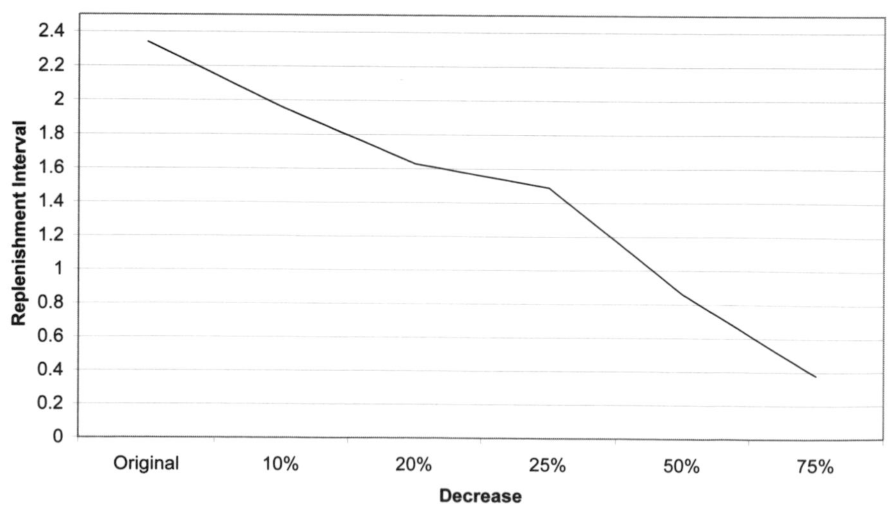

buffers for finished goods kanbans, make sure that you can deliver on the customer requirements (or your promises) in order to maintain customer satisfaction.

You can be aggressive with the internal and supplier buffers if you maintain a finished goods inventory buffer. The finished goods inventory can serve as the buffer for stock out of internal parts and supplier raw materials.

Internal Lead Times

Internal lead times refer to the process times to replenish parts. It also includes process constraints, such as chemical reaction times, cure or drying times, or inspections., Look at the process and size the buffer realistically to allow time for these activities to occur. Also, look at the lead times of your internal suppliers and factor in their lead times to resupply your process.

Supplier Lead Times

When looking at the lead times from the supplier, consider their production timeline as well as transportation time. Also, look at the supplier's reliability, quality, and delivery record when establishing their lead times. Don't pressure your suppliers into accepting unrealistic lead times. Don't put your production process in jeopardy (and ultimately customer service) by forcing fairytale commitments. To create a win–win environment, tell your supplier the target goals and let them accept the lead times.

When considering product transportation, also look at the transportation cost. You need to trade off the cost of holding inventory versus having more frequent deliveries. This analysis needs to consider the impact of partial shipments on your transportation budget and the space requirements to hold the larger quantity of material. (We will discuss options for minimizing freight costs due to partial shipments in Chapter 9.)

Comfort Level

Finally, determine your own desired inventory comfort level. Essentially, how much inventory do you need to sleep soundly at night? Here is where you need to be very careful that you don't let your desire for comfort make you into an inventory glutton.

When determining your inventory comfort level, use the previously collected data to challenge your beliefs about the necessary buffers. Is there fat in the process that causes you to overcompensate? What about any "hidden factory inventory"—such as multiple containers of material being staged at a downstream operation while still maintaining a control point?

Once again, look at how large of buffer the current operation uses. If you're not carrying extra material now, then why will you need it in kanban scheduling? The buffer requirements will be an excellent discussion topic for the team.

Determining the Final Buffer Size

When you have addressed these items, determine a final number for your buffer. Realistically look at the various items and determine if the events will occur in series or randomly to determine the final number. Essentially, will the buffers be additive or will one quantity be sufficient.

Calculating the Number of Kanban Containers

When you have determined how much buffer you require, then you are ready to calculate the final kanban container quantities. To calculate the number of containers, add together the buffer quantity and the replenishment interval, then multiply this number by the adjusted production quantity, and finally divide by the container capacity. Figure 4-18 shows the mathematical equation.

To determine all the container quantities, repeat this calculation for each of the production part numbers produced by the proc-

Figure 4-18. Equation for calculating the container quantity.

$$\text{Container Quantity} = \frac{(\text{Buffer Quantity} + \text{Replenishment Interval Quantity})}{\text{Container Quantity}}$$

Where:

$$\text{Buffer Quantity} + \text{Replenishment Interval Quantity} = (\text{Buffer} + \text{Replenishment Interval}) \times \text{Adjusted Production Requirement}$$

ess. Figures 4-19 and 4-20 show buffer assumptions and the container calculations for the examples in Figures 4-9 and 4-10.

Perform a Reality Check

When your calculations are complete, the hard part is done. You now need to look at the results of these calculations and assess their reality. At this point don't let funky numbers stop the process. If you get results that look strange, then step back and look at the assumptions. Follow the steps outlined below to drive out the culprit.

When you look at the final calculations, ask yourself these questions:

- ❑ Do the calculated quantities look like my current process?
- ❑ Does the inventory remain the same or decrease?

If you answer No to one of these questions, then you need to review your data to determine how you arrived at these numbers. Conversely, if you answer Yes, then you should also check your data to determine whether the new quantities look is unrealistically low.

(text continues on page 68)

Figure 4-19. Container calculations for the example in Figure 4-9.

Schedule Interval: Daily

Part Number	Part Name	Interval Production Requirement	Adjusted Production Requirements	Time Required for Production (in minutes)	Buffer	Replenishment Quantity	Container Size	Buffer Container Quantity	Replenishment Container Quantity	Comments
A	Red Carnival Ring	500	515	129	515	1030	500	2	3	
B	Blue Carnival Ring	800	825	200	800	1650	50	16	33	

1 x 515

2 x 515

515 / 500

1030 / 500

Replenishment Interval = **1.58 or 2**

Average Inventory= $\frac{\text{Replenishment Interval + Buffer}}{2}$

= (2+ 1) / 2 = **1.5 Days**

Buffer Assumptions:

Safety Stock	1
Advertised Delivery Commitment	0
Process	0
Total	**1**

Since we have simple process with a quick changeover and a reliable supplier, we will hold one day of buffer inventory for safety stock and customer orders.
--we will not consider the 15 minute cooling time as needing buffer
--note we gain some buffer by scaling up our replenishment interval to 2 days from 1.58.

Figure 4-20. Container calculations for the example in Figure 4-10.

Schedule Interval: ____________

Part Number	Part Name	Interval Production Requirement	Adjusted Production Requirements	Time Required for Production (in minutes)	Buffer	Replenishment Quantity	Container Size	Buffer Container Quantity	Replenishment Container Quantity	Comments
3502		500	531	17	1063	1594	100	11	16	
3503		750	806	31	1611	2417	100	16	24	
3504		350	388	31	776	1164	100	8	12	
3505		250	269	4	537	806	100	5	8	
3506		500	537	9	1074	1611	100	11	16	
3507		500	531	17	1063	1594	100	11	16	
3508		1200	1237	47	2474	3711	100	25	37	
3509		1000	1074	98	2148	3222	100	21	32	
3510		900	932	27	1865	2797	100	19	28	
3511		100	107	3	215	322	100	2	3	

Replenishment Interval = **2.34 or 3**

Average Inventory= $\frac{\text{Replenishment Interval + Buffer}}{2}$

= (3 + 2) / 2 = **2.5 Days**

Buffer Assumptions:

Saftey Stock	**1**
Process	**0**
Supplier	**1**
Total	**2**

We have more complicated process due to all the part numbers but have a quick changeover and low downtime, we will hold one day of buffer inventory for safety stock and customer orders.
--we have no process curing requirements
--we added a day to finished products because we have an unreliable supplier.
--note we gain some buffer by scaling up our replenishment interval to 3 days from 2.34.

Some of the common pitfalls with initial calculations include:

- ❑ Container sizes force added inventory
- ❑ Incorrect production data—production requirements, scrap, downtime, and changeovers
- ❑ Incorrect buffer assumptions
- ❑ Incorrect capacity assumptions

The errors associated with each of these areas revolve around using data that reflects "what we think happens" versus "what really happens."

Container Sizes

When looking at the container-sizing issue, you are trying to determine whether the containers are too big. When the containers are too big, holding parts in full container quantities gives you added inventory. In this situation, you are experiencing a rounding error. You will see this error if your calculated days-on-hand inventory is much higher than the inventory levels for the other parts. Another tip-off to this problem will be a kanban quantity that requires only one container, but increases days-on-hand inventory levels. Don't be fooled by the container number—look at the quantity of parts being held.

To solve this problem, select smaller containers that hold fewer parts. If new containers are not an option, then look at storing less in each container to lower the quantity. If you decide to hold less inventory in the same containers, then make sure that all the containers hold the same quantity to maintain uniform counts. Also, if you select this option, consider modifying the existing carts to hold fewer parts to ensure that everyone loads the same amount.

To illustrate the impact of the containers being too big, let's revisit the container calculations in Figure 4-19. Part A's container quantities are much different from part B's. They are produced with the same mold and only differ in color. Could this be a calculation error? With a container quantity of 500, we must hold over one extra day of production. Therefore, the container for part A should be resized. Figure 4-21 shows the effects of the resized container.

Incorrect Production Data

Once you rule out containers as a culprit, determine whether you are using the correct production data. If you are using incorrect production requirements, you will either inflate or reduce the required run time. Check your current build plans and forecast. Have you used old data or artificially high requirements that drove up the production requirements? Also, review your scrap numbers for accuracy:

- ❑ Are the scrap quantities out of date?
- ❑ Has one scrap rate been applied in a broad brush when the different part numbers really have their own unique scrap rates?

Next, review your downtime data: Have you used real data or guessed? The downtime data will affect the time available for changeovers and can drive your replenishment interval to be negative. In the real world, a true negative replenishment interval means that you have a capacity problem. Therefore, when you calculate a negative replenishment interval, ask yourself: Am I running overtime or stocking out the customer?

The same issues apply to changeover data as for the scrap and downtime data. Are you using the real data or estimates? Did you use the same changeover times for all the parts when they are really different? Remember that since you are building a bank of time that allows you to cover all the changeovers, high changeover times result in higher replenishment intervals and higher inventories.

Incorrect Buffer Assumptions

The next item to consider is lead time. When assessing lead times ask these questions:

Figure 4-21. Corrected kanban quantities for Example 1.

Schedule Interval: Daily

Part Number	Part Name	Interval Production Requirement	Adjusted Production Requirements	Time Required for Production (in minutes)	Buffer	Replenishment Quantity	Container Size	Buffer Container Quantity	Replenishment Container Quantity	Comments
A	Red Carnival Ring	500	515	129	515	1030	***50***	***11***	***21***	New container quantity with resized containers
B	Blue Carnival Ring	800	825	200	800	1650	50	16	33	

Buffer Container Quantity (A): $\frac{515}{50}$ — Replenishment Container Quantity (A): $\frac{1030}{50}$

Replenishment Interval = **1.58 or 2**

Average Inventory= $\frac{\text{Replenishment Interval + Buffer}}{2}$

= (2+ 1) / 2 = **1.5 Days**

Buffer Assumptions:

Safety Stock	1
Advertised Delivery Commitment	0
Process	0
Total	**1**

Since we have simple process with a quick changeover and a reliable supplier, we will hold one day of buffer inventory for safety stock and customer orders.
--we will not consider the 15 minute cooling time as needing buffer
--note we gain some buffer by scaling up our replenishment interval to 2 days from 1.58.

- ❑ Did you use the lead time you would like to have or what you really need?
- ❑ Do you really need all the contingencies you have planned for in the buffer inventory?

Take a good look at the buffer and make sure you are comfortable—not extremely overweight!

Incorrect Capacity Assumptions

The last item to consider is the capacity issue. If you must produce on a six- or seven-day schedule to support your customer's five-day schedule, then you must adjust the production requirements accordingly to account for this disconnect. Essentially, if your customer is on a daily schedule, then sum the weekly requirements and divide by six or seven to get your daily production requirements. Without scaling the requirements, you inflate the customer's requirements.

If you must produce on a six- or seven-day schedule to support your customer's five-day schedule, then make sure your buffer reflects this production disconnect. Your buffer must allow you to keep the customer supplied even though they will pull at a greater rate than you can replenish during their workweek. Finally, assess if this is a long-term situation to determine whether you need additional capacity to match your demand.

Reconciling the Problem

Take a systematic look at each of these factors to see why your calculated quantities do not parallel how you currently produce. Also, remember that the door swings both ways, so do not automatically accept your calculated kanban quantities being dramatically reduced. As a rule of thumb, review your numbers if the calculated quantities drop by more than 10 to 15 percent.

Once you have finalized the kanban quantities, then you and your team are ready to design the kanban's structure, which is the subject of Chapter 5. The rest of this chapter discusses an approach that does not utilize such in-depth calculations, looks at sizing supplier kanbans and at calculating the savings from implementing kanban scheduling.

An Alternate Method for Sizing Your Kanban

A second method, which yields results without as much data collection or calculations as the first method, is to make your current production schedule quantities the kanban quantities. This method does not lead to inventory reductions, but does have several advantages for organizations that want to move out quickly on kanban scheduling. The advantages of this method are that it:

- ❑ Reduces data collection requirements and implementation time, since you simply make your existing schedule quantity the kanban quantity
- ❑ Eliminates worries over incorrectly calculating the quantities, since you already know that the current schedule supports the production requirements

Although you do not engage in the same in-depth calculations as the first method, you should still follow the suggestions presented later in Chapter 9 when considering reductions in the kanban quantities. By following these suggestions, you ensure that you are not creating a problem that costs more than the savings. (Remember, there is no free lunch—to reduce quantities some action must take place!)

For those organizations that have problems with following the schedule and are either underproducing or overproducing, you may find that this kanban will reduce your total inventory. The kanban can insert the necessary control if you design controls on containers and storage area. Figure 4-22 contains an example of this method using the data from Figure 4-10 (ten-part number) example.

Note that the quantities in Figure 4-22 differ from those calcu-

Figure 4-22. Example of the alternate method for sizing your kanban.

Based on your years of experience you decide to set up the kanban to run everything once per week. Using the same data as in Example 2, you figure your adjusted production requirements and determine the number of containers in your kanban. You decide to maintain a buffer of 2 days to protect yourself from stockouts and as a safety factor.

Schedule Interval: ____________

Part Number	Part Name	Interval Production Requirement	Adjusted Production Requirements	Time Required for Production (in minutes)	Buffer	Replenishment Quantity	Container Size	Buffer Container Quantity	Replenishment Container Quantity	Comments
3502		500	531	17	1063	2657	100	11	27	
3503		750	806	31	1611	4028	100	16	40	
3504		350	388	31	776	1939	100	8	19	
3505		250	269	4	537	1343	100	5	13	
3506		500	537	9	1074	2685	100	11	27	
3507		500	531	17	1063	2657	100	11	27	
3508		1200	1237	47	2474	6184	100	25	62	
3509		1000	1074	98	2148	5371	100	21	54	
3510		900	932	27	1865	4662	100	19	47	
3511		100	107	3	215	537	100	2	5	

Required Pieces for 5 days:

531	x 5	=	2657
806	x 5	=	4028
388	x 5	=	1939
269	x 5	=	1343
537	x 5	=	2685
531	x 5	=	2657
1237	x 5	=	6184
1074	x 5	=	5371
932	x 5	=	4662
107	x 5	=	537

Required Pieces for 2 day Buffer:

531	x 2	=	1063
806	x 2	=	1611
388	x 2	=	776
269	x 2	=	537
537	x 2	=	1074
531	x 2	=	1063
1237	x 2	=	2474
1074	x 2	=	2148
932	x 2	=	1865
107	x 2	=	215

lated by Method 1 (shown in Figure 4-20). The increased quantities reflect the difference between this method versus the calculation method—you have arbitrarily picked the kanban quantities and have not modeled the kanban after your system's capability. Therefore, you have not optimized the batch size—you still have excess production in the system.

Supplier Kanbans

When extending kanbans to suppliers, you need to assess their ability to resupply your process. This assessment should include: shipment intervals, delivery time, quality issues, reliability issues, and demand fluctuation. In terms of calculating their replenishment interval—don't bother. Don't dig into their data unless your initial discussions with the supplier on kanban quantities makes them want to add safety stock to your inventory. Otherwise, relay your requirements to them and let them accept the requirements.

Don't bully your suppliers into accepting your desired kanban plans—it is a recipe for disaster. You must work with them to develop a plan that they can support. Once you have a mutual agreement on the kanban quantities, then follow the steps outlined in Chapter 5 to develop a mutually agreeable design to control the kanban between your operation and your supplier.

If you encounter resistance when dealing with suppliers on establishing kanbans, determine whether their resistance is based on lack of knowledge or unwillingness to change. If you value the supplier, then you should consider attempting to educate them on the benefits of kanban. On the other hand, their resistance may be a signal to consider changing suppliers.

Setting Up Supplier Kanban Quantities

To develop the kanban quantity, look at the delivery interval. This becomes the maximum replenishment quantity. In other terms, if you get a weekly delivery, then the replenishment interval must be one week. As you might suspect, this delivery interval may be an opportunity for improvement. To reduce the interval, you must look at your needs and the cost, then communicate these desires to your supplier. Once again, get the supplier to accept these new requirements, don't force them.

When considering a decrease in the delivery interval, which means receiving more frequent shipments, don't forget to consider transportation cost. You may end up decreasing inventory while dramatically increasing transportation cost. We will address some creative ways to reduce the delivery intervals in Chapter 9 when we discuss continuous improvement.

To determine your buffer for a supplier kanban, consider the delivery time, quality level, reliability level, and demand fluctuation. To handle the first three items, use your historical data on the supplier's performance. Also, determine whether the buffer created to cover the demand fluctuation will cover these items. As a rule of thumb, the kanban safety stock should not be greater than the current safety stock.

To handle demand fluctuation, consider your current order variation. To assess variation, calculate an average and standard deviation of your last ten orders or some other representative timeframe. (Once again we remind everyone not to be intimidated by the statistics terms and use the canned functions found in most spreadsheet programs.) Look at the standard deviation to determine how much the quantities vary over time.

If the demand fluctuation for the product is greater than 25 to 30 percent, then seriously *reconsider* the implementation of kanban and stick with forecasting. Additionally, in situations of extreme demand fluctuation, wait until you have successfully implemented several internal kanbans before taking it on.

If the standard deviation is 5 percent of the average or less, then don't worry about demand fluctuation. In this case, create a buffer to just cover delivery, quality, and reliability.

If the demand fluctuation exceeds 5 percent, then use a confidence interval to size the buffer. The confidence interval is a statistical factor that predicts the likelihood of an event occurring. We would suggest using the confidence intervals generated for a normal distribution. To use the confidence interval to size the buffer, simply multiply the standard deviation by the confidence interval. This quantity will become your safety stock. Typically, we recommend a confidence interval of 90 to 99 percent depending upon the impacts of stocking out.

To eliminate the phobia associated with the use of statistics by mere mortals, we have listed confidence intervals for 85 percent to 99 percent in Figure 4-23. Additionally, to further explain this concept, Figure 4-24 shows an example of a buffer based on various confidence factors.

Notice in the Figure 4-24 example how the buffer gets smaller as you decrease your confidence interval. Therein lies the heart of selecting safety stock confidence interval—how much risk can you afford versus how much inventory do you want to hold?

From our experience it is best to perform a quick stock out analysis to see whether the calculated buffer would have supported the demand used to calculate the quantity. To perform this analysis:

- ❑ Subtract the demand quantity for each part number from the shipment (or average order) plus the calculated buffer.

Figure 4-23. Confidence intervals for sizing the kanban buffer with demand fluctuation.

Confidence Interval (based on a normal distribution)	**Value**
99%	2.326
97.5%	1.960
95%	1.645
92.5%	1.440
90%	1.282
87.5	1.150
85%	1.036

Figure 4-24. Calculating a buffer where demand fluctuation exists.

Calculating a Buffer Where Demand Variation Exists

Product	wk 1	wk 2	wk 3	wk 4	wk 5	wk 6	wk 7	wk 8	wk 9	wk 10	wk 11	wk 12	Average Usage	Standard Deviation
A	300	250	275	350	325	310	305	285	295	285	305	300	299	25
B	700	740	800	735	750	790	785	800	725	745	775	750	758	32
C	500	560	600	625	550	575	525	565	610	635	550	580	573	40
D	900	935	950	890	880	975	940	935	980	925	955	960	935	32
E	775	800	795	785	805	840	835	810	820	790	825	800	807	20

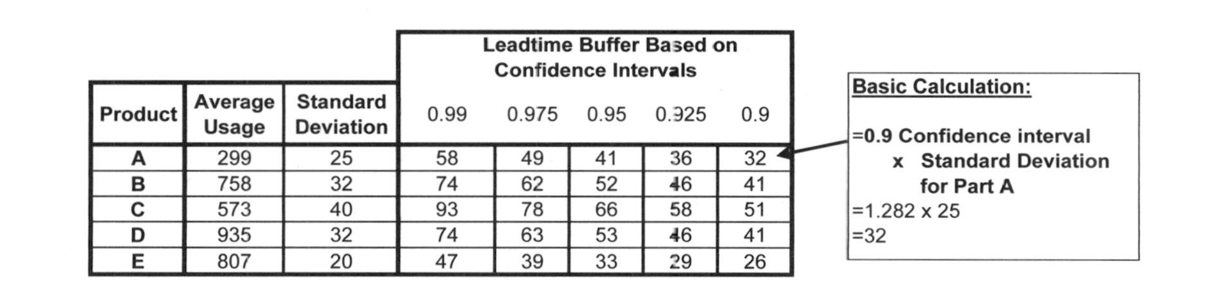

Product	Average Usage	Standard Deviation	Leadtime Buffer Based on Confidence Intervals 0.99	0.975	0.95	0.925	0.9
A	299	25	58	49	41	36	32
B	758	32	74	62	52	46	41
C	573	40	93	78	66	58	51
D	935	32	74	63	53	46	41
E	807	20	47	39	33	29	26

- ❑ Repeat this operation for all the demand quantities used to calculate the average shipment and buffer.
- ❑ Now look at the results to see whether the on-hand quantity (shipment plus buffer) went negative or close to negative.

If the on-hand quantity goes negative, then reassess the confidence interval used to calculate the buffer and make changes as appropriate. Figure 4-25 shows an example of the proposed analysis using the data from the example in Figure 4-24. Notice how stock outs occur more frequently in the example as the confidence interval decreases.

Finished Goods Kanbans

Follow the same advice for setting up finished goods kanbans as for the supplier kanban. Look at the customer demand and its fluctuation. However, in this case, you will need to assess your own delivery, quality, and reliability. Once you have that information, use the calculation method to calculate the kanban quantities.

If you have extreme demand fluctuation, again consider forecasting production versus kanban scheduling. Remember, two of your goals should be customer satisfaction and on-time deliveries that maintain customer satisfaction and manage cost.

Finally, follow the steps outlined in Chapter 5 on designing the controls for the kanban. Also, carefully consider any plans for making a finished goods kanban your first implementation project. You do not want to develop kanban implementation experience at the customer's expense.

Calculating the Benefits of Proposed Kanban

Once you have completed sizing the kanban, you may want to calculate the savings from implementing kanban. Typically, most senior managers will ask what the plant gains by implementing this sys-

Figure 4-25. Stock-out analysis using Figure 4-24 data.

Stock Out Analysis For Various Confidence Levels

Stockout Analysis with 99% Confidence Interval

Product	wk 1	wk 2	wk 3	wk 4	wk 5	wk 6	wk 7	wk 8	wk 9	wk 10	wk 11	wk 12
A	57	107	82	7	32	47	52	72	62	72	52	57
B	132	92	32	97	82	42	47	32	107	87	57	82
C	166	106	66	41	116	91	141	101	56	31	116	86
D	110	75	60	120	130	35	70	75	30	85	55	50
E	78	53	58	68	48	13	18	43	33	63	28	53

Stockout Analysis with 97.5% Confidence Interval

Product	wk 1	wk 2	wk 3	wk 4	wk 5	wk 6	wk 7	wk 8	wk 9	wk 10	wk 11	wk 12
A	48	98	73	***-2***	23	38	43	63	53	63	43	48
B	120	80	20	85	70	30	35	20	95	75	45	70
C	151	91	51	26	101	76	126	86	41	16	101	71
D	98	63	48	108	118	23	58	63	18	73	43	38
E	71	46	51	61	41	6	11	36	26	56	21	46

Stockout Analysis with 95% Confidence Interval

Product	wk 1	wk 2	wk 3	wk 4	wk 5	wk 6	wk 7	wk 8	wk 9	wk 10	wk 11	wk 12
A	40	90	65	***-10***	15	30	35	55	45	55	35	40
B	110	70	10	75	60	20	25	10	85	65	35	60
C	139	79	39	14	89	64	114	74	29	4	89	59
D	88	53	38	98	108	13	48	53	8	63	33	28
E	65	40	45	55	35	0	5	30	20	50	15	40

Stockout Analysis with 92.5% Confidence Interval

Product	wk 1	wk 2	wk 3	wk 4	wk 5	wk 6	wk 7	wk 8	wk 9	wk 10	wk 11	wk 12
A	35	85	60	***-15***	10	25	30	50	40	50	30	35
B	104	64	4	69	54	14	19	4	79	59	29	54
C	131	71	31	6	81	56	106	66	21	***-4***	81	51
D	82	47	32	92	102	7	42	47	2	57	27	22
E	61	36	41	51	31	***-4***	1	26	16	46	11	36

Stockout Analysis with 90% Confidence Interval

Product	wk 1	wk 2	wk 3	wk 4	wk 5	wk 6	wk 7	wk 8	wk 9	wk 10	wk 11	wk 12
A	31	81	56	***-19***	6	21	26	46	36	46	26	31
B	99	59	***-1***	64	49	9	14	***-1***	74	54	24	49
C	124	64	24	***-1***	74	49	99	59	14	***-11***	74	44
D	76	41	26	86	96	1	36	41	***-4***	51	21	16
E	57	32	37	47	27	***-8***	***-3***	22	12	42	7	32

tem, so you need to be prepared to address the question. The kanban savings come from:

- ❑ Reduced inventory
- ❑ Reduced carrying cost
- ❑ Reduced space
- ❑ Reduced obsolescence cost

To calculate the savings, look first at the calculated inventory versus the current inventory to determine the inventory reduction. This inventory reduction translates into reduced inventory carrying cost. To calculate the reduced carrying cost, provide the inventory reduction information to your accountants and they can do the calculations.

The space reduction savings will be based on the other potential uses for the freed-up space. This savings will take the form of cost avoidance because the new construction or leased space will not be required. However, the identification of the space reduction may have to wait for the next phase and the design of the controls. Additionally, you can only assign a dollar savings to the space reductions if you have some other use for this space.

The reduced obsolescence cost will be a future cost avoidance rather than a hard cost. This figure will be based on history and the expectation of not making the same mistakes again.

One last item on calculating cost savings is how you should respond to the management question of: Can you reduce the inventory further without making process improvements? Remember that stock outs can also cost money and that stock outs become more likely as the inventory is reduced.

On the other hand, the cost of a stock out is determined by where the stock out occurs. If you have a safety stock of finished goods, then your customer is protected from minor supply disruptions from your internal and external suppliers. Thus the finished goods safety stock can allow you to be aggressive with internal kanban sizes while minimizing the risk of customer stock outs.

So before you get too aggressive, remember the downside. Remember that part of your plan should be to reduce quantities after you have the kanban operating successfully, so don't worry about being conservative in the early days of the kanban.

What About Economic Order Quantities vs. the Calculated Kanban Quantity?

Many opponents of kanban like to discuss the need for economic order quantity (EOQ) calculations to determine whether the kanban quantities are correct. EOQ theories essentially attempt to calculate the batch size that minimizes the total cost. EOQ theory, however, does not consider the amount of inventory that can accumulate in the attempt to minimize the batch cost. EOQ supporters want to make these calculations to justify not doing kanban. Appendix E contains a detailed discussion of EOQ versus kanban and shows the benefits of kanban.

Regardless of the potential savings from using the EOQ model, you do not achieve the operational benefits of kanban scheduling without implementing kanban. Additionally, you have to store the inventory calculated by the EOQ model somewhere even if you have a lower batch cost. Therefore, when looking at the benefits of kanban, look beyond the raw dollar savings to the other benefits, such as flow, improved quality, empowerment of the operators, and space requirements.

Using the Workbook

The CD-ROM *Workbook* contains the kanban calculation form to help with the calculations for the kanban size. Use this form to calculate your kanban quantities. The workbook also contains the answers to the examples in Figures 4-9 and 4-10. Additionally, to facilitate the use of the equations, the *Workbook* and Figure 4-26 contain a summary of the equations presented in this chapter.

Summary

In this chapter you learned how to calculate the kanban quantities for your process. We proposed two methods for determining the quantities:

1. Calculate the optimal kanban quantity based on your current process data.
2. Use the current schedule quantity to set up the kanban.

Both methods have decided benefits. Method 1 allows you to optimize the kanban quantities based on the current state of the process, which requires accurate data gathering to make sure you get true results. Figure 4.26 summarizes the equations for using this method, and Figure 4.27 ties these equations to the replenishment interval worksheet.

If the initial results do not look correct when using Method 1, then look at these areas for possible errors:

- ❑ Container sizes force added inventory
- ❑ Incorrect production data—production requirements, scrap, downtime, and changeovers
- ❑ Incorrect buffer assumptions
- ❑ Incorrect capacity assumptions

Method 2 allows you to avoid the calculations and quickly determine the kanban quantities. However, this method maintains the potential excesses of the current schedule and achieves no calculated inventory reductions.

Regardless of which method you select, when reducing the kanban quantities, use the techniques presented in Chapter 9 to make the reductions. Remember that there is no free lunch, so don't arbitrarily reduce quantities. See Figures 4-14 through 4-17 for examples of how the continuous improvement process can dramatically affect the kanban quantities.

Figure 4-26. Summary of equations for using Method 1 to calculate the kanban size.

$$\text{Adjusted Production Requirements} = \frac{\text{Average Production Order}}{(1 - \text{System Scrap})}$$

$$\text{Adjusted Production Requirements} = \frac{\text{Average Production Order}}{(1 - \text{Process Scrap})\,(1 - \text{Downstream Scrap})}$$

$$\text{Available Time} = \text{Total Time in a Shift} - (\text{Planned and Unplanned Downtime})$$

$$\text{Available Time (Continuous Processes)} = \text{Total Time in a Shift} - (\text{Time for Planned Maintenance, Cleaning, and Breakdowns})$$

$$\text{Time Required for Production} = \text{Sum}\ (\text{Adjusted Production Requirements} \times \text{Cycle Time Per Part})$$

$$\text{Time Available for Changeovers} = \text{Total Available Time} - \text{Time Required for Production}$$

$$\text{Replenishment Interval} = \frac{\text{Total Time } \textit{Required} \text{ for Changeovers}}{\text{Total Time } \textit{Available} \text{ for Changeovers}}$$

$$\text{Container Quantity} = \frac{(\text{Buffer Quantity} + \text{Replenishment Interval Quantity})}{\text{Container Quantity}}$$

Where:

$$\text{Buffer Quantity \& Replenishment Interval Quantity} = (\text{Buffer} + \text{Replenishment Interval}) \times \text{Adjusted Production Requirement}$$

Figure 4-27. Application of the forms to the replenishment interval worksheets.

Schedule Interval: ______________

Part Number	Part Name	Interval Production Requirement	Adjusted Production Requirements	Time Required for Production (in minutes)	Leadtime Quantity	Replenishment Quantity	Container Size	Buffer Container Quantity	Replenishment Container Quantity	Comments

Multiply the interval production requirements by the scrap levels using the equations in Figure 4.2 or 4.3 to calculate the adjusted Production Requirements

Adjusted Production Requirements x Cycle Time Per Part

$$\frac{\text{Buffer Quantity}}{\text{Container Size}}$$

Adjusted Production Requirements x Buffer

Adjusted Production Requirements x Replenishment Interval

$$\frac{\text{Replenishment Quantity}}{\text{Container Size}}$$

Replenishment Interval = ________

Buffer Assumptions:

$$\textbf{Average Inventory} = \frac{\text{Replenishment Interval + Buffer}}{2}$$

When you begin the process of implementing supplier kanbans, use demand data to develop the order quantity and buffer quantity. Follow the steps layed out in the chapter to calculate these quantities. Once you have these quantities, conduct a quick stockout analysis to confirm the appropriateness of the buffers.

When implementing supplier kanbans, make sure that the supplier agrees to your plans. To develop the kanban quantities, use the information in this chapter to determine the necessary buffers. We also propose use of confidence intervals to handle demand variation.

Use the same process proposed for the supplier kanban to size finished goods kanbans. Do not make a finished goods kanban your first project since learning kanban at the customer's expense may not be the wisest move.

When you have the kanban sized, look at the potential savings. Savings can come from inventory reductions, space reductions, carrying cost reductions, and elimination of obsolescence cost.

Review Appendix A if you have concerns about how EOQ compares to the proposed calculation process. Appendix E proposes an EOQ model and contrasts EOQ versus kanban. Regardless of the potential savings from using the EOQ model, you do not achieve the operational benefits of kanbans without implementing kanban. Additionally, you have to store the inventory calculated by the EOQ somewhere even if you have a lower batch cost.

Finally, the form in the CD-ROM *Workbook* will help you calculate the replenishment interval, buffer, and container quantities for your kanban.

CHAPTER

5

DEVELOPING A KANBAN DESIGN

Many people think they only need to figure out the size of the kanban and they are ready to start up their kanban. Unfortunately, once they calculate the kanban size they are only partially ready. To successfully implement a kanban requires not only setting container quantities, but also the development of a design, deployment of the design, and training of the design. This chapter and the next two chapters will address these three topics. Thus our process flow expands, as shown in Figure 5-1, to include designing the kanban.

When we think of kanban design we should think about three things:

1. Selecting the signaling mechanism for the kanban
2. Developing the rules for operation of the kanban
3. Creating the visual management plans for the kanban

Figure 5-1. The next step in the implementation of kanban scheduling: the kanban design.

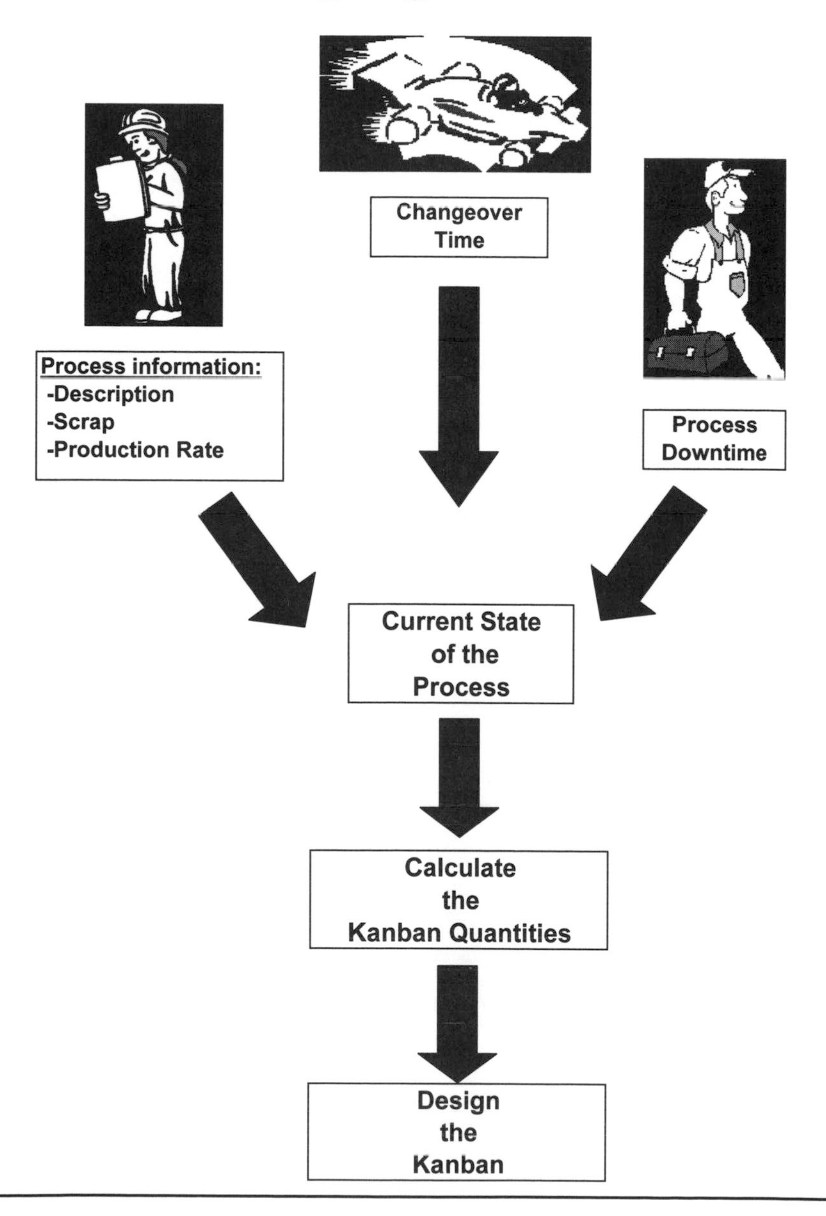

These three items will ensure that you have a design that can be successfully implemented. Consider each activity as an integral step on the road to successful implementation.

Setting up the scheduling signal means to develop a signal that tells the production operators when to:

- ❑ Produce parts
- ❑ Change over
- ❑ Stop production

This signal replaces the traditional production schedule. The signal can be cards, buggies, objects on a fixed board, etc. The only requirements for selecting a signal are that it must be unambiguous, readily understood, and maintainable.

The rules you develop for the kanban will drive its operation. They will be the guidance that allows the operators to control the production schedule. The rules should include directions on sequences, decision points, and anything else that will help production operators make the right decisions. Spell out who will perform what task, when to get help, who to go to for help, and what these "helpers" will do when contacted. The rules should use pictures and diagrams to facilitate understanding. Remember: if you want something to happen, then it better be in the rules.

Once you have developed a signal mechanism and the rules, you will need to determine how to communicate this information. The information should be communicated through your visual management plan. The visual management plans should include: putting up signs, marking or taping floors, posting the rules, posting job aids, etc. Your goal should be that anyone who walks into the production and material storage areas should immediately be able to determine the status of production, what needs to be produced next, and where to get parts. Additionally, your visual management plan should communicate all the other "everybody knows" stuff—because everyone doesn't know.

Team Activity

Although you may have skated on involving the entire team in the previous steps, don't do it in the design phase. By creating a design as a team you will increase buy-in and are more likely to create a design that addresses all the issues.

The team will be able to identify the roadblocks to the success of the program. A successful design will answer the team's concerns and questions. When the design achieves this objective, then you're on your way to a successful kanban implementation.

Also, consider the kanban a work in progress. As you operate the kanban and gain more information, make changes that will:

- ❑ Improve its operation
- ❑ Integrate in new information
- ❑ Correct the loopholes that prevent flow

Don't be afraid to change kanban quantities when the calculated amounts do not let the preferred production sequence occur as planned.

Develop a Concept That Works for Your Organizational Culture

As you embark on the design, keep the culture of your organization in the back of your mind. Organizational culture will play a big role in implementation success. Consider the level of empowerment that exists in the production operation. Then consider past history. Use this information to develop a scheduling system that fits your culture. Do not select a signal just because you "saw it" somewhere else and it looked neat. Make sure you carefully consider how the production operators will manage the signal and their ability to make decisions based on the signals provided. Use these guidelines when selecting the scheduling signal:

- ❑ Keep the signals simple
- ❑ Make sure that each signal only directs one course of action
- ❑ Don't have duplicate signals
- ❑ Make the signals easy to manage

Kanban Cards

When most people think of kanban they automatically think of kanban cards, probably because the Toyota Production System relies heavily on the use of cards for their signals. But, be aware that many people have strong feelings about the use of cards as signals because of bad experiences with losing the cards or the cards being mismanaged.

What are these mystical items called kanban cards? They are essentially pieces of paper that travel with the production item and identify the part number and amount in the container. The cards can include other information, such as who to call for service or when to take the cards back to the production department. The cards are typically about the size of the old computer punch cards, but they can be any size that works for you. We also recommend that they be brightly colored so that they are easy to spot as they make their way through the process. Figures 5-2 and 5-3 show examples of two kanban cards.

The kanban card serves as both a transaction and a communication device. Kanbans that use cards usually follow this simple routine:

1. A card is placed with the completed production container (typically, in a protective sleeve of some sort).
2. The container with its kanban card is then moved into a staging area to wait for use.
3. When the container is moved to a production work center for

Figure 5-2. Kanban card used between processes in the same factory.

Part Number:	*80800-14898*
Part Name:	10 V Power Supply
Production Line:	Line A
Container Type:	Plastic 12 × 14
Container Quantity:	20
Storage Location:	Portable Radio Line
Production Operation:	**50**
Bin Location:	**C-3**

use, the kanban card is pulled from the container to signal consumption.

4. The kanban card is then placed in a cardholder, or kanban post, to await transit back to the production line.
5. When the kanban card returns to the production line, it is

Figure 5-3. Parts ordering kanban card used between supplier and customer.

Part Number:	*80800-14898*
Part Name:	10 V Power Supply
Supplier:	Smith Electronics
Vendor Number:	133345
Container Type:	Plastic 12 × 14
Container Quantity:	20
Delivery Interval:	Daily
Storage Location:	Portable Radio Line
Production Operation:	**50**
Bin Location:	**C-3**
Delivery Location:	**Dock 5**

placed in a cardholder that has been set up to provide a visual signal for operation of the line. (Figure 5-4 is a picture of a cardholder rack.)

6. The kanban card sits in the cardholder waiting to be attached to a completed production container.

Although the cards are conceptually simple, many people have had varying levels of success with the cards. In their rush to emulate the system used by the Toyota Production System, many "would be" practitioners have applied a one-size-fits-all philosophy and ended up with failures or logistics problems when trying to manage the cards. The inappropriate use of the cards and the unjustified shrinking of their inventories drove many materials and production managers crazy trying to keep up. These horror stories also became the seeds of the opposition to kanban and a cornerstone of the MRP production scheduling craze.

Figure 5-4. Kanban cardholder rack.

So if cards are so bad, then how do you make them work? To be successful with kanban cards, you must make it easy for people to pull the cards. If you set up the kanban so that people have to backtrack, then they will forget from time to time. The key to utilizing the cards is to put the card post in the path of the material's flow. Also, make sure the rules specify who picks up the cards and how often to ensure the cards make a round trip. For example, if the parts are staged at the production cell, then place the card post at the first operation in the cell.

When you make kanban cards convenient to use and specify the return loop, kanban cards work just fine.

Are There More Options Than Just Kanban Cards?

Luckily, the answer to the above question is a resounding yes. The kanban signal can be anything that makes sense to your production operation and conveys a clear replenishment signal. As with the kanban cards, always put the signal in the path of the material flow and have a plan for getting the scheduling signals back to the production operations. Some of the more common methods (and variations of these options) are discussed below to give you ideas for your own implementation:

- ❑ Look-see
- ❑ Kanban boards
- ❑ Two-card system
- ❑ Faxbans (or e-mails)
- ❑ Electronic kanban
- ❑ Warehouse racks
- ❑ Move/production kanban

These options and their variations are by no means the only options available. When looking at possible designs, open yourself and your team to all possibilities. Be creative—invent new options of your own or springboard off of our suggestions to create your own variation. (By the way—send us a picture and description of any new ones you create or any new variations of our suggestions. We also want to keep expanding our knowledge.)

Look-See

Whenever possible, your kanban signal should rely on the most reliable sensor—your eyes. This form of kanban signal, called a "look-see," consists of visual signals such as floor markings or signs that tell you at a glance when to replenish the item. The basic rule with a look-see signal is that if you can see the yellow signal, then it's time to replenish the item. The red, or danger, signal is also integrated into this scheme. Look-see signals greatly aid in the implementation of the kanban supermarkets discussed in Appendix B. Figure 5-5 shows an example of a look-see scheduling signal.

A special case of the look-see signal is the use of containers as the signal. The container is specifically marked to show the part number and the production quantity. When the container returns to the production process, it goes back into the queue. When you have accumulated a certain quantity of containers, this constitutes

Figure 5-5. Look-see scheduling signal.

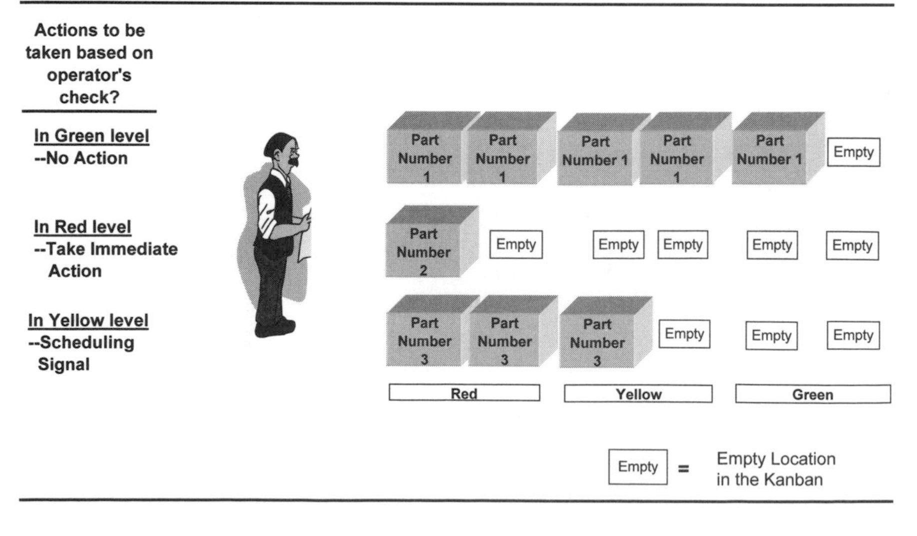

the yellow scheduling signal. The production operator will know what and how much to put into the container based on the information or standards set for the specific part number. Figure 5-6 shows a container used as a kanban signal.

Under very limited conditions, you can also set up a look-see kanban using warehouse racks. The racks can be painted or numbered to correspond to provide look-see signal. However, unless visibility can be maintained, this option can be tough to manage in a quick scan mode due to the typical size of racks. Forget this option if you are trying to cover several rows of racks or have conditions that hinder seeing the top rows. Instead, consider the card option discussed in the next section.

Another special case of the look-see signal is flow lanes. The flow lanes offer visual management of production material while managing stock rotation at the same time. Flow lanes are essentially aisles that the product travels down toward the production process.

Figure 5-6. Container used as a kanban signal.

The product enters the flow lane from the back and moves forward in its lane. You will interpret the schedule signals just like any other look-see kanban.

The lanes, while very visual, can be hard to keep straight if you make them too long. This problem can be avoided by putting guides in the aisles (as shown in Figure 5-7) or using flow racks (as shown in Figure 5-8).

The guides are typically angle iron strips, sheet metal frames, or rails that have been attached to the floor. The guides allow the containers to move only in the specified direction.

The flow racks (or angled roller conveyors) use gravity to move the containers forward as the previous container is removed from the flow lane. The roller conveyor is readily available and can be found in most material handling or industrial sales catalogs. However, as the flow racks get longer and the containers get wider and

Figure 5-7. Flow lanes with guides to control movement of containers.

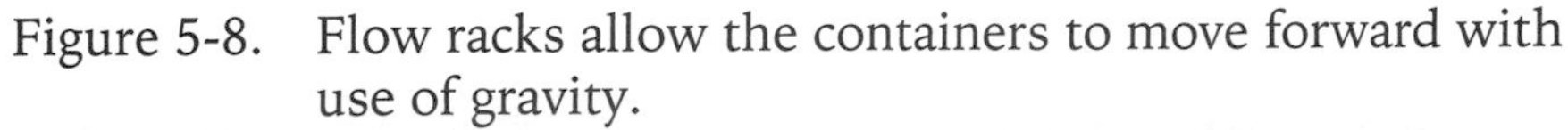

Figure 5-8. Flow racks allow the containers to move forward with use of gravity.

heavier (such as pallet size), then the price tag for the flow racks can get very big.

If floor storage space is in short supply, flow racks can be purchased as stacked rows. This option will require you to answer a number of questions about container size and weight. Therefore, if stacked flow racks have appeal, contact a material handling specialist for assistance.

One other item to consider when setting up your flow lanes is to be sensitive to the number of rows from which product can be pulled. You may defeat the stock rotation benefit if you allow too many choices, as for example if the operators withdraw the containers closest to their operation, leaving the material staged further away to age. There is no stock answer for this, but use common sense and talk with your operators.

Kanban Boards

The kanban boards are a variation on the kanban cards. Instead of the cards, the board simply utilizes magnets, plastic chips, colored washers, etc. as the signal. The objects represent the items in inventory. However, instead of chasing cards around the building, you are moving the objects around on a board. The movement of the objects corresponds to the production and consumption of full containers of product. The process works like this:

- ❑ As a container of product is completed and moved into inventory, an object gets moved into the inventory section of the board.
- ❑ When the container is consumed or moved to a staging area for consumption, then an object gets moved into the awaiting production section of the board.

To determine what gets produced next, you look at the board and follow the rules.

Figure 5-9 graphically shows an example of the movement of objects on a kanban board. Notice how only the bottom of the board contains the red, yellow, and green signals? This allows for only one scheduling signal—even though the number of colored cells in the top and bottom sections is equal. Figure 5-10 shows a picture of a kanban board that uses magnetic pieces for scheduling signals.

The pieces used to the show board status and product movement are not limited to magnets. In fact, kanban boards using chips, washers, etc. can actually simplify movements on the board. The simplification comes from collapsing the "awaiting production" area of the board, as shown in Figure 5-11.

Kanban boards work best when two conditions exist in the relationship of inventory storage and the production process:

1. The board can be positioned in the path of the flow of *all* the material to the customer (similar to the card system)
2. The board can be positioned so that the production process can see it and follow the visual signals

Figure 5-9. Kanban board set-up and operation.

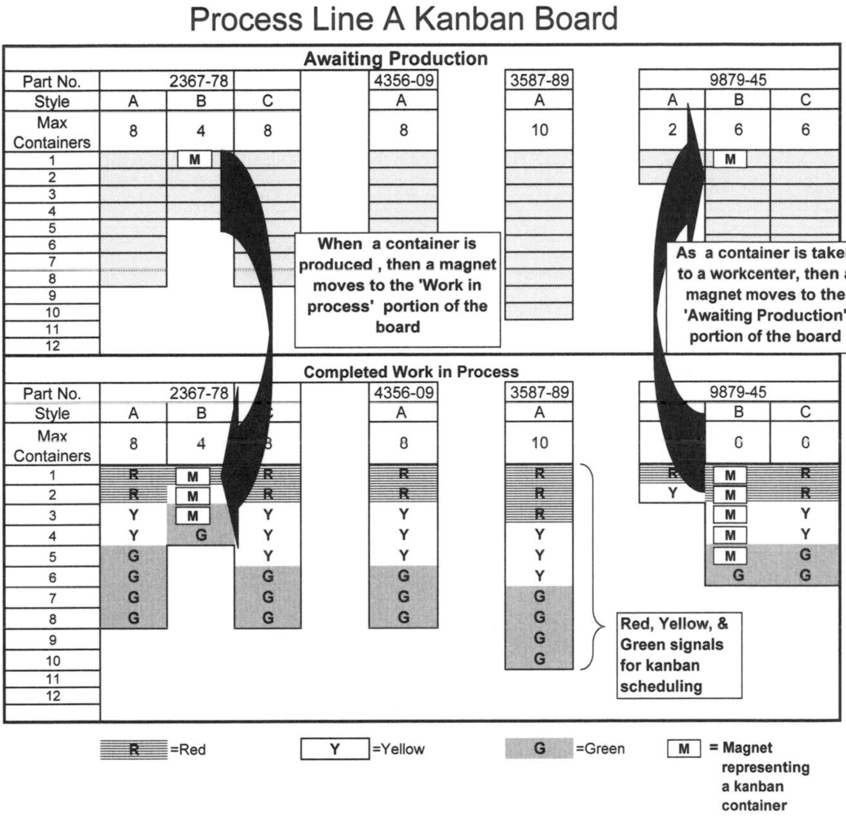

Process Line A Kanban Board

Awaiting Production

When a container is produced, then a magnet moves to the 'Work in process' portion of the board

As a container is taken to a workcenter, then a magnet moves to the 'Awaiting Production' portion of the board

Completed Work in Process

Red, Yellow, & Green signals for kanban scheduling

R =Red Y =Yellow G =Green M = Magnet representing a kanban container

If these conditions can be met, then the board works wonders. It is visual and provides an up-to-date schedule status. It also eliminates one of the major objections to the kanban cards—people forget to return the cards to the card racks. The board also makes it easy to add and subtract containers. In fact, if these two conditions can be met, then we recommend boards as our first choice for a scheduling signal.

Two-Card System

A two-card kanban system works well in situations where product rotation is also an issue. This system, which is a hybrid of the kan-

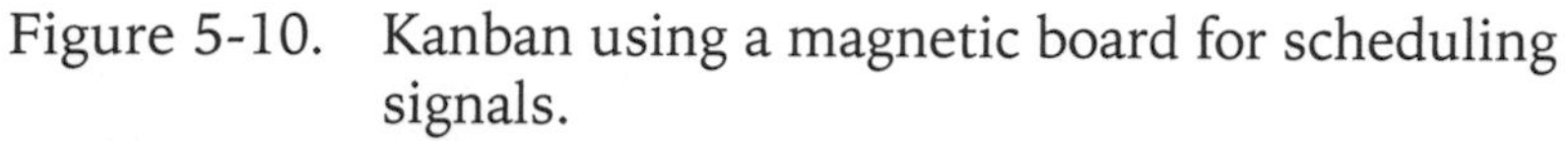

Figure 5-10. Kanban using a magnetic board for scheduling signals.

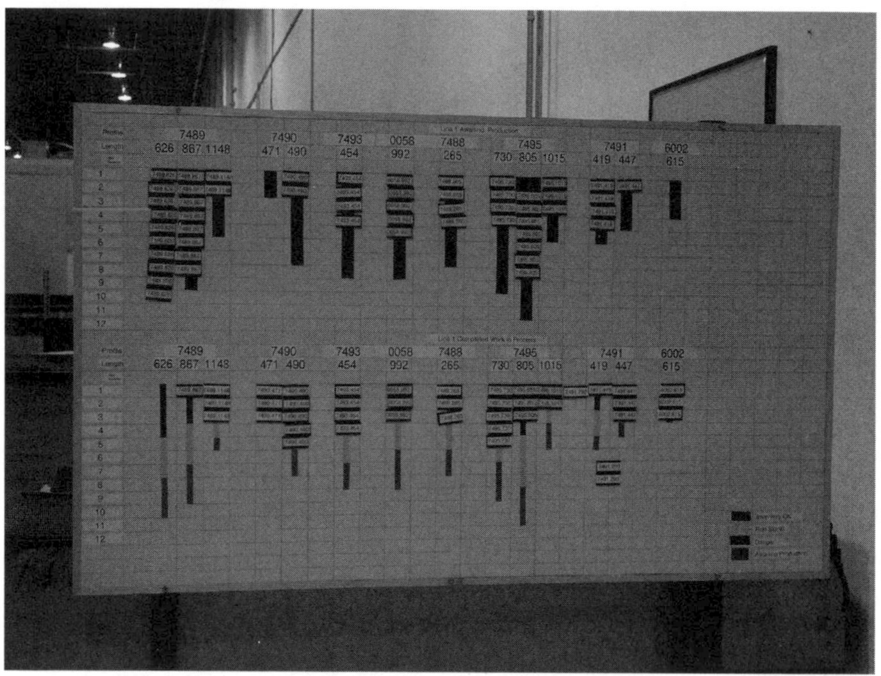

ban board and the kanban card racks, uses two companion kanban cards to signal location and product age. It is typically used for large items where flow racks are not utilized. The two-card system works like this:

- ❑ When product is produced or received from a vendor, two cards are pulled from a kanban card rack and filled out:
  - One kanban card goes with the container
  - The second kanban card goes into a special first-in, first-out (FIFO) box.
- ❑ Whenever a container of this product is needed, a material handler goes to the FIFO box and pulls out the bottom card.
- ❑ The material handler then goes to the location written on the card and pulls this product for the production operation.

Figure 5-11. Kanban using plastic chips.

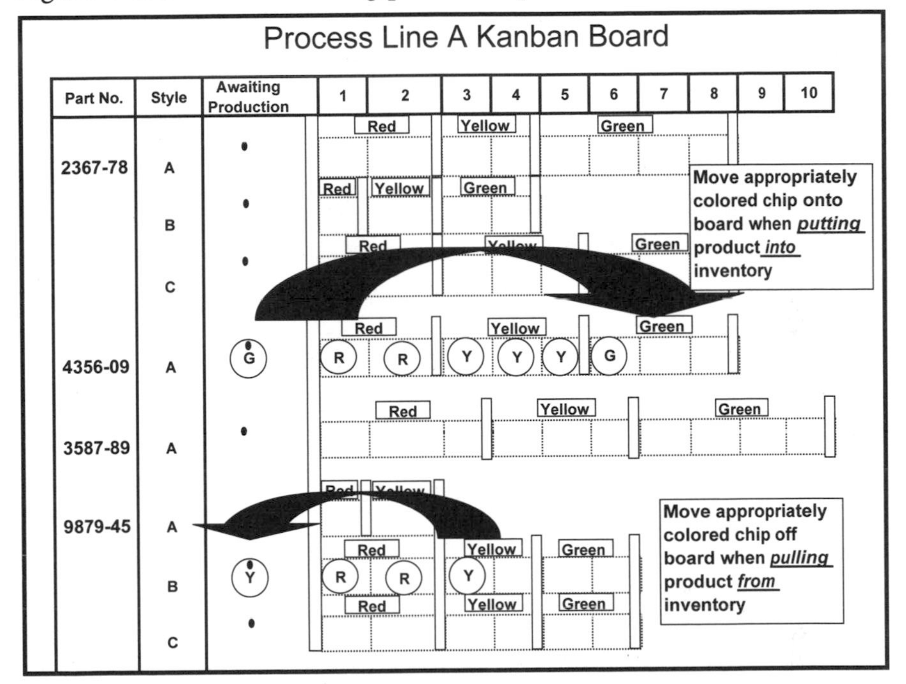

- The material handler then takes both cards and places them in the kanban card racks, which show the schedule signals for production or reorder.

This system, if maintained, allows pallet size items to flow while managing product rotation. It works especially well when used for floor stacked items. As you might suspect, detailed rules and training play a large part in the success of this kanban system. Figure 5-12 shows the FIFO box used for this kanban. Figure 5-13 shows an example of the cards used for a two-card kanban.

Faxbans (or E-mails)

Faxbans (or their twenty-first-century cousin—e-mail) are just a special variation of the kanban card system. They are used to order

Figure 5-12. FIFO box used for the two-card kanban system.

replenishment of products within large plants, from off-site warehouses, or from vendors. This system works as follows:

- ❑ You set up a preset replenishment notification time with the recipient (for example, 12 PM each day).
- ❑ You then look at your requirements and fax or e-mail the order before the appointed time.
- ❑ The recipient then fills the order and delivers it at agreed-to time and intervals (for example, at 7 AM the next day for the previous day's 12 pm order).

Figure 5-13. Example of the cards used for a two-card system.

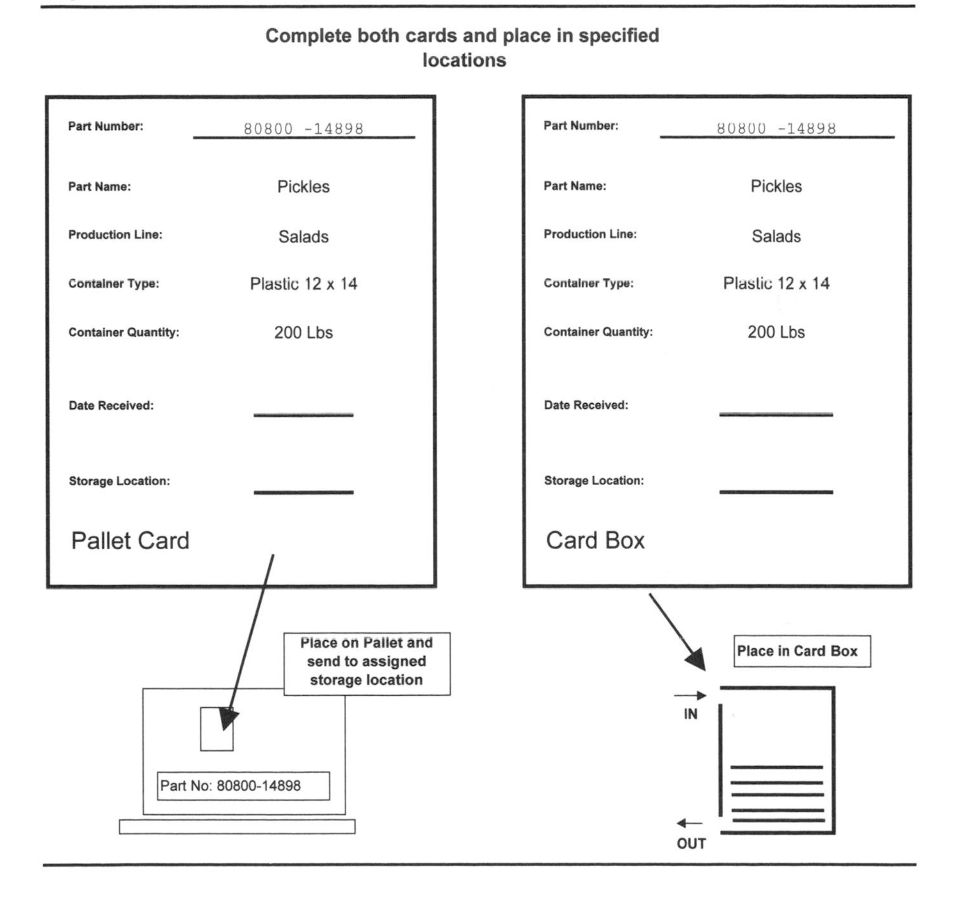

The system is a means of communicating usage requirements over a predetermined interval. The delivery times are typically short—under one week and, more than likely, under one day. The system helps cut down on the time wasted trying to manage purchasing organization bureaucracies, which allows for shorter lead times. The system requires preplanning and coordination. Because this system is faceless, make sure you plan on backup personnel to keep it going during absences and vacations.

The format of the fax sheet (or e-mail) should be agreed to by both parties. This sheet becomes the vehicle for communication and it should not be subject to interpretation. The typical sheet includes date, time, routing instructions, part numbers, and order quantity. These sheets should be preprinted or set up as a template on a word processor program to control uniformity and speed up the information transfer process. It is also helpful to include an area on the form for special information or instructions. Figure 5-14 shows an example of a typical faxban sheet.

Electronic Kanban

Electronic kanban is a term many people use when trying to avoid kanban implementation. They try to pass off their MRP systems as

Figure 5-14. Typical faxban sheet.

Smith Brothers Manufacturing
10101 ABC Street
St. Louis, MO 76890

Date: ____________________

24 Hour Delivery Faxban Order Sheet—
Please deliver quantity ordered for tomorrow to the dock door listed at the specified time. If you have any questions, then call Jack Jones, Purchasing Manager, at (555) 555-5555.

Vendor: Acme Supply
Fax # 555-444-4444

Please ship the following items:

1. 6—100 Foot coils of #12 Wire, red insulation
2. 4—Cartons of P/N 234567 switches.
3.
4.
5.

Deliver to: Dock door 7
Delivery Time: 8:30 AM

a kanban system because they are keeping their inventory levels at four to five days. However, as previously stated, a kanban only exists when production is based on usage (or demand). Therefore, since forecast systems do not meet this requirement, MRP scheduling systems do not meet the requirements to be called a kanban.

With this differentiation out of the way, we can now discuss what an electronic kanban really is. A true electronic kanban is a high-tech version of the faxban. It automatically transmits requirements or allows suppliers to access the customer's inventory status and ship replacement material. These systems are not conceptually difficult, but implementation can be complex. The systems are typically developed by larger companies that want to simplify their ordering process. They tend to be one of a kind and are tailored to a single company and its applications. Participating suppliers must be able to log into the system to receive the data. Therefore, the implementing company must be ready to provide assistance to their vendors.

Warehouse Racks

Earlier in the chapter we discussed using racks as a look-see signal. At that point we said this was a limited option and to use racks only if the area in question was manageable.

However, racks are an effective storage method that should not be avoided as a candidate for implementing kanbans when paired with an effective control mechanism. Racks simply need to have a companion tracking system to allow easier visual management of the storage space.

Any of the previously mentioned systems will work with the rack storage. The kanban cards, kanban boards, two-card system, or electronic kanban will help maintain status of the production items kept in the storage racks. With special emphasis on layout of the scheduling system, product rotation can also be integrated into the kanban structure.

However, as your storage space grows, we especially recommend using some sort of electronic kanban to maintain inventory levels. The summation capability and review format allow for easier transmittal of replenishment orders while still allowing you to manage visually. Again, the uniqueness of these applications can sometimes lead to the need for outside programmers for implementation; for example, cost can be an issue!

Move/Production Kanban

The move/production kanban was first introduced by Toyota to handle kanbans between work centers. This kanban utilizes a production kanban to signal production and a move kanban to order material from storage. This kanban is very useful when one work center supplies common parts to numerous other work centers.

To explain the sequence, envision two work centers, A and B:

- Work center A supplies work center B.
- The parts from work center A are stored in a warehouse or supermarket until needed by work center B.

In a move/production kanban, when work center B needs another container of parts, it removes the move kanban card from the container and sends it to the warehouse. At the warehouse, a production kanban card is removed from the full container and replaced with the move kanban card from work center B. The production kanban card is then sent to work center A to authorize production of more parts. The full container with a move kanban is sent to work center B. Figure 5-15 shows this relationship.

Note that the system can be confusing and needlessly compli-

Figure 5-15. Move/production kanban steps.

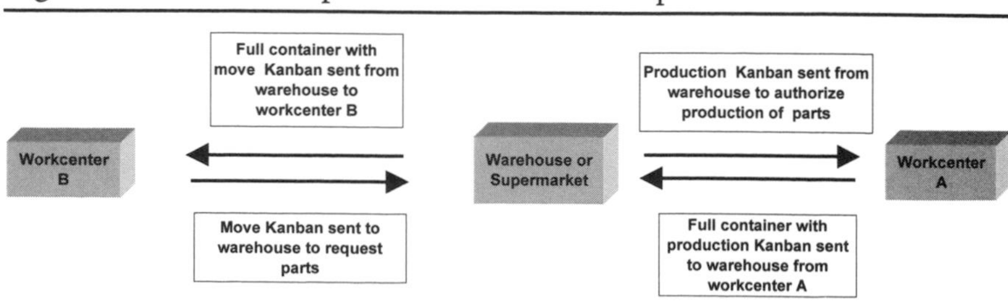

cated when a work center supplies only one work center. However, when this work center supplies multiple work centers, it can be very useful. Figure 5-16 shows the relationship of one work center supplying multiple work centers.

Determining Schedule Signal Logistics

Once you have selected the scheduling signal, you need to determine the signal and material logistics. You, and your team, need to determine how material and the kanban signal will move from the production process to downstream customers. You will also need to determine how the signal will make it back to the production process.

Figure 5-16. Move/production kanban with one work center supplying multiple work centers.

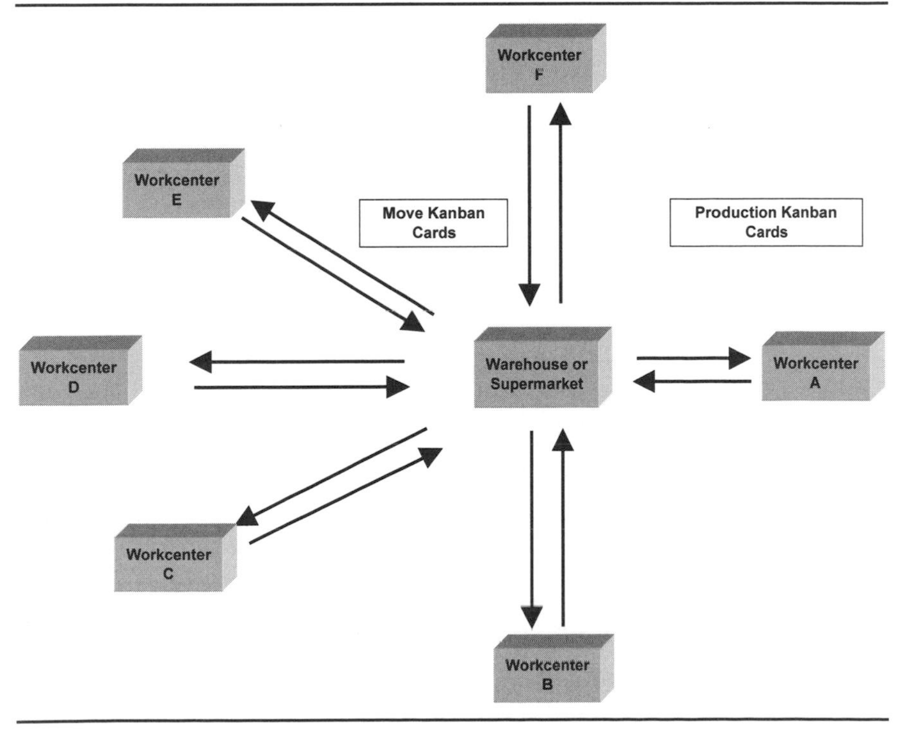

If you have not already done so then this is the perfect time to take a fieldtrip to the production process. During this fieldtrip, walk the path of the materials. Start at the production process and follow the same path the material takes to its customer. Look for stops, staging problems, and convenient ways to move the signals. Take this opportunity to determine the who, what, and when of the process. As Figure 5-17 shows, you must create a continuous loop of material and signals flowing from the production process to the customer and back again.

One of the first logistic decisions will be how the material will be staged or whether you need to change how you currently stage your production material. Consider how the layout facilitates maintenance of the kanban cycle when making the staging decision. Also, do you want to keep the material in one spot or dispersed to the customer cells? Consider how your organization manages material storage and stage the material where the highest kanban discipline will be maintained.

Consider the logistics of how the material moves into and out of the staging area. Look at the rotation issues and the ability to maintain order in the staging area.

When you have made the staging decision, make a drawing of the final layout. The drawing does not need to be fancy—use a CAD drawing, MS Excel, or just a simple pencil drawing. The drawing helps to explain the flow and can serve as a training aid later. Figure 5-18 shows an example flow diagram drawn with MS Excel.

As part of the design, you and your team will also need to decide where the scheduling signal will be located. When making this decision, remember the intent of the signal is to provide information for the production operators to make scheduling decisions. With this in mind, locate the scheduling signal as close to the operation as possible and in a very visible position. At the same time, position the scheduling signal so that you "pull" material through the production process instead of "pushing" it.

Make sure the signal location is also convenient to keep updated as production occurs. For kanban cards signal, locate the card post forward of the material storage area. This step will help in keeping the signal updated.

Figure 5-17. The kanban design must create a continuous flow of materials and signals.

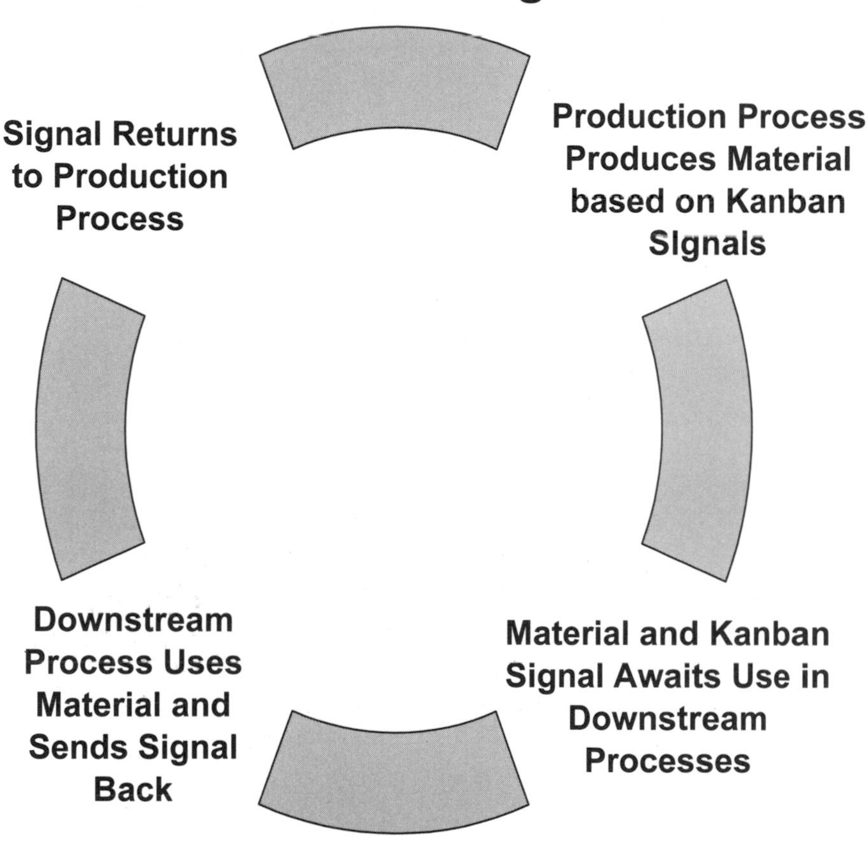

Develop Rules for the Kanban

Once the team has selected a kanban signal, it's time to develop the rules that govern its operation. The rule should address:

Figure 5-18. Kanban flow diagram.

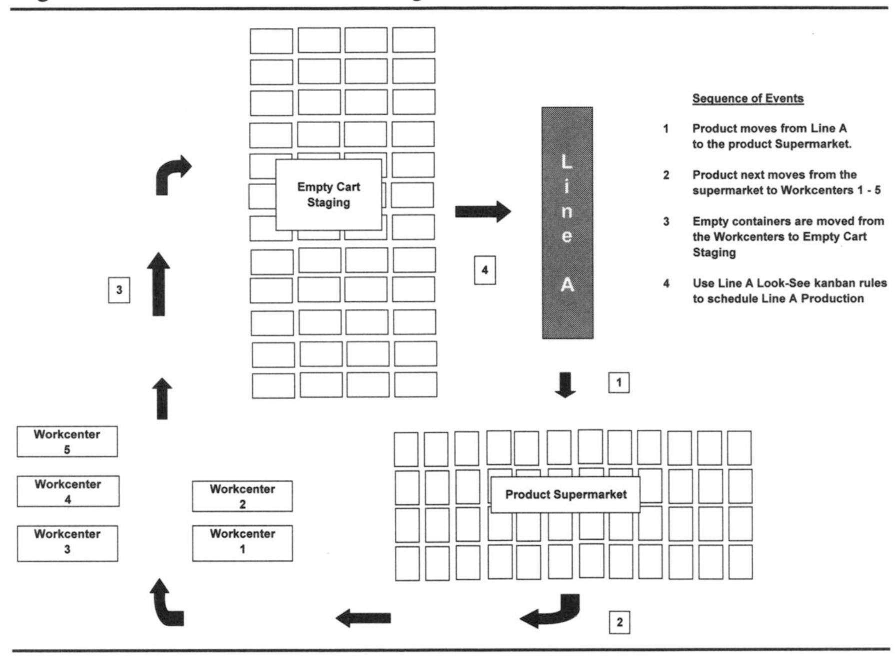

- ❑ The part numbers covered by the kanban
- ❑ How the design works—how the cards, magnets, etc., move
- ❑ The meaning of the scheduling signals and how to interpret them
- ❑ Any scheduling rules of thumb (if required)
- ❑ The preferred production sequence (if one exists)
- ❑ Who to go to and what the "helpers" should do when contacted
- ❑ Any special quality or documentation requirements

Remember, you are drafting the rules to communicate how to run the kanban and to allow the process operators to schedule the line. The only way the production operators can take over scheduling the line is by the rules providing clear direction and scheduling guidance.

The rules should be specific and designed to make sense for

your operation and the process. The rules should assign responsibilities by function (avoiding names) and should not allow buck-passing of responsibility. Finally, never forget this basic thought when developing the kanban rules: *If you want something to happen in a certain way, it better be spelled out in the kanban rules!*

When you discuss how the pieces of the kanban will be manipulated, be specific:

- ❑ If this happens, then do this.
- ❑ The kanban card will be placed in ______ when ______ occurs.
- ❑ Move the magnet to the ______ when this occurs.
- ❑ When ______ happens, call ______ at ext. ______.
- ❑ Complete this form and fax to ____________.

Once again, if you want the signals to move in a specific way, then you must tell everyone. Also, don't forget to tell everyone who, how, and when the scheduling signals (kanban cards, containers, faxbans) get back to the production process.

When you draft the scheduling rules make them easy and unambiguous to follow. Think through possible misconceptions and correct them so they will not occur. Spell out what signals a normal changeover. Spell out what signals an emergency changeover. Seek feedback to make sure that everyone else is as clear about how to interpret the signals as you and your team.

Additionally, the scheduling rules should contain clear-cut decision rules. The decision rules should help the production operators make consistent production scheduling decisions based on the stated priorities. The rules should provide rate information, if applicable, to allow the operator to develop production expectations. The decision rules should contain instructions on when and whom to call for help. Also, the rules should include all the "everyone knows this" items that everyone seems to forget from time to time. If you want the operators to schedule the line based on demand, then you have to give them the tools to do it.

If a preferred scheduling sequence exists, then list the preferred sequence in the rules. When developing a preferred sequence, specify the sequence in terms of normal operations. Potential items that can drive preferred sequences might include changing between paint colors, common raw materials, or common operational equipment. Whatever it might be, if you use these factors to schedule the line today, then include them in the rules by defining a preferred operating sequence. Also, make it clear that the schedule will deviate from the preferred sequence when red signals appear.

The rules should clearly state what the operators do when they get a red signal. The red signal is meant as a danger warning. Many people think red means hit the emergency stops and immediately change over. However, red means that a stock out will occur and action needs to be taken as soon as possible. Set the red levels at a point where you have time to react, not just to watch the kanban crash and burn.

Finally, use the kanban rules to develop a scheduling system that does not allow backsliding. Don't allow hidden forecast or MRP systems to really control the kanban. Make the production operators and the production managers use the scheduling signals to determine the schedule position and make decisions. Later, if you discover backsliding, figure out what is happening and make the necessary changes. Figure 5-19 shows a draft set of rules for the ten-part number example from Chapters 3 and 4.

Create a Visual Management Plan

Now that you have completed the design, it's time to design the visual management items for the kanban. The visual management plan will explain the kanban to everyone and visually instruct/remind everyone how the kanban operates. The basic goal of your visual aids should be to answer the questions that pop up on a daily basis: Where do I get this from, where do I move that, which color buggy contains which part, is there a color scheme, do we have anymore of this part?

Figure 5-19. Kanban rules for the ten-part number example from Chapters 3 and 4.

1. **Empty containers will serve as the signals for Scheduling Line 1.**
2. **Scheduling rules:**
   - Fill all the containers with the same profile before switching to the next profile unless a red signal occurs.
   - Look at the control point for empty buggies to determine the next item to be produced. Select the next profile that has exposed the yellow blocks.
   - If more than one profile is in the yellow zone (and no red signals exists), then run profiles (with containers in the yellow zone) in this sequence:

1. 3502	6. 3503
2. 3505	7. 3504
3. 3508	8. 3506
4. 3509	9. 3507
5. 3511	10. 3510

   - If a red signal occurs, then notify a supervisor and begin making plans to change over to this profile.
     - The supervisor should confirm this is a valid red signal before changing over.
   - When no yellow (or run) signals exist, then notify the supervisor and prepare to shut down the line.
3. **Movement of containers.** The attached drawing shows the flow of containers for this kanban. (Reference Figure 5.15)
   - Line A technicians will move containers from Line A to the product storage area.
   - Work center operators will return the empty containers to the empty container storage area.
4. If you receive rejected material, then contact your supervisor immediately. All rejected material will be treated as consumed product until released from quality hold.
5. If you have any questions regarding these rules, then see your supervisor or the materials scheduler.

From experience, we know that you cannot overcommunicate with signs, colors, arrows, lines, etc. Essentially, think about the questions someone could have about the kanban, then develop visual answers to these questions. Also, consider when and where people will be when they have these questions, then place the answers in those locations.

Make your visual aids colorful and easy to read. Use these tips when developing visual aids:

- ❑ Keep the colors consistent with existing color schemes
- ❑ Avoid red—typically associated with safety or quality
- ❑ Avoid yellow—typically associated with safety
- ❑ Use large print for hanging signs and wall signs
- ❑ Avoid excessive words on your signs—people don't read signs, they glance at them

Make forms and signs easy to update. To give homemade signs a professional look, use a word processing program to create the signs and hang them in Plexiglass holders, such as the one shown in Figure 5-20. Whenever you create signs or forms, don't forget to determine who will update them and under what circumstances.

Also, don't forget to consider ISO 9000 implications of the signs and forms. To make sure you don't run astray of these requirements, keep the people responsible for compliance in the loop. Work with them to achieve your desired outcome while still meeting their requirements.

If you plan to mark out your staging areas with lines, then consider using tape to mark the lines initially. Once you're happy with the layout of the staging areas, flow lanes, etc., paint permanent lines.

The same advice applies to floor markings. Initially, temporarily laminate paper signs and tape them on the floor. When you're certain that the signs are the ones you want and in the right location, make them into permanent signs.

Figure 5-20. Kanban rules for the ten-part number example from Chapters 3 and 4.

Develop an Implementation Schedule

Complete the design process by developing an implementation schedule. This schedule, which documents the steps required to transform your design into reality, must allow enough time to:

- ❑ Coordinate the final plan
- ❑ Purchase materials
- ❑ Install kanban signals and visual management
- ❑ Make the transformation from the current scheduling system to the kanban scheduling system
- ❑ Conduct training

The implementation plan is where the rubber hits the road. Assign members of your team to purchase the needed materials and to fabricate the necessary items to set up the kanban. Make sure that someone writes the required workorders, gets signs or boards hung, gets stands fabricated, and so forth, to support the schedule. Also, make sure to record all these plans so that you can track implementation progress.

Figures 5-21 and 5-22 show the same draft implementation schedule, but use different formats. These two formats illustrate a basic point: get decisions documented and don't get hung up on style.

Coordinate the Kanban Plan

Once you have an action plan, then you are ready to discuss coordination of the kanban design and how the production process will transition to kanban scheduling. When you consider the coordination process, consider who needs to approve, concur with, or understand the design. People who are probably interested in the plan include the plant manager, the materials manager, the production managers and supervisors, the material handlers, and (last but not least) all the production operators. Once you have determined who needs to buy into the plan, then determine how and what to communicate with them. Also, determine whether there is any specific order you want to follow—each organization has its own coordination path, so follow yours.

As you proceed through the coordination process, be prepared for feedback that might change your plans. As a matter of fact, on the first two or three kanbans you implement, expect the rules to undergo several revisions as people begin the transformation to kanban scheduling. Address the feedback—use what you can and discard the rest. As a courtesy, when you reject suggestions, always explain why you did not accept the suggestion. Finally, to help in implementation, plan the coordination process so the rules are finalized before the start of training.

Figure 5-21. Draft implementation schedule in Gantt chart format.

Action Plan: Compressor line 1 Kanban plan

Start Date: September 1

Champion: John Gross & Ken McInnis

Action Steps	Who	Days	1	2	3	4	5	6	7	8	9	10	11	12	13	14	% Complete 20	40	60	80	100
Coordinate Plan	Bob	2																			
Fabricate Kanban Board	Mike B.	10																			
Order Sign Holders	Jack	1																			
Make Signs	Bill	1																			
Hang Signs	Sally	3																			
Train Production Operators	John	1																			
Train Material Handlers	Ken	1																			
Conduct Dry Run	Team & 2nd shift	1																			
Start Kanban Scheduling	1st shift																				

Figure 5-22. Draft implementation schedule in table format.

Action	*Who*	*How Long (In Days)*	*When*
Coordinate Plan	Bob	2	Sept 1–2
Fabricate Kanban Board	Mike	10	Sept 1–10
Order Sign Holders	Jack	1	Sept 3
Make Signs	Bill	1	Sept 4
Hang Signs	Sally	3	Sept 8–10
Train Production Operators	John	1	Sept 11
Train Material Handlers	Ken	1	Sept 12
Conduct Dry Run	Team's 2nd shift	1	Sept 12
Start Kanban Scheduling	1st shift		Sept 13

Identify Who Needs Training

A subject closely related to the coordination process is training. As was true with coordination, you need to identify who needs training and what type of training. When making this list you should consider not only production operators, but also who will move the material and who will use the material. As a good rule of thumb for making this list, consider training everyone who touches the product. Figure 5-23 lists people to consider when making the training list. Also, note that not everyone needs to be trained to the same level and detail.

The subject of training is so important that we have devoted Chapter 6 to the subject. For now, we'll just say that it's key to the successful implementation and is often overlooked.

Develop a Transition Plan

The last part of the implementation plan is to determine how you will physically transition to kanban scheduling. Some of the questions that you need to consider are:

Figure 5-23. Who needs kanban training?

- ❑ Will this be a running change?
- ❑ Will you need to build inventory to meet the kanban requirements?
- ❑ Will you need any special coverage to oversee the change—such as sending the scheduler to third shift for the night the change occurs?

To answer these questions, use the team. By seeking their inputs you not only develop a cross-functional answer, but you also plant the seeds of coordination and cooperation. Additionally, remember to consider the customer when you make this plan. You do not want to misstep and fail to support the customer (who doesn't care how you schedule).

Special Cases

As you begin to implement more and more kanbans, you will encounter constraints or unique situations (manning, product mix, quantities, etc.) that complicate the implementation of kanban. When you encounter these situations:

- ❑ Look for commonality in the process
- ❑ Look for unique decisions rules
- ❑ Review your current informal scheduling rules for the process
- ❑ Look at the frequency of the various unique parts

Once you have looked at the problem from these angles, make a determination of whether you:

1. Can implement a kanban
2. Can implement a combination scheduling system
3. Cannot implement a kanban

We have not defined combination scheduling in our previous discussions. *Combination scheduling* occurs when you place part of the process on kanban scheduling and manually schedule the special case parts.

When analyzing special cases, one method for clarifying the current scheduling rules is by making a decision flowchart that explains how you currently schedule the production process. The flowchart forces you to write down all those unspoken rules that you now use to control the production process. Once you have these rules written down, study them for ways to commonize or simplify the scheduling process to turn these rules into kanban operating rules.

Additionally, look at the production process for ways to consolidate or redistribute the parts to simplify the problem. Once you have simplified the problem, then you may find that the problem gets smaller or that it creates an opportunity to use the questions above to create a kanban design.

When you encounter special cases, don't be discouraged. Analyze the problem and apply the questions above. When you come up with a solution, make sure the kanban rules reflect these decisions. Also, after thoroughly analyzing the problem, don't be afraid to make the decision to not implement a kanban for this process (or these processes). The following sections look at some special cases and suggest ways to implement the kanbans.

Low Demand Mixed with High Demand

What do you do when the production process has several lower demand items? For example, the process has three parts that run monthly versus ten parts that run weekly? In this case, recognize the difference and set up the buffer inventory and kanban schedule quantity to produce the low volume parts at their current interval. Don't be concerned that these parts are out of sync with the other parts that run daily or weekly. By making these changes, you can allow the process to proceed in an orderly flow without having to implement a combination scheduling system.

Variable Manning Requirements

What if the production process has different manning requirements for different parts? First, look for the opportunity to consolidate parts with similar production manning requirements on the same line (lines) in order to eliminate the manning variance. Next, look at the possibility of implementing a combination scheduling system on those lines that still have variable manning requirements. Also, look at the possibility of prioritizing which parts on which lines get the available manpower, and establish a backup product on the line that does not get the extra manning.

More Than One Line Produces the Same Part

What do you do when a production process produces overflow parts for another production process that is over capacity? First, set a standard production quantity for the overflow parts on the secondary line. Next, create rules for the secondary line that requires the production operators to look at the primary line's kanban for its schedule position when making changeover decisions. These rules should instruct the secondary line to change over to the overflow part when the primary line is at a predetermined level.

Using the Workbook

Use the CD-ROM *Workbook* to help document the design. The design forms will serve as an outline to lead you through the design planning, rule formulation, and the visual management plans. The required training form will help to make a list of who needs to be trained. Additionally, action items forms and action plan forms will provide a format for assigning action items and documenting the coordination and transformation plans. (Training elements will be covered in Chapter 6 of the CD-ROM *Workbook*.)

Summary

Once you have determined the kanban quantities, the next step is design of the kanban scheduling signal. This chapter provides several design options for your consideration, adoption, or modification. Whatever signal you select or create, make sure it fits the culture of your organization.

When you have determined what type of scheduling signal you

will utilize, then develop rules to control the operation of the kanban. The rules should include the following items:

- ❑ The part numbers covered by the kanban
- ❑ How the design works—how the cards, magnets, etc., move
- ❑ The meaning of the scheduling signals and how to interpret them
- ❑ Any scheduling rules of thumb (if required)
- ❑ The preferred production sequence (if one exists)
- ❑ Who to go to and what the "helpers" should do when contacted
- ❑ Any special quality or documentation requirements

Remember, you draft rules to communicate how to run the kanban and to allow the process operators to schedule the line. The only way the production operators can take over scheduling the line is by having rules that provide clear direction and scheduling guidance.

After you have the rules developed, develop a visual management plan to communicate how the kanban operates. Anticipate what questions are likely to arise from people operating and supporting the kanban and develop a visual management plan that answers their questions and guides them.

Finally, develop an implementation plan for deploying the kanban. The plan should address laying out the kanban, coordinating the design, training all participants, and the actual transformation from the current scheduling system to kanban scheduling.

CHAPTER

6

TRAINING

Chapters 4 and 5 helped you to size and design your kanban. You created the framework for controlling the operation of the line and allowing the operators to manage their schedule based on the rules you created. Now comes the time to start the deployment of your design. The deployment of the kanban will consist of training everyone who is involved in the operation of the kanban and in the set-up of the kanban itself—signals, control points, signs, etc.

This chapter discusses creation of training material and training implementation. Our focus will be on developing the necessary material to explain how the kanban operates and what actions each participant performs. We will also develop a game plan for getting this training done before we implement the training.

In Chapter 7 we will discuss the actual startup of the kanban. However, if you do not train the people who must operate and interact with the kanban, then long-term success is questionable. Figure 6-1 shows how our kanban process flow expands to include training.

Figure 6-1. Expanded kanban process flow.

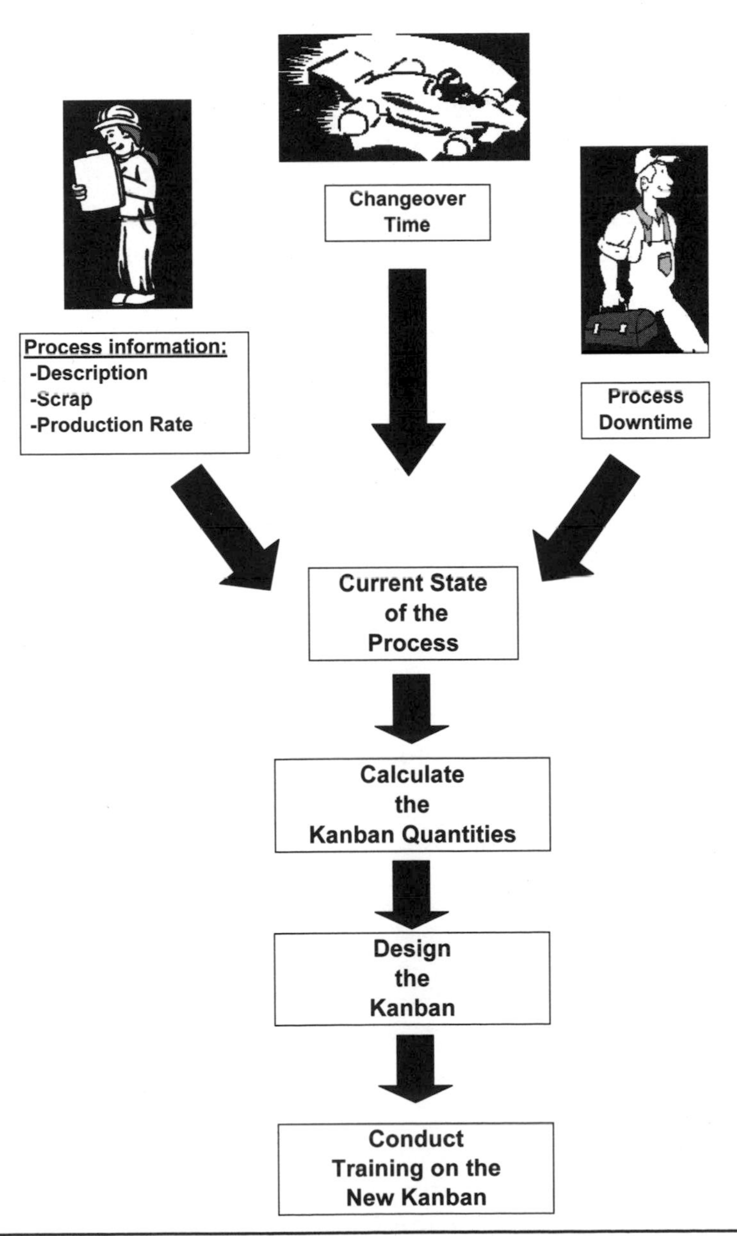

Developing Your Training Material

Using the training list you developed in the last chapter to identify who needs to be trained, determine what type of training they need to fulfill their part of the operation.

For example, the material handlers probably don't need much training on making scheduling decisions. However, they will need to understand how you want the material to move and how to handle the scheduling signal—moving the magnets or chips on a board, for example.

When creating the training, focus on how the kanban will work. We suggest the following outline for training:

- ❑ Kanban basics
- ❑ How kanban will work
  - What is the signal?
  - How will the material move?
  - Review of the rules
- ❑ What are the scheduling decisions and the rules for making the decisions
  - Use example of different schedule conditions to teach how and what decisions to make
- ❑ Discuss when to call for help and what to do specifically when encountering a red signal
- ❑ Conduct a dry run

Although this list seems long, if you prepare properly and focus the information, then you can convey all this information in seven to ten charts. Figure 6-2 shows the layout of a draft presentation.

Kanban Basics

When talking about kanban basics, avoid a lengthy discussion of kanban theory. Instead keep the discussion focused on what kanban

Figure 6-2. Draft presentation layout.

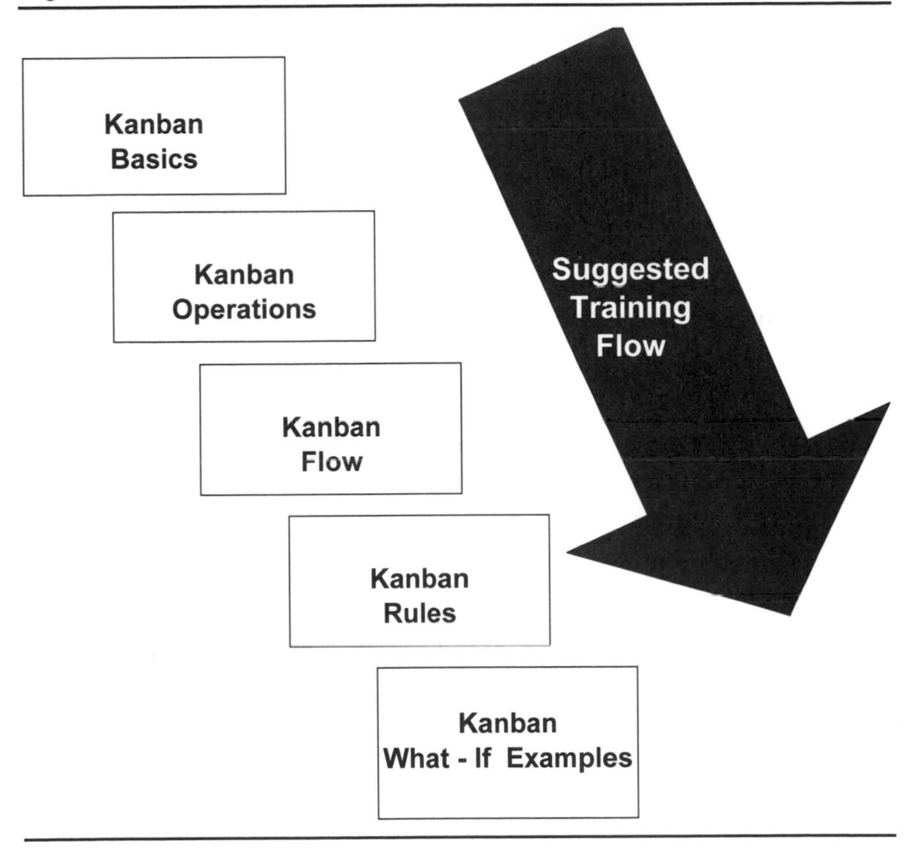

is and what it will do for them. Some of the points that you should include:

- ❑ *Kanban is demand-based scheduling.* You supply product based on usage.
  - They will no longer receive a schedule. The kanban signal will be their schedule.
  - Use this opportunity to tell the operators that you will train them on how to use the kanban schedule and you will be there to help get them started.
- ❑ *Kanban scheduling is more than just an inventory reduction*

strategy—it improves flow, reduces or eliminates unexpected schedule changes, and allows them to control the line's operation.

Figure 6-3 shows examples of two training charts for covering the topic of kanban basics.

Kanban Operation

Next move on to how the kanban will operate. Be specific about what the kanban signal is and how it moves through the process. Discuss in detail how the signal moves. Also show an example of the scheduling signal. Make a diagram that shows this flow. Use the

Figure 6-3. Training charts for kanban basics.

What is Kanban?

—Kanban is demand-based scheduling

—It matches use (or demand) to production

—It replaces forecasted schedules

—Operated by operators instead of schedulers

—Scheduling done with pre-established rules

Kanban Benefits

—Reduces inventory

—Improves material flow

—Simplifies operations

—Allows visibility into the schedule

—Reduces or eliminates *unexpected* schedule changes

diagram and the scheduling signal to reinforce how the signals flow. Finally, discuss *what-if* scheduling decisions. Figures 6-4 to 6-9 show potential charts for the ten-part number example using the rules and the flow diagram from Chapter 5.

If you are using a board of some type, then have a picture of the board. As an alternative, create a diagram of the board's layout to use during training. The picture or the diagram will make a good visual aid and help in discussing the scheduling decisions.

Discuss the rules for operating the kanban. Go through each rule to make sure everyone understands the rules and their meanings. As you discuss the rules, be sensitive to any confused looks or verbal feedback from the group being trained. Their confusion means that something needs to be clarified or modified. Do not be afraid to make changes if that will help to create a successful launch. (If you do make changes, then make sure you coordinate the changes and revise the documentation.)

Once everyone understands the basic flow and how the kanban will operate, it's time to explain how the scheduling process will work. After explaining the process, walk the operators through the various signals. Develop what-if scenarios that force the operators to make decisions. Ask them what decision they would make and then discuss why they made that decision:

Figure 6-4. Training chart for kanban operations.

Line 1 Kanban Operation

—Empty containers are the kanban signal

—Use the preferred sequence to determine which item to run next.

—Run full containers

—If a red signal occurs then contact the supervisor before changing over

—Questions—see your supervisor or the materials scheduler

Figure 6-5. Training chart for kanban flow diagram.

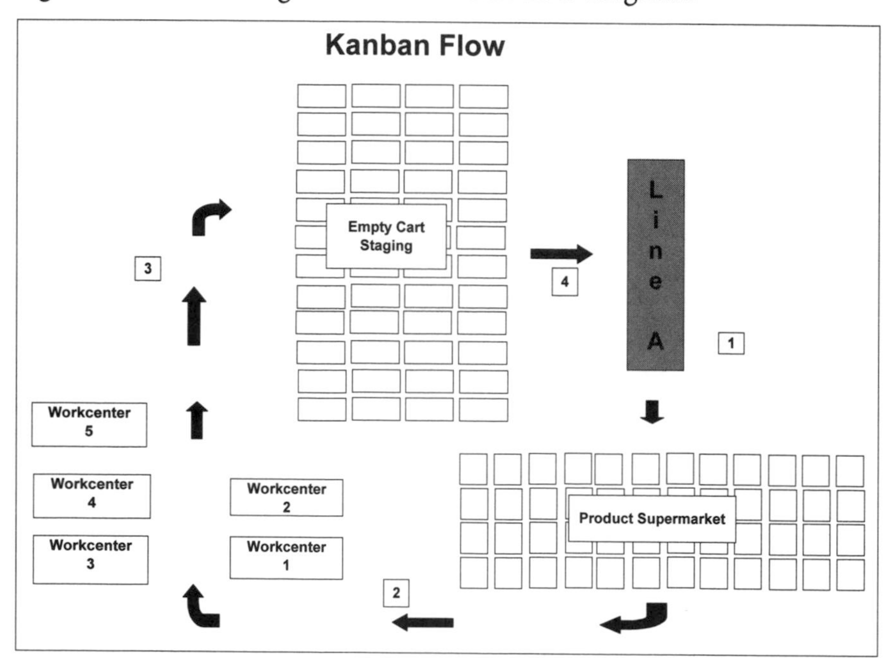

<u>Sequence of Events</u>

1 **Product moves from Line A to the product Supermarket.**

2 **Product next moves from the supermarket to Workcenters 1 - 5**

3 **Empty containers are moved from the Workcenters to Empty Cart Staging**

4 **Use Line A Look-See kanban rules to schedule Line A Production**

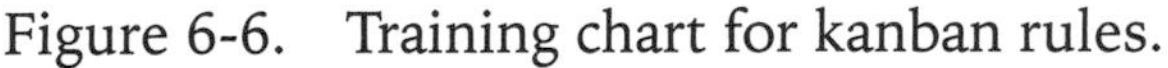
Figure 6-6. Training chart for kanban rules.

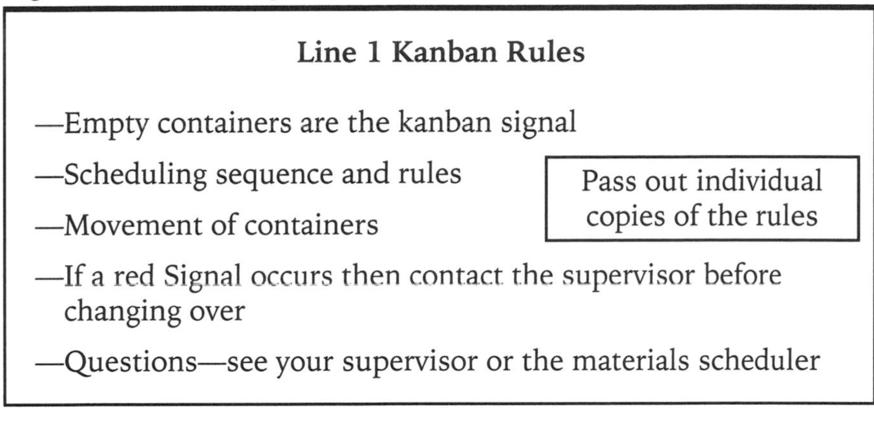

- ❑ If they made the correct decision, congratulate them.
- ❑ If they made the wrong decision, explain what they should have done.

Avoid being critical. You want them to take ownership of the process, not be paranoid that they will make the wrong decision. Develop enough scenarios so that you can go through the process several times—you want the operators to become comfortable in the decisions they will make.

Finally, discuss under what conditions operators should call for help. These are the "1 percent of the time occurrences" that require additional help. (If you included all the what-ifs in the kanban rules, then they would be ten to twenty pages long.) When one of these events pops up, then the rules should instruct the operators whom to contact. Also, make sure the contact person knows what they should do when contacted.

A special case requiring help is the red, or danger, signal. This signal, which most people think means to hit the panic button and stop the presses, is meant as a warning. The red signal, if properly used, warns the operators of impending danger so that corrective action can be taken. Therefore, tell the operators what to do when

Figure 6-7. Training chart for kanban what-if: Example 1.

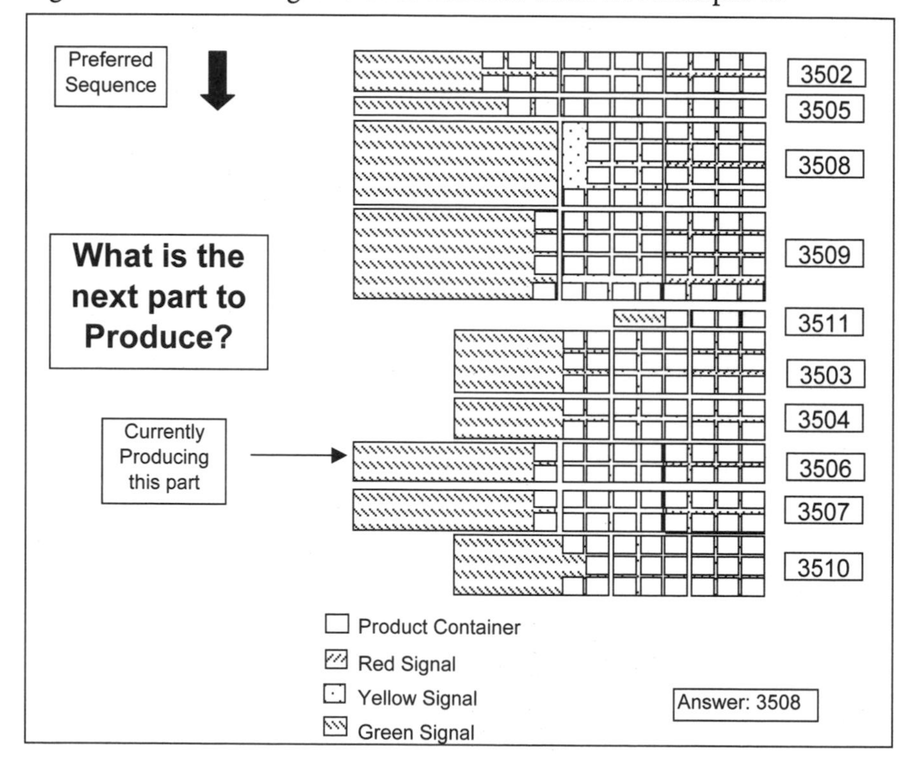

the red signal occurs. If they are to contact someone or take a specific action, then tell them who or what it is!

Conduct a Dry Run of the Kanban

Remembering that Murphy was an optimist, consider conducting a dry run of the kanban. The dry run becomes particularly important for kanbans with materials located over a large geographical area or in multiple staging areas. This dry run should involve representatives from the various groups that must operate or support the kanban. The intent of the dry run is to:

- ❑ Look for flaws in the design
- ❑ Make sure that everyone understands their role

Figure 6-8. Training chart for kanban what-if: Example 2.

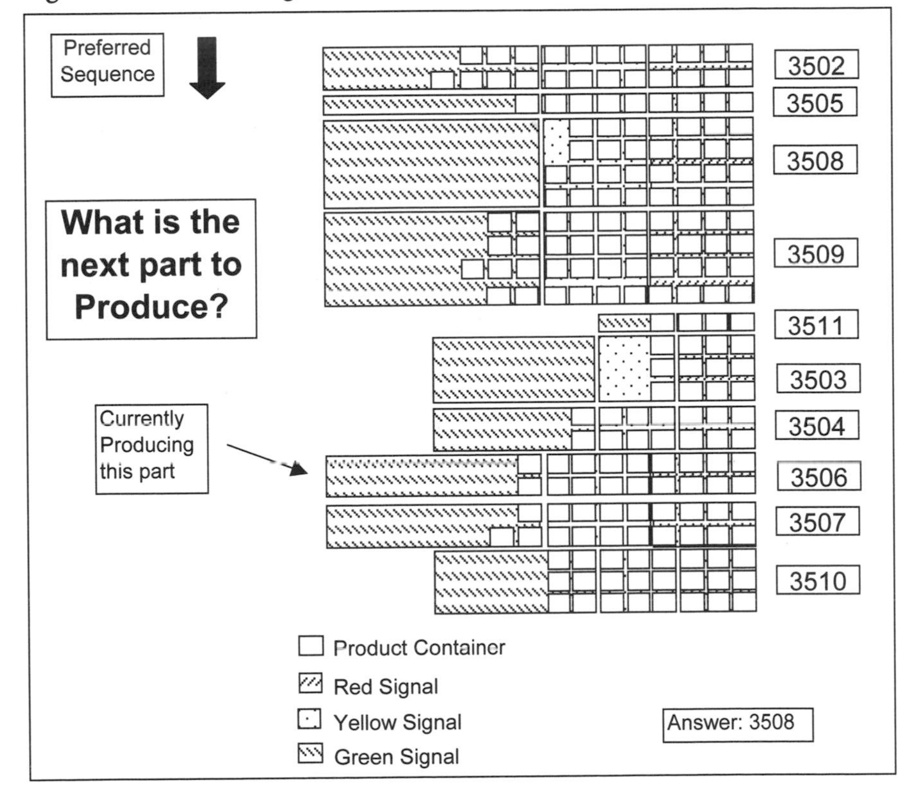

When you conduct the dry run, make sure you have prepared training information—the rules and the flow diagram. Set up scenarios with your scheduling signal and discuss how the participants will react to each scenario. If completion of the various actions requires movement of the cards, magnets, or chips, then have the appropriate person do so.

The intent of the dry run is to make sure that everyone understands their role and to discover any flaws in the plan. You cannot achieve these goals by sitting in a classroom or an office. The key to a successful dry run is working through the signals and learning from the actions and comments.

Therefore, take your group out and touch the hardware! If the dry run does not take place in the area where the kanban will take

Figure 6-9. Training chart for kanban what-if: Example 3.

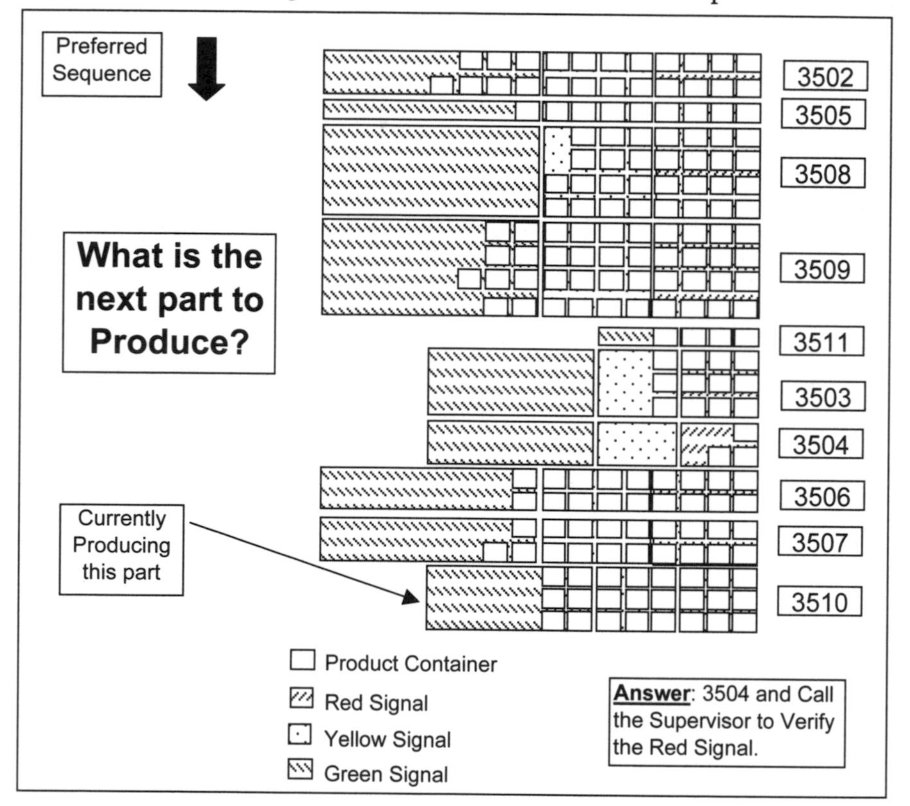

place, then it isn't a dry run. Lastly, don't miss the opportunity to modify the design now and avoid costly mistakes and miscommunications after the kanban has started.

Listen to the feedback from the dry-run participants. Be sensitive to their verbal and nonverbal communication on:

- ❑ What they don't understand
- ❑ What they don't like
- ❑ What mechanisms they find awkward

As you identify these items, discuss them with the group and determine what needs to change. Once you have made a decision, then trial it with the group. If it proves out, then revise the documentation and conduct any necessary retraining.

If you follow this basic outline you should be ready to provide the necessary training. Although the proposed training is short and to the point, it remains focused on the main training objective—preparing people to operate the kanban.

Serving as a Coach and Mentor

The last thing to remember as you roll out the training is that your role is to be a coach and a mentor. For many people, implementing kanban is a big step. Many operators have become dependent on the daily or weekly schedule. For many of them it is the first time they have had to make decisions on a consistent basis at work. (Don't be surprised if more than one person asks who's going to put out the schedule.) On the flip side, many production managers and supervisors are used to calling all the shots. So when we transfer control of the line to the production operators, we have made a big culture change for the entire organization.

Therefore, you must coach and mentor all levels of the organization. Be sensitive to their concerns and fears. Also, like any good coach, don't be afraid to be tough if the need arises.

Remember the bottom line on the coaching and mentoring—if you want them to own the process, then you'd better prepare them to take ownership.

Using the *Workbook*

The CD-ROM *Workbook* sheets are designed to identify who needs to be trained and to help you create an outline for the proposed training. Follow the training outline form to create focused training, which allows the operators to take ownership of the production schedule. Additionally, the *Workbook* includes the PowerPoint slides presented in this chapter for you to use as a starting point.

Summary

Training is one of the last steps before startup of the kanban. The goal of your training program should be to provide everyone who must operate or support the kanban the information and tools necessary to successfully operate the kanban. To achieve this goal, use the memory jogger in Chapter 5 (Figure 5-23) and decide what type of training each associate needs. Keep the training focused on the operation of the kanban. Keep the theory parts of the training brief and relevant. We suggest following this outline to achieve the best results:

- ❑ Kanban basics
- ❑ How kanban will work
  What is the signal?
  How will the material move?
  Review of the rules
- ❑ What are the scheduling decisions and rules for making the decisions
  Use example of different schedule conditions to teach how and what decisions to make
- ❑ Discuss when to call for help and what to do specifically when encountering a red signal
- ❑ Conduct a dry run

Finally, don't forget your role as a coach and mentor. If you want the operators to take ownership of the kanban, then you need to give them the information and tools to do so!

CHAPTER

7

INITIAL STARTUP AND COMMON PITFALLS

Well, here we are. We have formed a team, sized the kanban, developed a design, and developed training. So what's left? Are we ready to start up our kanban? (Well, almost!)

Before we go live, we need to take care of several items to ensure a successful implementation. We need to:

- ❑ Confirm the design is implemented
- ❑ Confirm training is complete
- ❑ Check the inventories

Once you have taken care of these items, you are ready to get on with the startup of the kanban. Therefore, our kanban process flow extends to include the startup and implementation step, as shown in Figure 7-1.

After you have started the kanban, then you need to watch for common pitfalls that disrupt the operation of the kanban. Consider

Figure 7-1. Modified kanban process flow.

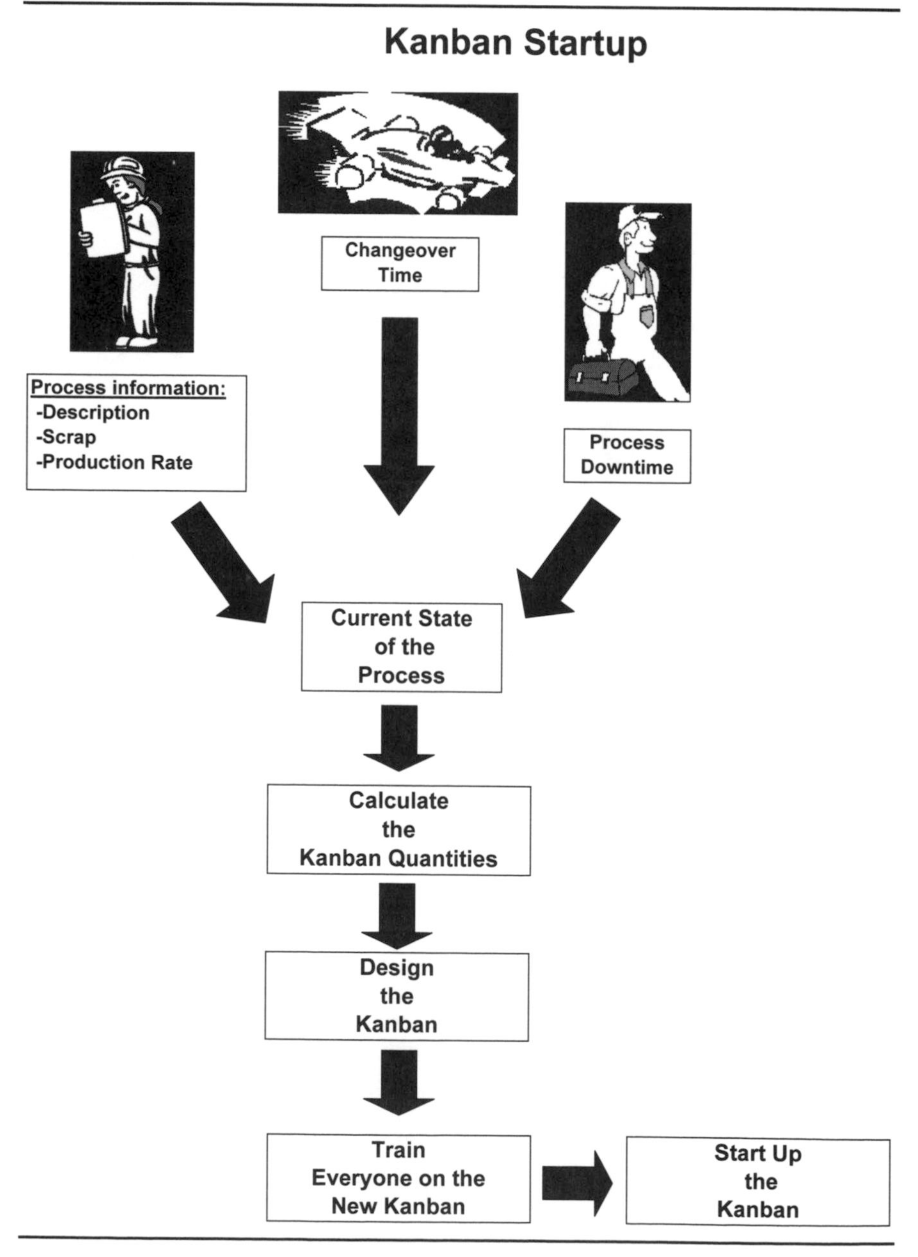

these pitfalls as growing pains of your adolescent scheduling process. Therefore, as you identify problems, correct the problem and remember your role as a coach and mentor.

Confirm That the Design Is Implemented

Before you start the kanban, make sure that you have implemented the kanban design. To make sure you're ready, verify the following items:

- ❑ Are the kanban signals completed?
- ❑ Are the rules posted?
- ❑ Is the visual management information posted?

Don't make a half-hearted attempt at implementation. Make sure these items are complete. Make sure that everything is posted and looks as originally intended.

Having the design implemented simplifies the process of changing from the current scheduling system to the new kanban system. It also makes the training portion considerably easier since the operators and supervisors can readily connect the implemented kanban with the design presented during training.

If you implement the kanban without all the pieces in place, then make sure that everyone knows about the future additions and changes. Also, make sure you have a work-around plan to handle deficiencies and have a firm date for completing the implementation. Finally, you must gain buy-in and support to manage the work-around from the associates. (In many cases, the simple act of open and honest communication coupled with delivery on the promised date will build the teamwork that makes the kanban successful.)

Confirm That Training Is Completed

Training is another key to implementing the design. Although the training content was covered extensively in the last chapter, it bears repeating that without training the associates will never take ownership of the kanban. Make sure you schedule and conduct the training. Also, make sure this training takes place on all affected shifts with all the participants—production operators, production supervisors, material handlers, etc. Finally, set up a dry run of the kanban to identify any shortcomings of the design and to make sure everyone understands the process.

Check the Inventories

Checking the inventories is the very last step before going live on kanban scheduling. In this step, determine whether your inventory level will support the transition to kanban scheduling. This assessment will determine whether you have enough inventory to let the system run on its own when you start the kanban.

If you have sufficient inventory, then you are ready to start. Stick to your original schedule and implement the kanban scheduling system. Make sure that everyone knows what the cutover date is and then do it. Congratulations!

If you do not have sufficient inventory, then develop an inventory plan that will get you to the required level. If you must slip the implementation date, then pick a realistic new start date and get started building the necessary inventory.

To develop the inventory assessment, conduct a physical count of all the proposed kanban part numbers. Next compare the inventory to the kanban quantities to determine whether you're at red, yellow, or green levels for the various production parts. Finally, determine whether the kanban as designed would operate properly at the current inventory levels. (Properly means in normal operational mode without scheduling intervention.) Once you have made this determination, then act accordingly—start the kanban or develop an inventory plan. Figure 7-2 shows an example of an inventory assessment for our ten-part number kanban.

As an alternate strategy, if you do not have sufficient inventory, then you can opt to manage the initial kanban production. If you

Figure 7-2. Startup inventory assessment.

Step 1 - Cycle Count

Step 2- Categorize Inventory into Red, Yellow, and Green Levels

3502
3505
3508
3509
3511
3503
3504
3506
3507
3510

Note that having the visual signals in place makes this a much easier task.

Step 3- Determine if the Kanban Will Operate Properly with the Current Inventory

After looking at the inventory and comparing build rates to estimated usage, we determined that we are OK!!
Start the Kanban!!

select this option, then make it short term. While this option is not desirable in the long term, it lets you get started with kanban.

When you manage the initial kanban production, you essentially set the sequence and the schedule of the production process using the kanban signals themselves. You basically create your own visual production schedule.

Although this is not an ideal strategy, in the short term it allows you to get the operators, material handlers, and any other participants using the kanban design. We only recommend this strategy when your kanban has goals other than just inventory reduction, goals that can't be achieved until you start the kanban. Examples of such goals might include creating flow between workcells or creating a product rotation system.

If you decide to manage the initial production, then make sure you have a plan for going into autonomous operations. Set a date and time that you communicate to everyone. When that date and time arrives, then let the kanban go—don't let the operators hang onto the crutch and don't let the schedulers nurse them along!!

There is one last little inventory item to check before going live: *the arrival of the raw materials.* Make sure that their arrivals do not impact the start of the kanban. As with the production inventory, make the appropriate decisions once you have the data.

Nothing Is Ever Perfect So Don't Wait—Just Do It!

One last thought to consider as you perform your last-minute checks and a dry run: Look at the readiness of the participants. If they are ready to start the kanban and no significant issues exist, then start the kanban. Nothing is ever perfect. Sometimes we can rationalize ourselves into inaction for an eternity by looking at all the little flaws. You should also remember your role as a coach and mentor. Do not let your own fears keep yourself and the team from implementation.

Startup Issues

As hard as it is to believe (because of the perfect design, excellent planning, and perfect training), you may run into startup issues. These issues usually arise from miscommunications, lack of clarity about roles and responsibility, or not understanding the training. As we said at the beginning of the chapter, take these startup issues in stride and make the necessary corrections. Do not let startup problems cause you to dismiss the benefits of kanban or lose faith in your ability to implement kanban. Once again, identify the problems and make corrections.

To help in getting through these pitfalls, we have listed four of the more common startup problems:

1. Production operators and supervisors weren't sure the kanban started
2. Production operators didn't follow the signals
3. No one knew what to run because the kanban had no yellow signals or too many red signals
4. Production operators cheated with the signals

To help you deal with these four problems, we have provided their causes and recommended solutions to counter them.

1. Production Operators and Supervisors Weren't Sure the Kanban Had Started

On the shift that starts the kanban, you may find that some or all the operators and supervisors didn't know that the kanban had started. This can occur because they didn't want to know (i.e., they are slow rolling you). Or they truly didn't know because there was a miscommunication. Regardless of what drives this situation, you can avoid it by clearly communicating the startup and any special conditions surrounding the startup. Communication means the posting of memos and having someone personally speak with the startup crew. Remember, you cannot overcommunicate and overcoordinate.

2. Production Operators Didn't Follow the Signals

Why don't production operators follow the kanban signals? This may result from one of two reasons:

- ❑ They do not understand the signals
- ❑ They have ignored the signals

To determine which is the cause, you will have to conduct your own investigation. Go about your investigation carefully, since your own behavior can be responsible for "the cause" moving from the first reason to the second (which is real bad).

If you determine that the production operators don't understand the signals, then you need to determine whether the design is unclear or whether the training failed. If the rules are unclear, then make the necessary changes to clarify the uncertainties and conduct retraining.

If you determine that the training failed, then determine how the failure occurred. Once you have the failure identified, make the necessary corrections to the training material and conduct retraining.

Also, be aware that this situation can occur with your material handlers. Just like the production operators, determine the cause and make the necessary corrections.

What do you do when the operators don't follow the signals? This is a special case, which goes beyond simple design flaws. When this situation occurs get the production managers and supervisors involved to resolve the issue. They will need to resolve the problem for you.

If you are the person who must resolve the problem, you will need to differentiate between operators not wanting to operate the kanban and operators using the kanban as an opportunity to support a different agenda. Once you have made this determination, then the path to correction will become clear. As with all situations of this nature, use your own judgment and proceed carefully.

3. No One Knew What to Run Because the Kanban Had No Yellow Signals or Too Many Red Signals

How do you handle the situation where no one knew what to run because there were no yellow signals or there were too many red signals? When this situation occurs, it results from the failure of the kanban's design. You can avoid this problem at startup by making sure the kanban is set up appropriately with adequate inventory levels that allow the process to proceed in an orderly process. If one of these situations occurs after startup, then it signals one of the following conditions:

- ❑ There are too many containers in the kanban (no yellow signals)
- ❑ There are not enough containers in the kanban (too many red signals)

Additionally, it identifies a weakness in the decision rules because either the operators were unable to make a decision with the data available, or no one understood when to call for help.

When you identify which deficiency occurred, make the necessary corrections and conduct retraining.

4. Production Operators Cheated with the Signals

What do you do when you discover the production operators are cheating with signals? First, be glad they understand the design well enough to cheat, then fix the loophole. To discover the cheating will most likely require auditing of the kanban is discussed in Chapter 8.

Using the Workbook

The CD-ROM *Workbook* will assist you in preparing for startup by helping you document your readiness. The inventory analysis worksheet will help you assess your inventory position by helping to determine your current inventory status.

Summary

Don't make a half-hearted attempt at starting your kanban. Look at these three items to make sure you have all your bases covered before starting:

1. Confirm the design is implemented
2. Confirm training is complete
3. Check the inventories

Once you are satisfied with the findings of the above items, then it is time to start the kanban. If you are not satisfied with your findings, then develop a plan to make the necessary corrections to get ready for startup.

Also, as you perform your last-minute checks and dry run, look at the readiness of the participants. If they are ready to start the kanban and no significant issues exist, then start the kanban.

Remember, nothing is ever perfect. Sometimes we can rationalize ourselves into inaction for an eternity by looking at all the little flaws. You should remember your role as a coach and mentor: Do not let your own fears keep you and the team from implementing the kanban.

Once you have made the decision to start the kanban, then watch for startup issues. Some of the common startup issues include situations where production operators:

- ❑ Weren't sure the kanban started
- ❑ Didn't follow the signals

- ❑ Didn't know what to run because the kanban had no yellow signals or too many red signals
- ❑ Cheated with the signals

Use the information in this chapter to help address these startup potential pitfalls. As you resolve these startup issues, always remember your role as coach and mentor. Also, use the CD-ROM *Workbook* to help in performing the inventory analysis.

CHAPTER

8

AUDITING THE KANBAN

Once the kanban has started, the next task becomes keeping it going and reducing the kanban quantities. The task of keeping the kanban going centers on the process of auditing and making corrections as problems are discovered. This chapter addresses the auditing function and proposes a process for implementing corrective action. Chapter 9 will address how to reduce the kanban quantities by implementing the continuous improvement techniques of Single Minute Exchange of Dies (SMED), Total Productive Maintenance (TPM), Preventative Maintenance (PM), 5s, scrap reduction, and buffer reduction. Our kanban process flow now expands to include auditing of the kanban, as shown in Figure 8-1.

By auditing of the kanban we mean verifying the kanban runs as designed. The plant material managers or schedulers usually perform this task.

The audit process consists of cycle counting and reviewing past production records. The cycle count will provide an up-to-the-minute

Figure 8-1. Expanded kanban process flow.

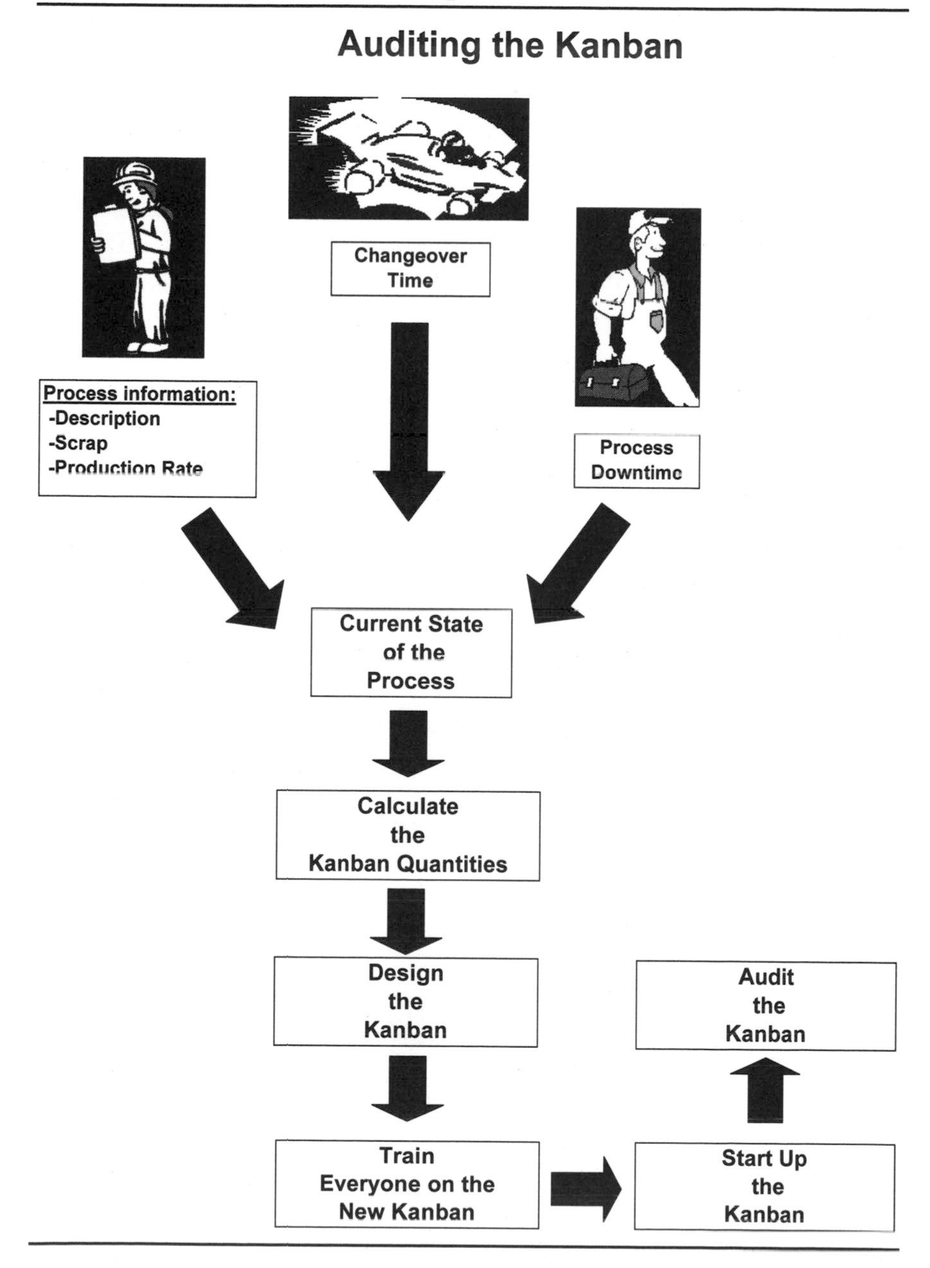

inventory that can be compared to the signals to make sure they match. The review of production records will confirm that the production operators are following the kanban signals. When auditors find a problem, they must implement the necessary changes or seek help to get the kanban back on track. When the correction is not obvious, problem solving will be required to identify and correct the problem.

The auditing function also includes making sure the kanban size is adequate to support any production requirement changes. To determine whether the kanban size supports production requirements, compare the current production requirement's forecast to the baseline quantities used to size the kanban. If the requirements have changed by 15 to 20 percent, then consider resizing the kanban.

Although auditing seems like a mundane task, most kanbans fail because no one initiated this function or let it slide over time. As a result, the kanban's problems never get corrected and production requirement changes never get addressed. Consequently, the kanbans become useless and the plant returns to its original forecast, or push, schedules. Figure 8-2 shows the relationship between auditing and assessing requirements to maintaining the kanban.

Formalizing the Audit Process

The first step to the audit process is to set up a regular schedule for conducting the audits. We recommend making this a daily procedure initially, and later reducing it to once or twice per week. The purpose of the audit is to get the kanban running and then keeping it running.

Use the audits to force the operators to run their kanban. Also, don't let the auditor become their mom or dad!

Auditing the Kanban

When auditing the kanban, look for the following items:

- ❑ Have any of the scheduling signals or pieces disappeared?
- ❑ Is the inventory correct (containers versus signals)?

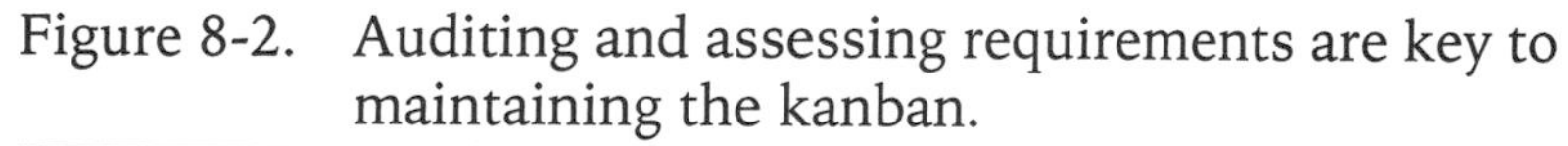

Figure 8-2. Auditing and assessing requirements are key to maintaining the kanban.

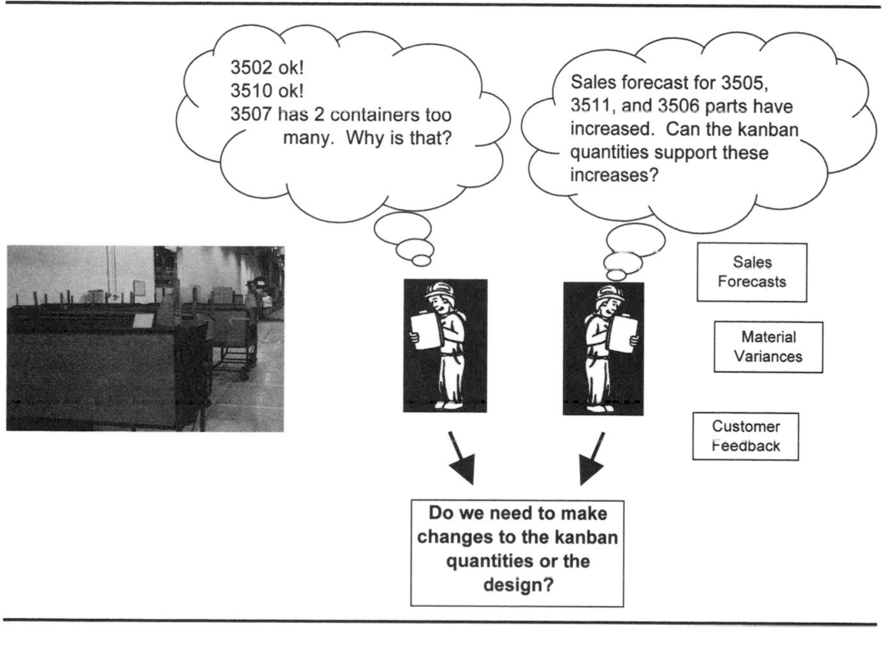

- ❑ Are the operators, material handlers, and customers following the design?
- ❑ Does anyone in the process have any questions or concerns?
- ❑ Do the original sizing assumptions and calculations still apply?

To determine whether any of these situations exist, the auditor must go to the kanban. With the exception of checking requirements versus the design, the audits cannot be conducted from the office.

We recommend that you also create standard forms to track the inventory and to track kanban compliance over time. Figures 8-3 and 8-4 show forms that perform these functions.

The audit will take the physical form of:

- ❑ Conducting a cycle count
- ❑ Counting the signals

Figure 8-3. Audit form.

Date/Time: ____________					Kanban Audit sheet
Part Number	Pcs/ Container	Total Containers	Cards In Rack	Cards Gone	Miscellaneous Comments

- ❑ Talking to the operators, material handlers, customers and their supervisors
- ❑ Checking the kanban design and size versus the long-term requirements

As you collect the data, compare answers to the above questions to determine:

1. Whether a problem exists
2. What the possible solutions are

Finding the Problem

How will you detect these changes? The audits or your analysis of future requirements will uncover the issues. In terms of the audit,

Figure 8-4. Completed audit summary form.

Week of: ____________

Summary of Audit

Process Line	Part Number	5/13	5/20	5/27	6/3	6/10	6/17	6/24	7/1	7/8	7/15	7/22	7/29	8/5	8/12	8/19	8/26	9/2	9/9
Line 1	A																		
	B										3		3						
	C										1								
	D																		
	E																		
	F																		
	G																		
	Week of --->	5/13	5/20	5/27	6/3	6/10	6/17	6/24	7/1	7/8	7/15	7/22	7/29	8/5	8/12	8/19	8/26	9/2	9/9
Line 2	A																		
	B																		
	C																		
	D																		
	E																		
	F						-1		-2										
	G								-3										
	Week of --->	5/13	5/20	5/27	6/3	6/10	6/17	6/24	7/1	7/8	7/15	7/22	7/29	8/5	8/12	8/19	8/26	9/2	9/9
Line 3	A		1																
	B																		
	C							4	-3				3						
	D	-1											2						
	E	2	-1			2		1											
	F					1													
	G							2											
	H					-1		1											
	Week of --->	5/13	5/20	5/27	6/3	6/10	6/17	6/24	7/1	7/8	7/15	7/22	7/29	8/5	8/12	8/19	8/26	9/2	9/9
Line 4	A		1										-6						
	B																		
	C																		
	D																		
	E		4		-1			2					-3						
	F	-1		-1				2					-1						
	Week of --->	5/13	5/20	5/27	6/3	6/10	6/17	6/24	7/1	7/8	7/15	7/22	7/29	8/5	8/12	8/19	8/26	9/2	9/9
Line 5	A												1						
	B												1						
	C								-15				16						
	D								-27										
	E								-2										
	F								-1										
	G								-1										
	H								-1										
Total errors found --->		3	4	1	1	3	1	6	9	0	2	0	9	0	0	0	0	0	0

(-) negative number shows that containers were missing
(+) positive number shows that there were too many containers

you will begin to see the kanban material stops flowing, the production flow will begin to jump around instead of roughly following the preferred sequence, or stock-outs become a regular occurrence.

If you find a problem, then begin your investigation into the cause. Don't consider failures in process discipline as failures in kanban scheduling. Do not stop kanban scheduling just because you find a problem—let the kanban keep operating while you figure out how the problem occurred.

When you find the problem, asks yourself and all the involved participants: What has changed? Also apply the 5 Whys and 1 How (or 5W1H) approach to determine the cause of the problem. When using 5W1H, ask *why* until you get to a root cause, then ask *how* this cause could have happened. As Figure 8-5 illustrates, the audi-

Figure 8-5. Problem solving to keep the kanban operating properly.

tor needs to put the pieces of the jigsaw puzzle together to understand how the problem occurred.

Once you know the answers to these questions, make the appropriate corrections. Even if the change is simple, make sure that you communicate and coordinate the change with all affected parties. (Don't forget the first rule of communication—you can't overcommunicate.)

When you begin to see problems occur, also go back to the original kanban sizing calculations. Review the assumptions and, if necessary, recalculate the kanban quantities using the changes. Once you have the new figures, coordinate these changes and implement the new quantities.

Assess the Impact of Changing Requirements on the Kanban

When the kanban assumptions change significantly, the kanban quantities must also change (or be resized) up or down. The direction of the change will depend on production requirement or demand changes. Note that these changes can be due to more than just changes in demand. Changes can occur when:

- ❑ Changes in process operating parameters (scrap, downtime, or changeovers) are causing capacity increases or decreases
- ❑ Lack of process control is forcing an increase in buffer inventory

Additionally, when changes (other than production requirements) force you to make increases in the kanban quantity, target these problems as a continuous improvement opportunity. Make sure that everyone understands why the kanban quantities increased and task them to develop an improvement action plan.

Another consideration is that you must keep track of cyclical demand for your products. For example, do you sell much lawn furniture in December? Or, when do you sell more barbecue sauce, in

December or July? If you have cyclical demand, then you will need to plan on the periodic recalculation of the kanban quantities to address these changes. When looking at cyclical demand, also consider the leveling of production to meet peak demand or developing alternate production items with opposite cyclical demand (for example, producing lawnmowers and snow blowers).

As you audit the kanbans, keep track of the number of times you must resize due to changes. If you are resizing the kanban more than three to four times per year, then go back to your original design and reassess it for sensitivity to the changing parameters of your business. You may need to change your buffer quantities to support production fluctuations. These types of assessments will come with experience. Just remember that you are implementing the kanban to improve production management and improve flow, not to complicate your operation.

Using the *Workbook*

The CD-ROM *Workbook* contains the audit form and the audit summary form for your use in setting up a formal audit process. The *Workbook* also has questions to guide you through the process of creating an audit plan.

Summary

Once you launch your kanban, it is time to create a process for auditing the kanban. Your goal must be to get the kanban started and to keep it running: Auditing will be the key to keeping it running.

The first step is to set an audit schedule. Initially, audit daily; then move to one or two times per week.

When you audit, you need to look for the following items:

- ❑ Have any of the scheduling signals or pieces disappeared?
- ❑ Is the inventory correct (containers versus signals)?

- ❑ Are the operators, material handlers, and customers following the design?
- ❑ Does anyone in the process have any questions or concerns?
- ❑ Do the original sizing assumptions and calculations still apply?

As you find problems, then use the 5 Whys and 1 How (or 5W1H) method to determine the root cause and to determine how the problem occurred. Once you know how the problem occurs, then make the necessary corrections.

Also, reassess the appropriateness of the kanban size and make corrections as appropriate.

CHAPTER

9

IMPROVING THE KANBAN

One of the basic tenets of kanban (and for that matter the entire Lean philosophy) is that once you implement, you should continuously improve the kanban by reducing the kanban quantities. However, the only way to reduce the quantities, without jeopardizing the customer is to improve the process or reduce your buffers. To improve the process you must reduce scrap, downtime, or changeovers. To initially illustrate this point, we presented four graphs in Chapter 4 that showed the impact of these process improvements on the calculated quantities. (Figures 9-1 to 9-4 show these same graphs.) Reducing the buffer requires you to address your safety stock and to reduce supplier lead-times.

Accordingly, we have developed this chapter to discuss how to improve these three process areas and to discuss options for reducing buffers. Our first recommendation, however, is to assess your process and determine which of the three process areas will make the most significant improvement in the kanban quantities. A sim-

Figure 9-1. Impact of reducing scrap on kanban quantities.

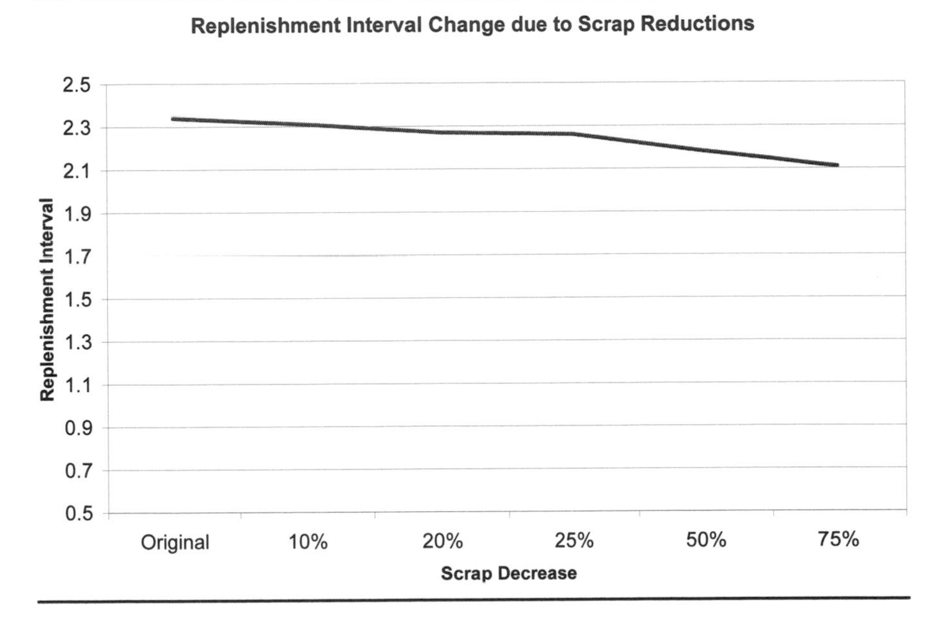

Figure 9-2. Impact of reducing downtime on kanban quantities.

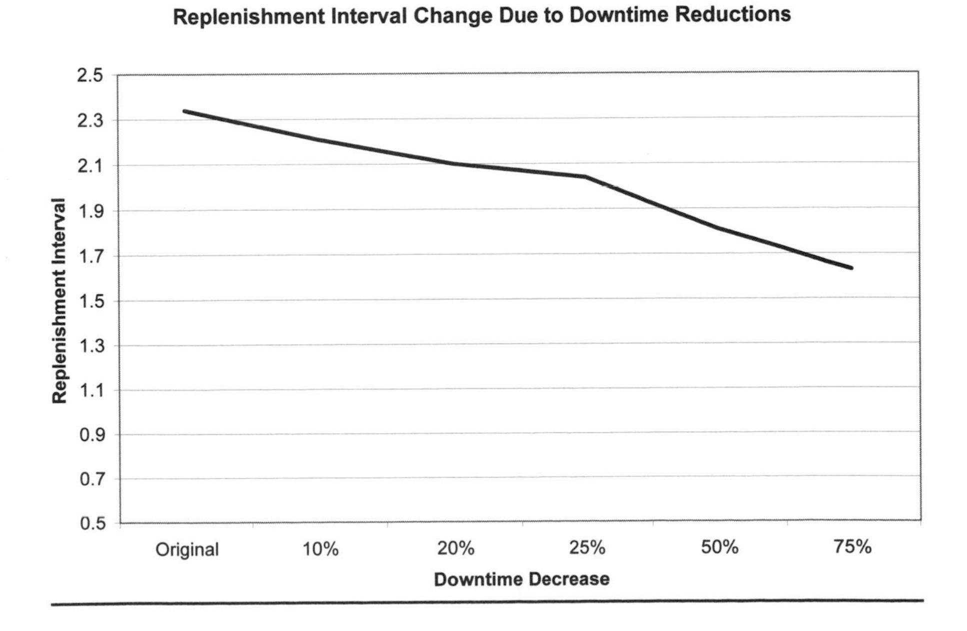

Figure 9-3. Impact of reducing changeover times on kanban quantities.

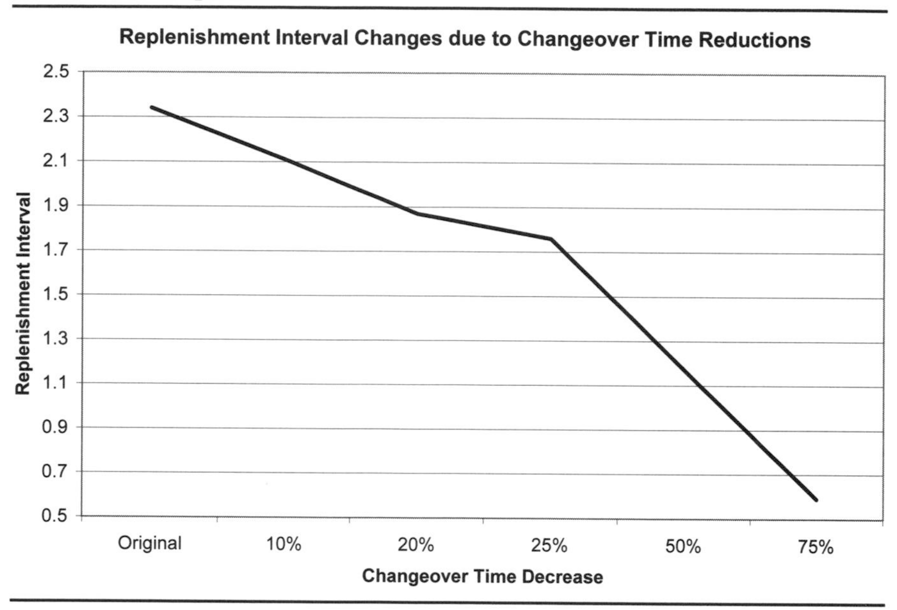

Figure 9-4. Impact of reducing all three factors on kanban quantities.

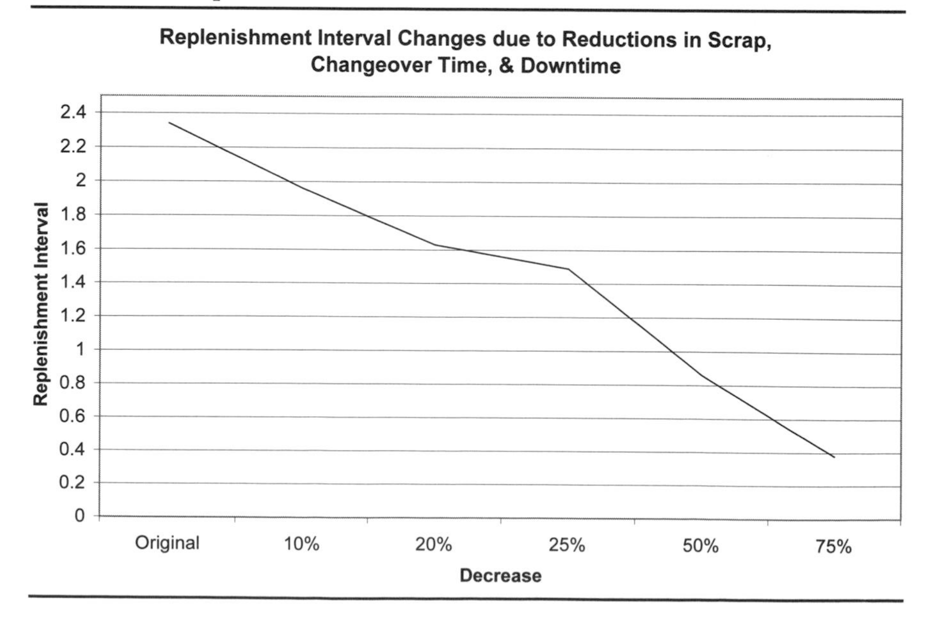

ple way to make this determination is to incrementally change each factor in your original kanban calculations to see how the replenishment interval changes.

Once you have determined where to focus, then we recommend you develop a systematic plan for improving the kanban. This plan should also include long-term goals for reducing kanban quantities. Hopefully, by establishing long-term goals, you will plant the seeds for a continuous improvement mentality (or culture) within your organization.

With the introduction of the continuous improvement step we have completed the process flow we started in Chapter 3 and have developed throughout this book. The completed process flow for implementing kanban is shown in Figure 9-5.

Note that the addition of this last step creates a continuous loop of improvement for the kanban. We created this loop in keeping with the philosophies of the Toyota Production System (or TPS). Remember, the driving concept behind TPS is to continually drive waste out of the process. Therefore, the process of improvement never ends.

Improving the Process

From our experience, the biggest improvement to the kanban replenishment interval, which in turn allows the biggest reduction in kanban containers, comes from reducing changeover times of the process. This statement is born out by our graphs, which also show that changeover times beat out reducing scrap and downtime. However, scrap and downtime reductions can lead to the biggest bang for the buck since improvements in these areas typically lead to savings in both inventory and scrap dollars. Therefore, we will address methods for improving all three areas.

Reducing Changeover Times

To reduce changeover times you need to:

1. Improve the actions that occur while the process is down for changeover
2. Perform as many changeover steps before the process stops

Figure 9-5. Kanban implementation flow.

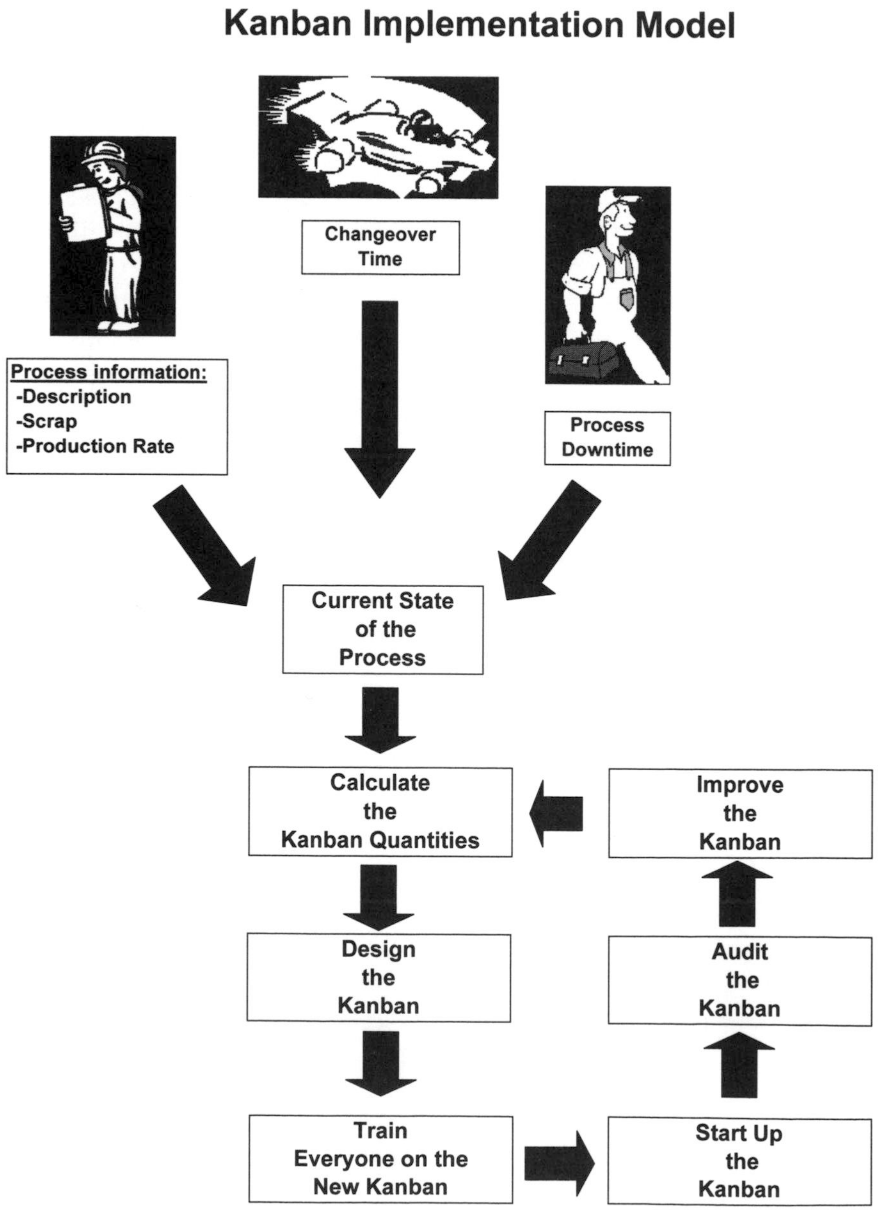

Kanban Implementation Model

Changeover Time

Process information:
-Description
-Scrap
-Production Rate

Process Downtime

Current State of the Process

Calculate the Kanban Quantities

Improve the Kanban

Design the Kanban

Audit the Kanban

Train Everyone on the New Kanban

Start Up the Kanban

Some of the actions to consider for improving the changeover include:

- ❑ Coordinate the activities of the changeover participants
- ❑ Eliminate wasted motion
- ❑ Eliminate travel
- ❑ Eliminate waiting
- ❑ Improve the startup activities

The best way to accomplish these two objectives is to conduct a quick changeover workshop, or SMED (short for Single Minute Exchange of Dies workshop). SMED workshops were pioneered by Shigeo Shingo to support the needs of the Toyota Production System.

A SMED workshop consists of vidcotaping a changeover, then dissecting the changeover to make improvements. During the review of the video, you breakdown the changeover activities into a series of steps so that you can identify activities that can be:

- ❑ Done before or after the changeover occurs
- ❑ Done faster
- ❑ Eliminated

The act of moving an activity to before or after the changeover is called making the action an "external" step. Making an action happen faster or eliminating the action completely is called "streamlining" the step.

Also, when reviewing the video, look for actions that are out of place, should be assigned to another person, or should be combined with another activity. These observations will form the coordination part of the workshop activities.

When reviewing the video for items that can be moved from an internal step to an external step, look at these areas for candidates:

- ❑ Travel back and forth for changeover parts
- ❑ Cleaning or 5s activities
- ❑ Alignment activities
- ❑ Attachments of hoses or cables

Most times these steps can be moved to an external step by prepositioning the changeover parts, creating new cleanup procedures, or fabricating new jigs (or duplicate jigs).

When reviewing the video for items that can be streamlined, look at these areas for candidates:

- ❑ Numerous nuts and bolts that need to be removed and reinstalled
- ❑ Confusing cabling
- ❑ Alignment activities
- ❑ Excessive movement at workstations
- ❑ Manhandling of fixtures

These items can often be streamlined by looking at the purpose of the activity. In most cases, the waste will become readily apparent to the operators participating in the workshop when they see themselves or their peers performing the changeover. To streamline the removal and installation of bolts and nuts, look at eliminating the number required (this action will typically require engineering and safety approvals), shorting of the bolt lengths, and utilizing speed nuts, ratchet handle bolts, or quarter turn nuts and bolts. (Figure 9-6 shows examples of speed nuts and ratchet handle bolts.)

To streamline the changeout of confusing wiring and inexact alignment issues, use visual management techniques. Such techniques as color coding, special fittings, and scribing of corner and centerline marks will help eliminate fumbling and mistakes. Fumbling and mistakes can also be eliminated by standardizing gaps between tools and fabricating spacers and jigs.

To eliminate excess operator movement during changeovers make sure that the operator has the tools required for the task within *easy reach* and make sure that the operator has a place to put the old changeover hardware. Prestaging tooling, 5s tool boards, and carts all help to eliminate unnecessary movement. Also, question any out of sequence activities, such as the operator suddenly leaving to go help someone else, or moving on to another activity without completing the current activity, or moving back and forth around

Figure 9-6. Examples of quick changeover hardware.

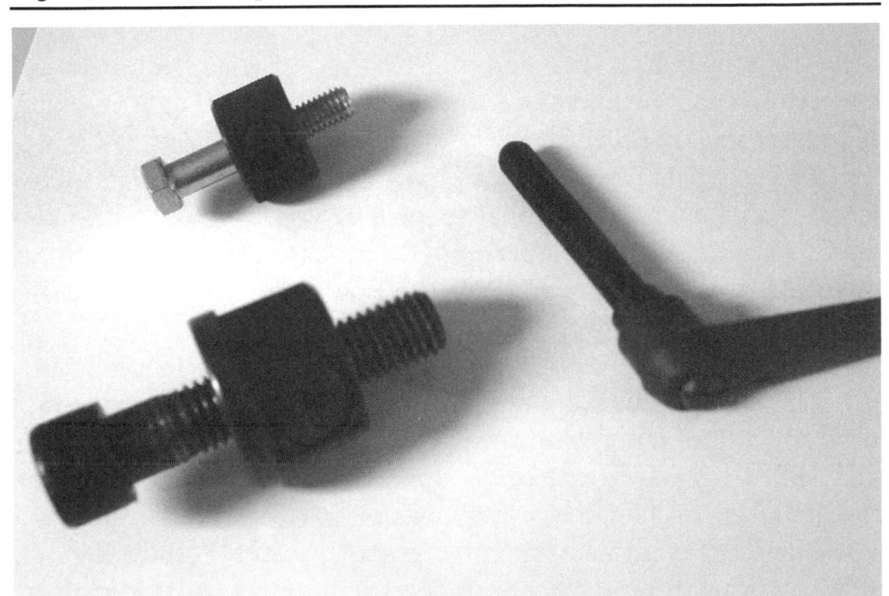

the machine without an apparent pattern. These observations may be opportunities to change the workflow or to reassign tasks to someone else. However, streamlining of these actions may also require the assistance of engineering or maintenance to modify the changeover tools.

Once you have reviewed the video (or videos) and documented your findings/improvement opportunities, it's time to create a new changeover. The new changeover design should be a choreographed plan of who does what and when during the changeover time. The new design should also incorporate all the changes you identified in the preceding steps.

In addition, before you start designing the new internal changeover, you will need to identify the external activities that will occur before the changeover starts. Make this a running list so that you can add to it as you proceed with creating the new changeover.

Start your new internal changeover at "time = 0" when the last good part has been produced. Now, operator by operator, create a timeline of the actions that each operator will perform. Each operator's timeline should incorporate the changes you identified while dissecting the video. This step is also the point where you use your observations about excessive travel to make sure that it is eliminated or properly timed in the new changeover.

As you create the timeline of the actions for each operator, look for waiting time and tasks that require two or more people to perform. Use the waiting to perform the tasks that require multiple people. Also, consider everyone's location to determine who is the best person to perform these tasks.

The last part of designing a new changeover is to design the process startup. This step represents a major opportunity to reduce time and to save scrap. Many people who are unfamiliar with kanban and SMED fail to recognize this opportunity. They misunderstand the definition of changeover includes not only the time for the physical changeover, but also the time to start up and produce the first good part at full rate. Therefore, a structured startup timeline reduces the time required for startup, which means less startup scrap.

The startup process should identify each person's activities: where they are, what they are doing, and with whom they are working. Just like the changeover workflow, develop a list of steps starting at the point where you are ready to start the process. Now proceed through the startup, listing the actions that need to occur and who will do them. Be specific about who does what in this step; often the main problem with startups is that the crew members are unsure of their responsibility and there are conflicting practices. Don't shy away from addressing the lack of standardization with workshop members—make them determine the "one best way" and put it in the workflow.

Once you have the changeover completed, then it becomes time to document the action items and develop a training plan. The action items should be clearly spelled out with timelines and people assigned for their completion.

For those readers who are unfamiliar with SMED workshops, this is an area where a consultant may be helpful. The consultant can make sure that team gets a usable video and can ask the questions that will get the answers for external versus internal and streamlining. Even if you hire a consultant initially, you can develop a training plan to develop your own internal capability.

Finally, for those readers who would like more information on SMED, we recommend you read Shigeo Shingo's book, *A Revolution in Manufacturing: The SMED System.*[1] This book documents the development of SMED theories and presents many useful ideas for reducing changeover times.

Reducing Scrap

Although reducing scrap may not yield as great a contribution to reducing kanban quantities as the reduction in changeover times, it has other benefits. By reducing scrap you not only reduce kanban quantities, but you save scrap cost, improve customer relations, improve quality, and improve operator morale. Additionally, reducing scrap may allow you to reduce your safety stock due to the resultant reduced process variability.

When attempting to reduce scrap, you need to determine whether the cause of the scrap is a lack of nonstandard operations and training or a technical issue. If the scrap is due to nonstandard work or lack of training, then no amount of technical expertise will create a sustainable reduction in scrap. To determine whether your problems stem from this lack of standardization and training, evaluate your standard work instructions, 5s status, training program, and visual management signs and markings:

- ❑ Do work instructions instruct operators on only "one best way"?
- ❑ Are operators trained to operate the process according to standard work?
- ❑ Do you have a training program?
- ❑ Are the operators periodically evaluated, or audited, for their compliance to standard work instructions?
- ❑ Are locations clearly marked for all tools and supplies?

- ❑ Do the signs clearly show the flow of work and material through the process?

If the answers to these questions are no, then start looking at how to make the answers yes. By creating standardization and training, you create a culture that can sustain the technical improvements.

To reduce scrap due to technical issues you will need data. The data will tell you where to focus and what to focus on. Experience tells us that in most processes, scrap follows the Pareto principle: 80 percent of the scrap is caused by 20 percent of the problems.

To follow this process, build a three-level Pareto to identify the root cause of your processes highest scrap cause or causes. Start by building a graph of the scrap causes for the target process. Rank the scrap causes from highest to lowest on the graph. Now identify the top one and two scrap causes for further investigation.

The next level of Pareto looks graphically at the causes of these top scrap items. Following the same format, identify the top items for further investigation.

Finally, repeat the process for those items identified in the previous graph. At this point you should have a fairly good idea of what's causing the scrap and be ready to develop solutions. Figure 9-7 shows the relationship of these graphs.

Once you have eliminated these scrap causes, then move onto the next scrap cause, using the same three-level Pareto process to eliminate these new items. Remember, the continuous improvement process never stops!

Reducing Downtime

Just like scrap reduction, downtime reduction requires a two-pronged approach:

1. Permanently repair the chronic failures and improve the equipment's general condition

Figure 9-7. Three-level Pareto to determine root causes.

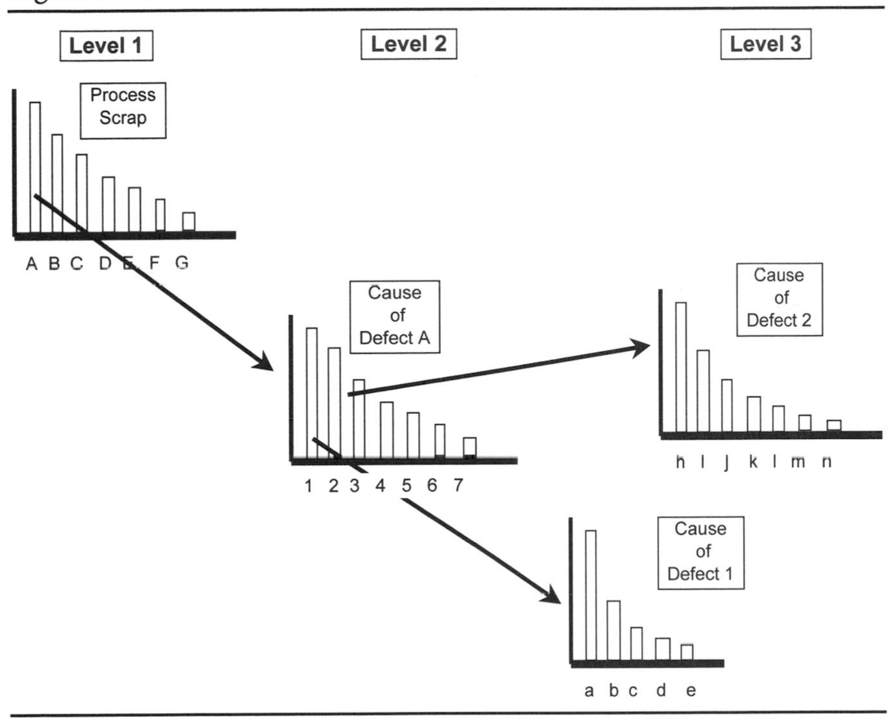

2. Institute periodic maintenance to keep the equipment in like-new condition

To achieve these two objectives, we suggest you conduct a total productive maintenance (or TPM) workshop for your process. The TPM workshop will allow you to systemically approach the elimination of downtime. The workshop steps consist of:

- Generating a repair and correction list that documents and tags all the maintenance problems (called an abnormality list or yellow tag event)
- Conducting a deep-cleaning event where all the operators physically remove machine guards to literally clean the entire machine—inside and out
- Generating an access and contamination list of areas that are

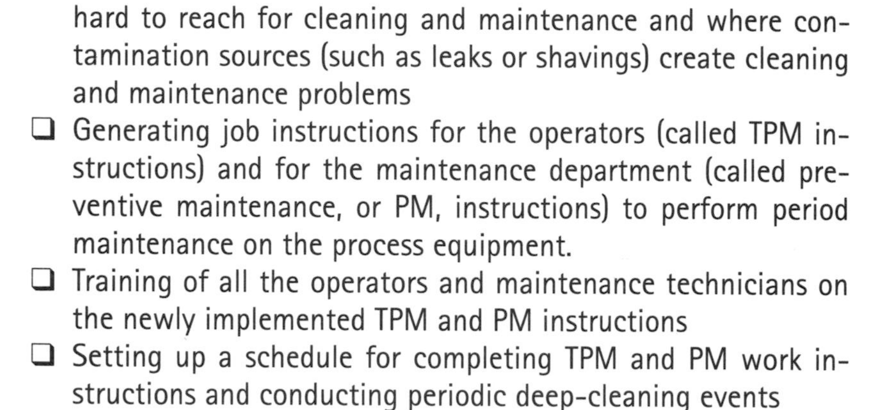

hard to reach for cleaning and maintenance and where contamination sources (such as leaks or shavings) create cleaning and maintenance problems

- ❑ Generating job instructions for the operators (called TPM instructions) and for the maintenance department (called preventive maintenance, or PM, instructions) to perform period maintenance on the process equipment.
- ❑ Training of all the operators and maintenance technicians on the newly implemented TPM and PM instructions
- ❑ Setting up a schedule for completing TPM and PM work instructions and conducting periodic deep-cleaning events

The TPM workshops may take place in a week or may take several weeks to complete—depending on the size of the process. The workshop should include a cross-functional team of operators and maintenance technicians. The cross-functional team ensures that you have adequate process knowledge and technical knowledge at the workshop. The cross-functional team also promotes buy-in from both groups while allowing both groups to understand the issues faced on a daily basis by the other group.

When developing the job instructions, look at the process as a system and determine the activities required to keep it running at peak performance. Many people approach this activity by asking what actions the operators can perform and what should be assigned to maintenance. They then proceed to develop the TPM instructions first.

By taking a systems approach, you ask what task must be performed to keep the equipment running at peak performance, how often these tasks should occur, and who can perform each task. Once you have made this list, then develop your TPM and PM work instructions. (For those readers who are not familiar with developing PM instructions, the book *Fundamentals of Preventive Maintenance* provides excellent information on developing PM work instructions and systems.[2])

The regularly scheduled deep-cleaning events will require scheduled downtime. These events are important to maintaining the like-new condition of the equipment and to identifying potential failures. The deep-cleaning activity allows not only for inspection opportunities, but for the operators to become more knowledgeable about how their equipment operates. Because you will regularly conduct deep cleaning, completion of the items on the access and contamination list is as important as the items on the abnormality list. These items make it easier to complete the deep clean and reduce the cleaning effort required.

Although after completing the first deep-cleaning event you may be dirtier than you have ever been in your entire life, the toughest part of the program will be its long-term conduct. To complete the action list and to perform the work instructions requires scheduling of downtime. However, the payoff will be worth the effort.

Incorporating Process Changes into the Kanban

As you make changes in one of the areas above, you will have the opportunity to reduce the number of containers in the kanban. To determine how many containers can be eliminated, follow the process model presented earlier in the chapter, in Figure 9-5. The steps to reducing the kanban quantity include:

- ❑ Recalculate the quantities with the new improvements.
- ❑ Assess whether the new quantities cause you to change your design.
- ❑ Communicate the changes to the operators and anyone else impacted by the changes.
- ❑ Make the changes and get started.
- ❑ Keep auditing!

As you move through the model, you may not need to make design changes or conduct massive training, but all these areas need to be thought through for continuity purposes.

Reducing Buffers

The last area to assess for opportunities to reduce your kanban quantities is in the area of buffer reductions. Treat buffers separate from the other improvement areas because the replenishment interval is determined without considering the buffer. Additionally, the buffer is usually set by past practice and gut feel, with little or no calculations. In fact, these lead times are often entered into MRP scheduling systems and never visited again. The areas for focus when looking at buffer reductions are safety stock assumptions and raw material lead times.

Reducing Safety Stock

We created the safety stock to cover downtime, quality issues, stock outs, and demand fluctuation. So as time goes on and you gain confidence, review the original assumptions and ask these questions:

- ❑ Were we too conservative?
- ❑ Have process factors (such as scrap, downtime, or changeovers) improved?

As you consider your answers to these questions, assess how many times you stocked out, how many times you hit red and had to make an emergency changeover, and how many times you had emergency quality problems. The answers to these questions will guide you in determining whether you can reduce your safety stock.

Reducing Raw Material Lead Times

When we say that we want to reduce our raw material lead-times, we really mean that we want more frequent deliveries of the material. The lead-time reductions can happen by the supplier either reducing the batch size to allow more frequent deliveries or making smaller shipments from the existing inventory.

In the simplest case, the supplier maintains an inventory of a common raw material and ships the raw material more frequently. Although this situation appears to be very straightforward, a pitfall exists with the increase in shipments. As you increase the shipments and decrease your WIP due to lead time, your transportation costs can skyrocket. Therefore, you must look at transportation costs as well as the WIP cost reductions when making this decision. As a matter of fact, since transportation can spiral out of control if not monitored, we recommend using transportation cost as a percentage of sales as a business metric.

One option to combat higher transportation cost is to use milk runs among multiple suppliers. *Milk runs* are shipments with multiple pickups or deliveries by the same truck on a prearranged route. A milk run can originate from a single supplier with deliveries to multiple customers, or it can deliver multiple items from different suppliers to the same customer. The intent is to optimize cost for shipment sizes that are smaller than a semi-trailer (or in shipping lingo, "less than a load").

This strategy is used daily by automobile manufacturers to reduce their assembly plant inventory levels. They have preset routes that pick up parts based on prearranged orders at their suppliers' plants for transport to the assembly plants.

To implement a milk run requires the creation of a route and a schedule for the trucks to pick up your materials. You can create this route or you can work with your trucking company to create the route. Whatever method you use to create a milk run, your goal will be to reduce inventory by having more frequent pickups without increasing transportation costs.

The alternate version of this idea would be for you to see whether your supplier has other customers in your area, and then have the supplier create the milk run. You could also check with companies in your area to see whether they have suppliers in the same region as your supplier and partner with these suppliers to create a milk run. Either of these options is feasible when all parties are cooperating. If you're considering multicompany milk runs, then don't be afraid to get your trucking company involved—after all, their job is transporting material from point A to point B.

The more difficult side of reducing the lead times of suppliers occurs when their lead times or current processes prevent them from making smaller deliveries without increasing their inventory. When they must increase their inventory, they increase their costs, which they ultimately pass on to you. Or in some cases, they may not be able to reduce batch sizes under their current process, and they will need to make changes in the process to accommodate your request.

In this situation, you will need to meet with the supplier and discuss what you have in mind. During this meeting, make sure they are aware of Lean concepts (you will be amazed how many manufacturers think that you are talking about weight loss) and the benefits of Lean manufacturing. They should already be aware of the changes you're undergoing because of your original discussions when you first set up the kanban.

Also, as part of this meeting, listen to any suggestions they have that could reduce the quantities or otherwise save money. Often, as customers, we may think we know the business better than the supplier. Likewise, suppliers may wonder why we want something that costs so much extra, but that no one else has ordered.

The outcome of such a meeting will be the supplier accepting or rejecting your request for reduced lead times. As we previously advised, you must let them make the decision. If you bully them into acceptance, then you run the risk of their agreeing to a schedule that they cannot support, and you end up suffering the consequences. If they reject the request, then determine why and take appropriate actions as a customer: Accept the answer, change suppliers, or work with the supplier to reduce the batch size incrementally

In terms of working with the supplier, this action can take several forms. You can refer them to training programs or to your consultants for implementation of Lean. If you have enough trained resources, you may even offer to help. If you offer to help, then you will want to work out a fee in advance. Typically the fee comes as a price reduction proportionate to the savings from changing the target process.

Incorporating Buffer Changes into the Kanban

The process outlined in Figure 9-5 also applies to reducing the kanban size for changes in the buffer calculations. The recalculation of the quantities is easier because you simply add buffer onto the replenishment interval quantities to determine the total number of kanban containers. When you have these quantities calculated, follow the process outlined in the previous section on implementing process changes.

Using the Workbook

The CD-ROM *Workbook* contains useful forms for identifying and prioritizing the area to focus on for continuous improvement. The *Workbook* will also help you create the framework for executing improvements strategies in each of the areas described in this chapter.

Summary

The last step in our kanban implementation model is reduction of the kanban quantities. The best way to reduce the quantities, without jeopardizing the customer, is to improve the process or reduce your buffer. To improve the production process you must follow a structured program to reduce changeovers, scrap, and downtime. Changing the buffer requires you to address your safety stock and to reduce the supplier lead times.

When looking at process improvements, prioritize the areas of focus before launching off in all directions. Using the graphs presented in Figures 9-1 through 9-4 as a guide, look at which improvements will lead to the biggest reduction in the replenishment interval.

To reduce changeover times, conduct a SMED workshop. The SMED workshop will help you analyze the changeover and develop improvements. The results of the workshop will be a choreographed changeover that has each participant's role mapped out.

To reduce scrap, determine whether the problem arises from lack of standardization and training or from a technical problem. If the issue is standardization and training, resolve these issues before placing heavy emphasis on the technical problems. A lack of standardization and training will prevent long-term technical solutions from being permanently implemented.

When you begin to focus on the technical issues to reduce scrap, use a structured data-driven process to find the root cause of the major technical issues. Because our experience shows that most scrap problems follow the Pareto principle, we recommend using three-level Paretos to determine the root cause.

To reduce downtime, conduct a TPM workshop. This workshop will help you identify areas for repairs and improvements to bring the equipment back to like-new condition and will help you set up a maintenance program to maintain this condition. When setting up the maintenance instructions, look at the whole process and what it will take to maintain the process: Develop instructions to achieve this outcome, and then assign responsibilities.

To reduce buffers, address the assumptions behind the safety stock and your raw material supplier's lead time. When looking at safety stock reductions, answer the questions presented in this chapter to determine whether you can reduce the quantities.

To reduce supplier lead times, work with the supplier to determine their ability to handle the reduced lead time. As you reduce shipment quantities, also watch your transportation cost to make sure you don't achieve smaller raw material inventories at the expense of skyrocketing transportation costs. The chapter presents several ideas on how to manage the transportation costs using milk runs.

When you work with suppliers who cannot reduce the ship

quantities due to their lead times or batch sizes, make sure they are aware of the concept of Lean manufacturing. If they do not embrace Lean or cannot support your goals for reducing raw material shipments without an increase in price, then you will need to make the appropriate business decisions for your operation.

Finally, whenever you have achieved a change in one of these areas, use the model in Figure 9-5 to implement the changes in quantities. The steps to changing the kanban quantity include:

- ❑ Recalculate the quantities with the new improvements.
- ❑ Assess whether the new quantities cause you to change your design.
- ❑ Communicate the changes to the operators and anyone else impacted by the changes.
- ❑ Make the changes and get started.
- ❑ Keep auditing!

As you move through the model, you may not need to make design changes or conduct massive retraining, but these areas need to be thought through to ensure continuity.

Notes

1. Shigeo Shingo, *A Revolution in Manufacturing: The SMED System* (Portland, Ore.: Productivity Press, 1985).
2. John M. Gross, *Fundamentals of Preventive Maintenance* (New York: AMACOM, 2002).

CHAPTER

10

CONCLUSION

Throughout the book we have developed a basic model (repeated in Figure 10-1) for the implementation of kanban scheduling. This model contains seven steps, listed in Figure 10-2, for implementing and maintaining the kanban. In keeping with the basic tenets of the Toyota Production System and Lean manufacturing, we have shown this model as a continuous loop of implementing and improving the kanbans. Today's competitive manufacturing environment requires this philosophy of continuous improvement and change to survive.

In Chapter 1, we also said that many people didn't implement kanban because of lack of understanding and fear of change. We hope that this book clears up the lack of understanding and that it gives you the means to address your implementation fears. We believe that the best way to address your fears is by developing plans that prevent these fears from occurring. This belief leads us to stress:

- Using current process data to calculate the kanban quantities
- Developing written kanban operating rules and visual manage-

Figure 10-1. Kanban implementation model.

Kanban Implementation Model

Process information:
-Description
-Scrap
-Production Rate

Changeover Time

Process Downtime

Current State of the Process

Calculate the Kanban Quantities

Design the Kanban

Train Everyone on the New Kanban

Start Up the Kanban

Audit the Kanban

Improve the Kanban

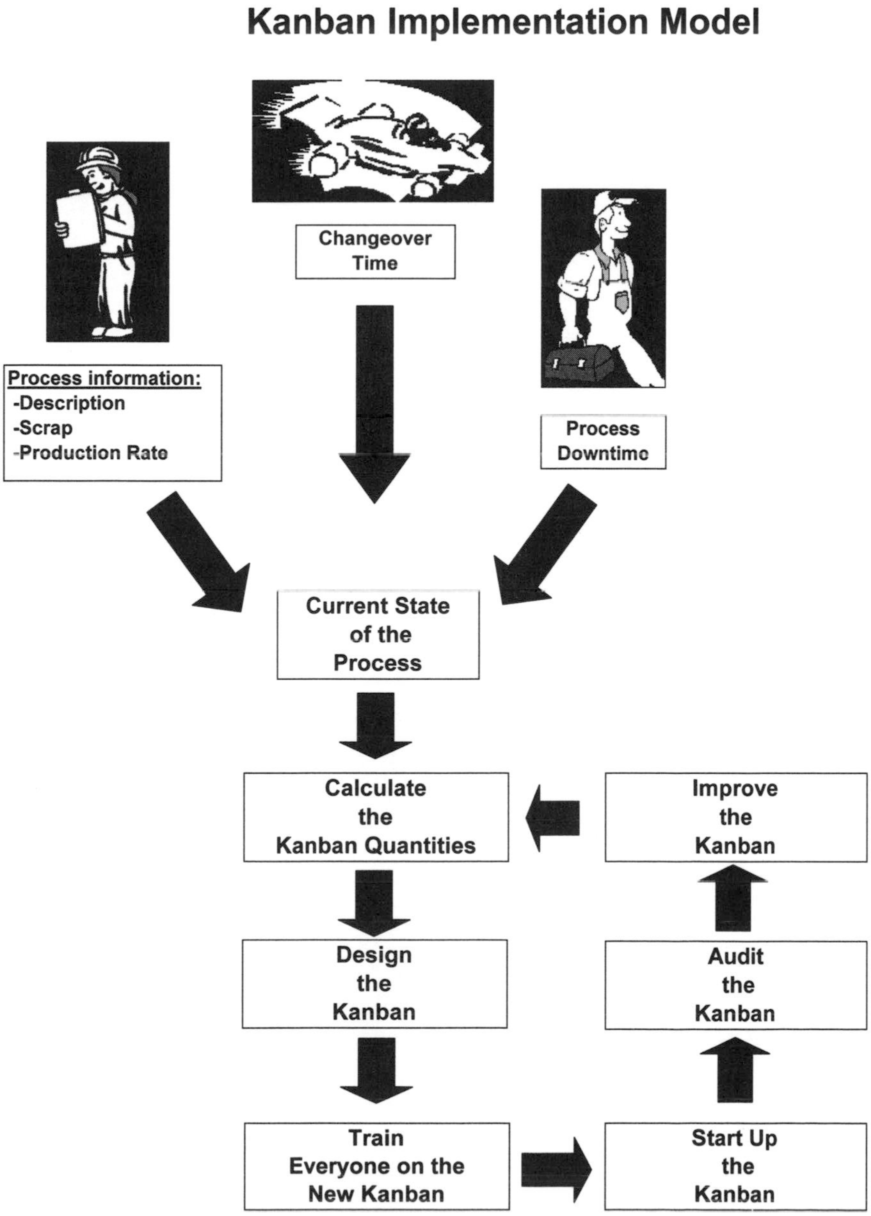

Figure 10-2. Seven steps to implementing kanban.

1. Conduct data collection
2. Calculate the kanban size
3. Design the kanban
4. Train everyone
5. Start the kanban
6. Audit and maintain the kanban
7. Improve the kanban

ment plans that spell out the when, where, and who of the kanban design

We also proposed several keys to successful implementation of kanban scheduling to help in formulating your kanban. These items are shown in Figure 10-3. Throughout the book we have built our concepts around these keys.

Figure 10-3. The keys to successful kanban implementation.

- Size the kanban to current conditions
- Adapt container size to allow flow
- Make kanban signals visual
- Develop rules that provide decision points plus checks and balances
- Train the operators to run the kanban system
- Set up audit plans to keep assumptions current and maintain system discipline
- Develop a phased improvement plan to reduce the kanban quantities

Finally, we know that the best way for you to develop an understanding of kanban is by implementation, or the proverbial: *Just Do It*!!

Therefore, use the steps in this book to help guide you through the process. As you encounter unique situations, use your team to develop solutions that address the issues. Thanks for your time. Good luck. Now get to work.

APPENDIX

A

MRP vs. Kanban

Although Kanban is an excellent execution tool, it is not intended as a planning tool. However, planning is where MRP-type systems excel. MRP systems work by taking a production forecast and turning it into a series of component forecasts. They do this by using bills-of-materials and routers, which break down each finished good into its basic components. MRP systems also use data on lead times and safety stocks to develop production schedules and raw material requirements. MRP systems excel at planning; however, they are data-intensive systems fraught with problems:

- ❑ Forecast error
- ❑ Labor intensive
- ❑ Systems intensive
- ❑ Resistant to change

Every forecast is a prediction of future demand based on present information. And, like weather forecasts, the farther out the forecast goes, the less accurate it is. Thus, when you plan your production and material schedules based on these forecasts, you will frequently have the wrong amount of material. If the forecast is high, you will schedule too much production, resulting in excess inventory and unnecessary work. If the forecast is low, you will miss customer shipments resulting in excessive expediting and overtime costs. Since the consequences of stock outs are higher (and more visible) than the consequence of excess inventory, most materials professionals choose to increase inventory levels to protect themselves ("just-in-case" inventory management).

MRP systems are also very labor intensive. Bill-of-materials and routers must be kept up-to date on every part in the system. Since there are always going to be errors (either in the bills and routers or in scrap and production reporting), cycle counts must be taken to correct the on-hand inventory levels. Accurate inventories are critical in a traditional MRP system, as errors lead to stock outs or excess inventory.

Since MRP systems are computer systems, they require special (and expensive) expertise to manage. This expertise takes the form of:

- Software experts (to constantly maintain, back-up, update, and monitor the software)
- Hardware experts, engineering experts (to create and maintain bills and routers)
- Materials experts (to run the system and execute its orders)

Once all of the files and systems have been created to run an MRP system, they also act as a strong disincentive to change. Every change means that a significant amount of work needs to be done to update the system. Thus, strong resistance to change (in particular the small, incremental changes necessary to achieve continuous improvement) develops in the organization.

Still, there are situations where MRP is useful:

- Ordering long lead-time items
- Generating forecasts

- ❑ Capacity planning
- ❑ Financial analysis

In cases where lead times are extremely long (such as when components must be shipped in from overseas), MRP forecasts may actually be a better solution than kanban. Generally, long lead-time parts also experience variance in transit times, and kanban systems rely on consistent transit times. Also, long lead-time items are usually accompanied by high freight costs. Since many MRP systems utilize EPQ models, they can be useful in keeping total system costs down (see Appendix E, EOQ vs. Kanban).

MRP systems offer an effective tool to turn production or sales forecasts into raw material component forecasts. The material components forecast is particularly valuable for companies with long lead-time items or complex supply chains. For example, tier-1 suppliers in the automotive industry are required to transmit material forecasts to all of their tier-2 suppliers. The tier-2 suppliers are likewise asked to transmit the same forecast data to their suppliers. When this is done throughout the supply chain, inventory can be minimized and the "bullwhip phenomena" minimized.

The "bullwhip phenomena" occurs when different firms in a supply chain modify forecast data before passing it down the chain. This distortion of data can result in huge swings in the amounts of inventory held in different stages of the supply chain, which leads to excess inventories, higher obsolescence costs, and slower responsiveness.

MRP systems can turn forecasts into capacity planning data. Thus, a firm can look into the future and resolve capacity issues (for both manning and equipment capacity). This information can also be used to make modifications to Kanban systems so it can support the new production requirements.

In order to track performance and report key financial information, an MRP system can be extremely useful. It can give detailed, real-time inventory information on raw materials, work-in-process, and finished goods that the accounting department needs to report plant performance. This information can also be useful to the plants' management team in tracking overall plant performance.

The shortcomings of the MRP systems, which we already discussed, are not as critical if the system is not used to execute production schedules and material purchases. Errors in the bill-of-materials, for example, will show up as inventory growth or shrinkage, but they will not lead to a stock out nor will they cost you sales. Thus, they still need to be addressed, but not with the same urgency. Also, the MRP system will not require as much detail in the areas of lead times, container sizes, and routings, since it will not be used to link operations or place material orders. Thus, it is possible to realize the benefits of MRP and Kanban at the same time as complementary management tools. The MRP system can handle the planning tasks, and Kanban can handle the day-to-day production scheduling execution, while preventing overproduction.

APPENDIX

B

KANBAN SUPERMARKETS

Implementing supermarkets in your plant can be a useful tool for transforming a manufacturing plant from a traditional operation to a pull system. In the traditional operation, raw materials are stored in a warehouse and issued to the floor per an MRP-generated schedule. In essence, a supermarket is a central storage location where raw materials are stored near their point-of-use, so customers can pull them as needed. It works just like the supermarket where you buy your groceries—hence the name. This system can help:

1. Minimize transaction costs
2. Facilitate visual management
3. Establish the framework to switch to a point-of-use kanban system

It can also be useful in overcoming resistance to a pull system, since it requires the production cells to obtain their own materials versus the materials department delivering it to them in large batches.

The first step in setting up a supermarket is to find a central location to hold the material. If the plant is large, several small supermarkets may be needed. The idea is to set up locations where all of the materials can be stored for easy retrieval as needed. In order to ensure proper stock rotation, the area needs to facilitate the proper flow of materials. Rotation is very important, since production employees will be pulling their own materials from the supermarket, and inventory rotation is not one of their primary concerns.

A simple way to accomplish this rotation is by installing flow lanes (using gravity-fed conveyor racks, if possible). The flow lanes work like this to ensure proper rotation: As materials are received, they are loaded onto the back of the conveyor rack. As needed, the customers then pull them from the front (see Figure B-1).

In order to make the supermarket and the rotation plan work, it may also be necessary to change some of the containers that materials are shipped in. The containers need to be small enough to be stored in the supermarket and pulled by production as needed. In order to minimize the quantity of materials on the shop floor, the quantity per container should be kept to a reasonable level (one shift's worth or less). This is particularly important if raw materials are issued from the supermarket to the floor. Since your inventory system may not track what has been issued, you want to keep the quantities of WIP to a minimum.

Attention also needs to be placed on keeping track of what is in the supermarket. Since (hopefully) you order your raw materials with a kanban system, the details of what is in the supermarket will mainly be used for financial tracking purposes. (For some suggestions on how to integrate kanban systems with inventory and MRP systems, see Appendix A.) The simplest way to track what is in the warehouse is to set up "supermarket" warehouse locations for each item. As materials are received in the plant, they are transported to and stored in the supermarket. At this point, they are received into the inventory system and scanned into the "supermarket" inventory location. As customers pull materials, they scan them out of the

Figure B-1.

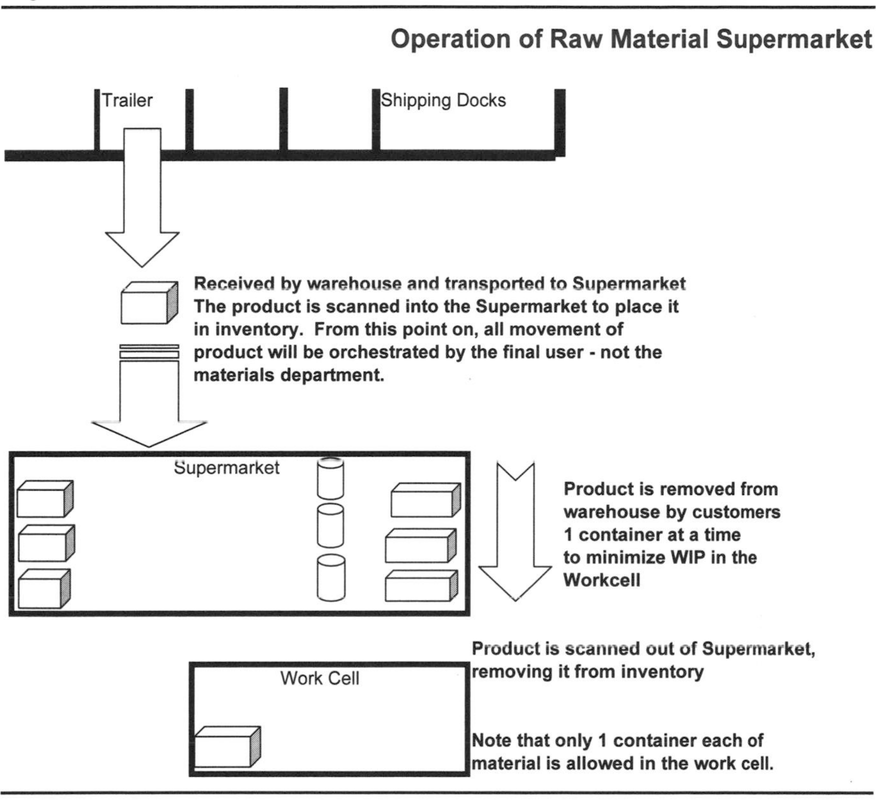

supermarket and into WIP. Thus, you have a simple method of tracking exactly what is in the supermarket. This method can be used with your MRP system or with a simple PC program (see Figure B-1).

Attention also needs to be paid to ensure the supermarket is laid out to allow visual management. Visual management is critical if you are using the supermarket to prepare the plant for the transformation to point-of-use kanbans. Therefore, at a minimum, every part in the supermarket needs to be labeled with:

- ❑ Supplier name
- ❑ Part number
- ❑ Internal customer

- ❑ Quantity per container
- ❑ Average daily usage

Additionally, visual markings (such as colored zones marked on the floor) and signs can be helpful.

Once a supermarket is installed and running, the transition to a point-of-use kanban system is simple. You can make this transition by building on two basic facts:

- ❑ You already have production operators pulling their own materials from the supermarket to keep themselves supplied.
- ❑ Your operators are experienced with visual management of their inventory levels.

At this point, follow this two-step process to implement point-of-use kanbans:

1. Move each of the raws to its point-of-use (within the production cell).
2. Design and install the kanban system for the production operators to order their own raw materials.

Supermarkets are a big improvement over the traditional warehouse system most companies use, and they facilitate the transition to a pull system. They get production operators into the practice of pulling their own materials as they need them, and they get them used to working with a visual system. Both of these activities can help reduce operator resistance to a pull system, which is critical in the successful transformation from traditional manufacturing to kanban.

APPENDIX

C

Two-Bin Kanban Systems

Two-bin kanban systems are a good tool to simplify material control. They make it possible to issue small items to the shop floor and basically "ignore" them until the pull signal (an empty bin) returns. This technique is especially useful in operations with a large number of parts. With a two-bin system you can place the small, inexpensive components into a two-bin kanban system. You can then focus your attention on managing the more expensive components (it is not unusual to find that 10 percent of your parts make up over 90 percent of your inventory dollars).

The first step to implementing an effective two-bin kanban system is to sort your raw materials by cost. A simple way to do this is to multiply the cost of each item by your average daily or weekly usage. Table C-1 shows a fictional product's parts list sorted in descending order by weekly usage in dollars.

The next step is to calculate the percentage of inventory value represented by each item, as shown in Table C-2. Once this is done,

Figure C-1.

Description	Weekly usage	Unit cost ($)	Weekly $
1 Drive	200	$300.00	$60,000
2 Motor	15	$2,500.00	$37,500
3 Harness	100	$140.00	$14,000
4 Fixture	45	$300.00	$13,500
5 Valve	130	$100.00	$13,000
6 Gage	12	$500.00	$6,000
7 Hose	100	$45.00	$4,500
8 Drive	12	$250.00	$3,000
9 Coupling	15	$150.00	$2,250
10 Belt	85	$25.00	$2,125
11 Fitting	40	$50.00	$2,000
12 Motor	5	$400.00	$2,000
13 Drive	5	$400.00	$2,000
14 Screw	2400	$0.50	$1,200
15 Belt	30	$35.00	$1,050
16 Coupling	150	$5.00	$750
17 Fitting	40	$15.00	$600
18 Belt	6	$80.00	$480
19 Adapter	3	$125.00	$375
20 Drive	5	$75.00	$375
21 Motor	70	$5.00	$350
22 Coupling	70	$5.00	$350
23 Drive	32	$10.00	$320
24 Charger	6	$50.00	$300
25 Belt	30	$10.00	$300
26 Fitting	5	$60.00	$300
27 Gizmo	50	$5.00	$250
28 Adapter	10	$25.00	$250
29 Charger	5	$40.00	$200
30 Belt	40	$5.00	$200
31 Charger	20	$10.00	$200
32 Belt	250	$0.50	$125
33 Motor	20	$5.00	$100
34 Gizmo	20	$5.00	$100
35 Adapter	20	$5.00	$100
36 Washer	20	$5.00	$100
37 Assembly	2	$50.00	$100
45 Gizmo	5	$20.00	$100
46 Seal	40	$2.00	$80
47 Tube	20	$4.00	$80
48 Pipie	160	$0.50	$80
49 Adapter	40	$2.00	$80
50 Screw	150	$0.50	$75
51 Clamp	300	$0.25	$75

52 Nut	300	$0.25	$75
53 Hose	5	$15.00	$75
54 Nozzle	5	$15.00	$75
55 Washer	30	$2.00	$60
56 Screw	30	$2.00	$60
57 Seal	20	$3.00	$60
58 Adapter	10	$6.00	$60
59 Nozzle	5	$10.00	$50
60 Belt	5	$10.00	$50
61 Screw	10	$4.00	$40
62 Seal	10	$4.00	$40
63 Belt	10	$4.00	$40
64 Adapter	40	$1.00	$40
65 Charger	40	$1.00	$40
66 Belt	40	$1.00	$40
67 Screw	10	$4.00	$40
68 Assembly	150	$0.25	$38
69 Adapter	140	$0.25	$35
70 Clamp	140	$0.25	$35
71 Gizmo	3	$10.00	$30
72 Charger	15	$2.00	$30
73 Washer	10	$3.00	$30
74 Pipie	10	$3.00	$30
75 Gizmo	440	$0.05	$22
76 Nut	40	$0.50	$20
77 Tube	400	$0.05	$20
78 Hose	20	$1.00	$20
79 Motor	40	$0.50	$20
80 Seal	5	$2.00	$10
81 Adapter	100	$0.05	$5
82 Gizmo	10	$0.40	$4
83 Charger	10	$0.25	$3
84 Gizmo	10	$0.25	$3
85 Adapter	10	$0.25	$3
86 Belt	160	$0.01	$2
87 Gizmo	40	$0.05	$2
88 Adapter	40	$0.05	$2
89 Charger	130	$0.01	$1
90 Tube	25	$0.05	$1
91 Screw	20	$0.05	$1
92 Charger	25	$0.04	$1
93 Belt	40	$0.02	$1
94 Clamp	160	$0.01	$1
95 Belt	75	$0.01	$1
96 Assembly	60	$0.01	$1
97 Assembly	10	$0.05	$1
98 Washer	10	$0.05	$1
99 Adapter	75	$0.01	$0

Figure C-2.

Description	Weekly usage	Unit cost ($)	Weekly $	% of total
Drive	200	$300.00	$60,000	**34.86%**
Motor	15	$2,500.00	$37,500	**21.79%**
Harness	100	$140.00	$14,000	**8.13%**
Fixture	45	$300.00	$13,500	**7.84%**
Valve	130	$100.00	$13,000	**7.55%**
Gage	12	$500.00	$6,000	**3.49%**
Hose	100	$45.00	$4,500	**2.61%**
Drive	12	$250.00	$3,000	**1.74%**
Coupling	15	$150.00	$2,250	**1.31%**
Belt	85	$25.00	$2,125	**1.23%**
Fitting	40	$50.00	$2,000	**1.16%**
Motor	5	$400.00	$2,000	**1.16%**
Drive	5	$400.00	$2,000	**1.16%**
Screw	2400	$0.50	$1,200	**0.70%**
Belt	30	$35.00	$1,050	**0.61%**
Coupling	150	$5.00	$750	**0.44%**
Fitting	40	$15.00	$600	**0.35%**
Belt	6	$80.00	$480	**0.28%**
Adapter	3	$125.00	$375	**0.22%**
Hose	5	$75.00	$375	**0.22%**
Motor	70	$5.00	$350	**0.20%**
Coupling	70	$5.00	$350	**0.20%**
Adapter	32	$10.00	$320	**0.19%**
Charger	6	$50.00	$300	**0.17%**
Belt	30	$10.00	$300	**0.17%**
Fitting	5	$60.00	$300	**0.17%**
Gizmo	50	$5.00	$250	**0.15%**
Adapter	10	$25.00	$250	**0.15%**
Charger	5	$40.00	$200	**0.12%**
Belt	40	$5.00	$200	**0.12%**
Charger	20	$10.00	$200	**0.12%**
Belt	250	$0.50	$125	**0.07%**
Motor	20	$5.00	$100	**0.06%**
Gizmo	20	$5.00	$100	**0.06%**
Adapter	20	$5.00	$100	**0.06%**
Washer	20	$5.00	$100	**0.06%**
Assembly	2	$50.00	$100	**0.06%**
Gizmo	5	$20.00	$100	**0.06%**
Seal	40	$2.00	$80	**0.05%**
Tube	20	$4.00	$80	**0.05%**
Pipie	150	$0.50	$80	**0.05%**
Adapter	40	$2.00	$80	**0.05%**
Screw	150	$0.50	$75	**0.04%**
Clamp	300	$0.25	$75	**0.04%**

Nut	300	$0.25	$75	0.04%
Hose	5	$15.00	$75	0.04%
Nozzle	5	$15.00	$75	0.04%
Washer	30	$2.00	$60	0.03%
Screw	30	$2.00	$60	0.03%
Seal	20	$3.00	$60	0.03%
Adapter	10	$6.00	$60	0.03%
Nozzle	5	$10.00	$50	0.03%
Belt	5	$10.00	$50	0.03%
Screw	10	$4.00	$40	0.02%
Seal	10	$4.00	$40	0.02%
Belt	10	$4.00	$40	0.02%
Adapter	40	$1.00	$40	0.02%
Charger	40	$1.00	$40	0.02%
Belt	40	$1.00	$40	0.02%
Screw	10	$4.00	$40	0.02%
Assembly	150	$0.25	$38	0.02%
Adapter	140	$0.25	$35	0.02%
Clamp	140	$0.25	$35	0.02%
Gizmo	3	$10.00	$30	0.02%
Charger	15	$2.00	$30	0.02%
Washer	10	$3.00	$30	0.02%
Pipie	10	$3.00	$30	0.02%
Gizmo	440	$0.05	$22	0.01%
Nut	40	$0.50	$20	0.01%
Tube	400	$0.05	$20	0.01%
Hose	20	$1.00	$20	0.01%
Motor	40	$0.50	$20	0.01%
Seal	5	$2.00	$10	0.01%
Adapter	100	$0.05	$5	0.00%
Gizmo	10	$0.40	$4	0.00%
Charger	10	$0.25	$3	0.00%
Gizmo	10	$0.25	$3	0.00%
Adapter	10	$0.25	$3	0.00%
Belt	160	$0.01	$2	0.00%
Gizmo	40	$0.05	$2	0.00%
Adapter	40	$0.05	$2	0.00%
Charger	130	$0.01	$1	0.00%
Tube	25	$0.05	$1	0.00%
Screw	20	$0.05	$1	0.00%
Charger	25	$0.04	$1	0.00%
Belt	40	$0.02	$1	0.00%
Clamp	160	$0.01	$1	0.00%
Belt	75	$0.01	$1	0.00%
Assembly	60	$0.01	$1	0.00%
Assembly	10	$0.05	$1	0.00%
Washer	10	$0.05	$1	0.00%
Adapter	75	$0.01	$0	0.00%
Total $			$172,136	

it is easy to identify which parts are valuable enough to merit significant management attention, and which are candidates for a two-bin system. In our example, the top fourteen items represent over 94 percent of the entire inventory cost. Our decision to take the top fourteen items was based on a simple visual analysis of the data—there is no need to develop complex rules for this type of analysis. A similar analysis of any data will present similar obvious cut-off points.

Using the top fourteen items as a break point, we can now devise a strategy to manage our two types of inventory. The bottom eighty-six items make up only 6 percent of our weekly inventory dollars. Generally speaking, these items will also tend to be small in size (being made up of items such as screws, bolts, washers, hoses, clamps, etc.). Obviously, we need to focus most of our management attention on the fourteen items that make up 94 percent of our inventory cost. Excessive levels of inventory on our top fourteen items would tie up large amounts of capital, while high levels of stock on the lower value items would have little effect on inventory dollars or floor space. A two-bin system will allow us to utilize this information to design a system that will prevent stock outs while managing our total inventory dollars.

For the expensive items, we would need to explore a variety of options to tightly control our inventory dollars and floor space utilization. Various forms of kanban, vendor-managed, and consigned inventory arrangements need to be considered. Again, we are going to implement a simple two-bin system for the balance of the raw materials, so that management attention can be devoted to these high dollar items.

The low value items (in our example, the bottom eighty-six) are good candidates for a two-bin system. As the name implies, this involves setting up two bins: one for use on the shop floor, and one in the storage area.

The container on the shop floor needs to be sized appropriately. The container needs to be small enough to fit at point-of-use, but big enough to minimize the frequency of replenishment. For example, if an item is purchased in minimum quantities of 50,000 items, it may not be appropriate to size the shop-floor container to hold that many parts. Maybe a container of 1,000 items would fit well in the work cell, and the remaining 49,000 parts would be stored in the warehouse. Since these items are of little value, they should be expensed as they are issued from the warehouse. Expensing these items keeps you from wasting time counting and tracking them.

The bin in the storage area needs to hold enough parts to cover the replacement time (order time plus transit time) of the part. Per our example above, it may need to be much larger than this. Again, if a particular part (say a custom bracket) only comes in quantities of 50,000, and this equates to ten weeks worth of usage, then that is how big the bin will need to be. When the bin from the shop floor is returned empty, it is filled from the warehouse stock and sent back to production. When the warehouse stock reaches the predetermined reorder point, a replenishment signal is sent to the supplier.

A two-bin system can also be utilized between a plant and its suppliers. For example, if you are purchasing chemicals or lubricants in large containers, you can set up a two-bin system between yourself and the supplier. When the empty bin is returned from production, the full one is sent to production and the empty one returned to the supplier. The supplier then ships you a full bin and begins production to refill the empty one he just received. (In this system, there would actually be three bins in the loop, one in the production cell, one in the warehouse, and one at the supplier plant.)

APPENDIX

D

ORGANIZATIONAL CHANGES REQUIRED FOR KANBAN

In order to fully realize the benefits of kanban, some decision making needs to be decentralized. To successfully implement kanban, the materials department must evolve from its traditional role of controlling production. This task can be tougher than it sounds, because some functions are difficult to decentralize. Typically, all material functions are coordinated by a materials department that:

- Generates the production and shipping schedules
- Coordinates raw material purchases and deliveries
- Controls material handling and storage systems

Since these activities occur in all parts of the plant, it is difficult for these activities to take place at the work cell level. It is critical for the success of Lean manufacturing, however, that control of these vital functions to be turned over to the work cell.

The solution lies in dividing the tasks between a centralized materials department and a series of empowered work cells. However, certain key tasks, such as vendor selection, price negotiations, and purchase order maintenance, need to be managed by trained materials professionals. With kanban scheduling, key tasks traditionally performed by the materials department, such as placing orders, warehouse layout, and vendor selection and evaluation, need to be transferred to the shop floor (see Figure D-1).

Functions of the Materials Department after Decentralization

One of the primary functions that must remain in the materials department to be handled by trained materials professionals is the coordination of vendor selection. The materials department needs to research potential vendors, qualify them, and present this information to the associates in the work cell. This activity must remain in

Figure D-1.

Materials Department	Shop Floor
• Generate Production Schedule • Order Raw Materials • Issue Purchase Orders • Select Vendors • Evaluate Vendor Performance • Maintain Materials System (BOM, Routers, etc.) • Generate Ship Schedules • Control Freight • Control Inventory Levels	• Schedule Attainment • Production/Scrap Reporting

the materials department for several reasons. For one, only materials professionals will have the knowledge necessary to locate, research, and qualify new vendors. For another, there are legal and ethical issues related to vendor selection that require training to be understood. Finally, by the materials department managing the vendor selection process, you prevent an uncontrolled proliferation of vendors that can dilute your pricing and negotiating leverage. This also allows the materials department to build long-term relationships with key vendors. Once a list of qualified vendors has been selected, it is up to the work cell to interview the potential vendors and make a selection.

It is critical that the work cell makes the final vendor decision, and that vendors understand that the work cell is the final decision maker. If this is not the case, the work cell will not expend any energy in building a relationship with the vendor. And the vendor, for his part, will not value feedback from the shop floor. The vendor will concentrate their attention on pleasing the materials department, whose critical issues may not coincide with those of the business unit.

A prime example of this conflict is a materials department switching to a lower cost supplier. Often, the opinions of the production department are not given enough weight. Consequently, a poor decision may be made because all of the relevant (non–price-related) costs are not considered.

Price negotiation and delivery arrangements are areas where the expertise of a materials professional is also necessary. Once the team has selected a vendor, the materials department needs to work with the selected vendor to arrive at pricing and delivery terms. The materials department can then issue a blanket purchase order, good for a specific time period, to the vendor. This purchase order can contain any legal terms or disclaimers deemed necessary. It can also be limited to a specific total quantity, to help minimize the risk of a work cell authorizing a vendor to overproduce material. The materials department can also set up shipping arrangements that are spelled out on the purchase order. The blanket purchase order allows the team to then release orders as required to support their production plans, without getting involved in the pricing and legal issues of purchasing.

The materials department should also be responsible for giving direction to all material activities in the plant. For example, the materials department should set targets for inventory levels. The targets are required to prevent individual departments from increasing inventory levels beyond those that are in the plant's operating budget. The materials department should also plan the training needed by the material coordinators in the work cells.

The final key function of the materials department in a decentralized system is maintaining the materials system. Any system, whether it is a simple pull system or a complex MRP system, needs to be maintained and developed by trained professionals. Maintenance of the routers, bill-of-materials, and invoicing/payment information all need to be kept up-to-date. The cost of training employees from each work cell to learn these functions is cost-prohibitive and could lead to a decline in the quality of the information.

Functions of the Work Cell

The key materials function of the work cell is production scheduling. The production schedule drives all other schedules (raw materials, subcomponents, staffing, etc.), so control of it is essential if the work cell is to truly manage itself. Making production scheduling a task of the team also helps create schedule buy-in. It also allows the team to tailor the production schedule to their unique requirements. The team also recognizes that the scheduling task is greatly simplified by transitioning to a kanban system.

If MRP is used to generate forecast and capacity information, then someone from the work cell needs to be trained on this system. Ideally, this person will be a full-time materials coordinator, who works as a member of the work cell team. This person is responsible for all of the materials functions that affect the work cell. Appointing one person to this task allows the company to limit the number of people that require training and creates a conduit for information flow between the work cell and the materials department

Two related functions of the work cell are controlling inventory levels and sending releases (orders) to the suppliers. Utilizing a visual kanban system facilitates this process. Floor space needs to be marked off to hold specific quantities of material. Ideally, two days or less of material should be held within the work cell. This will enable the employees of the team to quickly evaluate their inventory status while leaving them time to react if levels fall below the preset minimum. If higher inventory levels are required, the material should be held in a defined inventory area located away from the work cell. (Note that sometimes "larger-than-ideal" quantities of materials need to be ordered to minimize freight costs.)

The work cell should also be involved in vendor selection, as noted previously. The materials department should present the team with a list of qualified potential vendors, and the team should make the vendor selection. As part of the vendor selection process, the team should also develop a written list of supplier expectations to be given to each vendor prior to issuing a purchase order. The team needs to evaluate vendor performance, determining which vendors get future business and which do not. The evaluation process must be heavily weighted toward the experience of the employees on the floor. If they are not happy with the performance of the vendor, then action needs to be taken regardless of how well the materials department rates the vendor's performance. Figure D-2 details the materials department's responsibilities after decentralization.

Materials Organization after Decentralization

By separating the tasks between the materials department and the shop floor, the benefits of decentralizing the materials function can be realized, while still operating in an efficient and professional

Figure D-2.

Materials Department	Shop Floor
• Maintain Materials System • Train SBU Materials Coordinators • Issue Blanket Purchase Orders • Qualify New Vendors • Control Freight-out • Generate Ship Schedules	• Generate Production Schedules • Order Raw Materials • Select Vendors • Evaluate Vendor Performance • Coordinate Freight-in • Control Inventory Levels

manner. The net result will be a considerably smaller materials department, supplemented by a series of empowered work cells. The work cells will also assume responsibility for controling their own material supplies, which eliminates a layer of bureaucracy between them and their suppliers.

APPENDIX

E

EOQ vs. Kanban

A kanban model can sometimes lead you to a solution that requires an unrealistic number of changeovers. Since kanban formulation logic only considers time and does not consider the cost of changeovers, the final calculation can result in a solution that minimizes run size and inventory levels but schedules a large number of changeovers. An EOQ model can be utilized to give you a different solution that can be used as a sanity check on the kanban solution. EOQ models seek to find an optimum solution by determining the mathematical minimum total cost, taking into account holding cost and changeover costs. Although some companies apply the EOQ model directly, its logic is also used in some MRP/ERP systems. There are significant differences in the solutions generated by each method (EOQ versus kanban).

Kanban seeks to minimize inventory by minimizing the replenishment interval, which essentially drives you toward increasingly small lot sizes. This means that as you improve efficiency (for example, through reduced changeover times or decreased downtime), the kanban model will utilize this extra time to reduce the replenishment interval (and thus increase the number of changeovers.)

The EOQ model, however, seeks only to minimize cost. It will use any improvement in efficiency to reduce total system costs. Thus, as you increase efficiency, the optimal solutions given by the two models will change.

EOQ Model

The goal of the EOQ model is to determine the optimum procedure for producing a given quantity of product that minimizes holding and set-up costs while preventing stock outs. In our simplified example, we will set up a two-day safety stock that provides us with a 100 percent certainty that there will not be any stock outs (wouldn't it be nice if it were that easy in real life?). The model assumes a rotational cycle. This means that it assumes that every product is only set up once during the production cycle, similar to the replenishment cycle used in kanban calculations. As you will see below, the EOQ model's focus on cost minimization can create unrealistic solutions. We will compare the results of the EOQ model with the kanban model in an analysis of a fictional company that manufactures plastic components on one machine.

In this analysis, our company makes nine different products, some in multiple lengths. In this model, we plan for a two-day safety stock to avoid stock outs (the cost of stock outs is zero). We also input line speeds and changeover time (changeover time for length changes only is zero).

This is a simple model to demonstrate how EOQ models work. There are many different variations that can be incorporated into this model to fit real-world situations. In this simple model, we are seeking the minimum total cost; balancing holding costs with set-up (or ordering) costs. *Set-up costs* (f) are calculated as the cost of a machine set-up, including both the scrap generated and the labor required to perform the set-up. *Holding costs* (h) are the cost of holding inventory, which includes the value of the capital tied up in inventory (calculated as the firm's cost of capital, which in this case we will assume to be 12 percent). If there is an alternate revenue-producing use of floor space occupied by the inventory, then this also needs to be included in the holding costs. For our example, we assume this is not the case.

Under our EOQ model, the minimum cost (and thus the optimum lot size) for a lot size equal to q^* occurs where it is possible to show that $q^* = \sqrt{2fd/h}$, where d equals the demand rate on an annual basis.

$$q^* = \sqrt{(2fd/h)}$$

In the analysis below, we examine the solutions offered by a kanban model and an EOQ model. We also examine the impacts of productivity changes on the solutions that each system generates. As you will see, the two models offer very different solutions. The EOQ model drives toward a solution with large inventories in an attempt to minimize total system costs. The kanban system drives to a solution with ever-shrinking lot sizes. In analyzing the different solutions, keep in mind that many of the benefits of the kanban system are difficult to quantify (more flexibility, reduced quality exposure, and employee empowerment). By its nature, the EOQ model seeks to minimize all quantifiable costs. Thus, the EOQ model will generally provide a solution that yields a lower *quantifiable* total cost than a kanban system. However, also keep in mind that both models are strongly influenced by the cost assumptions used. The value of floor space and the cost of capital, for example, both have a large impact on the EOQ solution.

For our kanban model, we created a spreadsheet to calculate the number of containers used to control production for individual products. Based on average daily requirements, production losses and secondary process losses, the spreadsheet calculates the adjusted daily requirement (the quantity of product to be produced to meet the average demand from the customer). Daily run-time requirements are then calculated by multiplying the adjusted daily requirement by the production cycle time required per piece. These run times are then summed to calculate the daily run-time requirement.

Available production time, daily run-time requirements, and total set-up time are used by the kanban spreadsheet to determine the production cycle. Available time is calculated by subtracting downtime, both planned and unplanned, from the total scheduled hours. Using the total run-time requirement and the available time, time available for set-ups is calculated.

Total Available Time − Total Run Time = Available Set-up Time

If this number is less than zero, there is no feasible answer and there is a shortage of capacity on the particular production line. If the number is positive, the total set-up time for the production cycle is divided by the available set-up time to determine the replenishment interval.

Days per Cycle = Total Set-up Time / Available Set-up Time

Based on the capacity of the containers for individual parts, the appropriate number of containers is calculated to match the buffer size of two days plus the production run quantity. Production run quantities of each part are calculated by multiplying the production cycle by the adjusted daily requirements. The production quantity plus buffer quantity divided by part capacity per container determines the total number of containers required to control production.

What advantages does this solution offer? The system minimizes the production cycle and gives the benefit of speed and flexibility. If demand is volatile and requirements for an individual part change, you can respond quickly, reducing the reliance on forecasts and the need for expediters to help adjust to schedule variations. This system also minimizes inventory and reduces the risk of obsolescence. These lower inventory levels reduce quality risks, since production defects may be detected earlier with fewer parts at risk. The use of the kanban signals also allows operators to schedule their own production activities, reducing the need for a large production control department.

The Effect of Productivity Improvements

Let's begin to examine the effects of productivity improvements on the different models. Lets assume a SMED program is launched that will reduce set-up time from 45 minutes to 23 minutes. Additionally, scrap costs incurred during set-ups are targeted for reductions from $100 to $75 per set-up. As reductions in set-up time are made, the kanban model drives closer to the theoretical optimum lot size of one piece. Unfortunately, it does this without consideration of changeover costs. If set-up costs are not reduced proportionally to set-up time reductions, the kanban model actually makes recommendations that increase costs by increasing the total set-up costs. The only consideration is time, with available capacity being fully utilized with additional set-ups. With the current planning model, the targeted SMED results will increase operating costs.

Let's also assume a TPM program is launched that reduces unscheduled downtime for the production lines. Current historical averages for downtime are 15 minutes of planned downtime per shift and 57 minutes of unplanned downtime. Unplanned downtime has been targeted, with a goal of 30 minutes of unplanned downtime per shift. As these efforts are made to increase available production time, the kanban system makes further reductions in cycle time (see Table E-1).

EOQ Model: Basic Cycle

The EOQ model optimizes the production system based on total holding and changeover costs. Unlike the kanban, the EOQ model is not concerned specifically with time unless a dollar value is attached to the time. Improvements in available time only shorten

Table E-1. Kanban cycle time.

	Cycle Time Days	Annual Holding Costs	Annual Setup Costs	Total Costs
Current	3.78	$5,418	$ 86,430	$ 91,847
After SMED	1.93	$3,663	$112,160	$115,823
After downtime reduction	2.04	$4,506	$159,906	$164,412
Nirvana	1.04	$3,663	$207,510	$211,173

the production cycle time by the improvement. So downtime reduction efforts only cause minor changes in the calculated cycle. Reductions in set-up costs have a direct impact on the calculated cycle; it becomes more economical to change more frequently, which also reduces average inventory levels and associated holding costs. But these changes are a result of total set-up costs, not just the time required for set-ups. Since our fictional company incurs significant cost in scrap material for each set-up, this is critical.

EOQ Model: Rotation Cycle

Table E-2 shows the calculated production cycles before any productivity improvements. Several products in our example share common set-ups, eliminating the set-up costs. These products are sequenced to avoid these unnecessary set-ups. This same sequence was also used in the kanban schedule. Total costs are significantly lower than the kanban system, but at higher inventory levels with longer production cycles. In efforts to achieve speed and low inventory levels, it appears as though the kanban model will incur significant additional costs. Remember, many of the benefits of the kanban system are difficult to quantify, so use judgment when viewing calculations that show that the kanban solution drives up costs.

As improvement efforts pay off in reductions to set-up costs, the total cost of the production system shows improvement. How-

Table E-2.

Buffer	2	days								
Setup Time	45	minutes								
Labor Cost	$ 19.00	per hour								
Scrap Cost	$ 250.00	per setup								
						Optimal Cycle Time, T* =			0.08	years
	No. of Working Days per week	5							19.84	days
	No. of Shifts per day	3								
	No. of Available Shifts per week	15								
	Planned Downtime/Shift	15	minutes					**Tmin =**	77.08	hours
	Available Time per shift	465	minutes						3.78	days
	Unplanned Downtime/Shift (Historic)	57	minutes							
	Adjusted Available Time per shift	408	minutes			Annual holding cost =			$ 38,708.00	
	Weeks per year	52				Annual set-up cost equals=			$ 16,456.00	
						Total annual cost =			$ 55,165.00	
	Holding cost	12.00%	annually			Total containers required =			452	

ever, the EOQ model calculates the reduction in cycle time based on the reduction of the total cost of changeovers, not just the reduction in time required. The improvements in equipment uptime, however, do not have a significant impact on the total cost (see Table E-3 for the production cycle after the implementation of SMED and TPM).

Production Constraints

Space requirements for inventory may become a constraint for the EOQ solution. Assume a container size of 3′ x 6′ (18 square feet). The EOQ solution requires an increase from 126 containers to 452, but reduces identified costs from $91,847 to $55,165. Assuming 75 percent utilization of floor space, this gives an increase in floor space requirements of 7,824 square feet. Depending on the available floor space in the plant, this may not be feasible. Again, if there were an identified alternative use of the floor space that would produce revenue, then this cost would need to be added to the model. Table E-4 shows the cycle times and total costs of the EPQ solutions.

Although the EOQ model seems to give a lower cost solution, you need to use caution when comparing the models. The EOQ model places no value on reductions in inventory (except for the minor reduction in holding costs), and no value on quality improvements, increased flexibility, or employee empowerment. With the kanban model, the value of the intangible benefits of speed, flexibility, and very low inventory levels need to be considered. Plotting the costs of scheduling options versus total cost as shown in Figure E-1 should be done during each planning cycle. This provides an easy method to evaluate the cost impact of planning decisions. Also note that as changeover time and cost approaches zero, both models will give very similar solutions.

The EOQ model also highlights the need to assess total cost when determining kanban quantities. Smaller batch sizes may produce larger total costs. Keep this thought in mind as you reduce kanban quantities.

Table E-3.

Buffer	2	days								
Setup Time	45	minutes								
Labor Cost	$ 19.00	per hour								
Scrap Cost	$ 250.00	per setup								
						Optimal Cycle Time, T* =			0.08	years
No. of Working Days per week		5							19.79	days
	No. of Shifts per day	3								
No. of Available Shifts per week		15								
	Planned Downtime/Shift	15	minutes					**Tmin =**	44.42	hours
	Available Time per shift	465	minutes						2.04	days
Unplanned Downtime/Shift (Historic)		30	minutes							
Adjusted Available Time per shift		435	minutes			Annual Holding cost =			$38,617	
	Weeks per year	52				Annual set-up cost equals=			$16,499	
						Total annual cost =			$55,117	
	Holding cost	12.00%	annually			Total containers required =			450	

Figure E-1. Total Cost

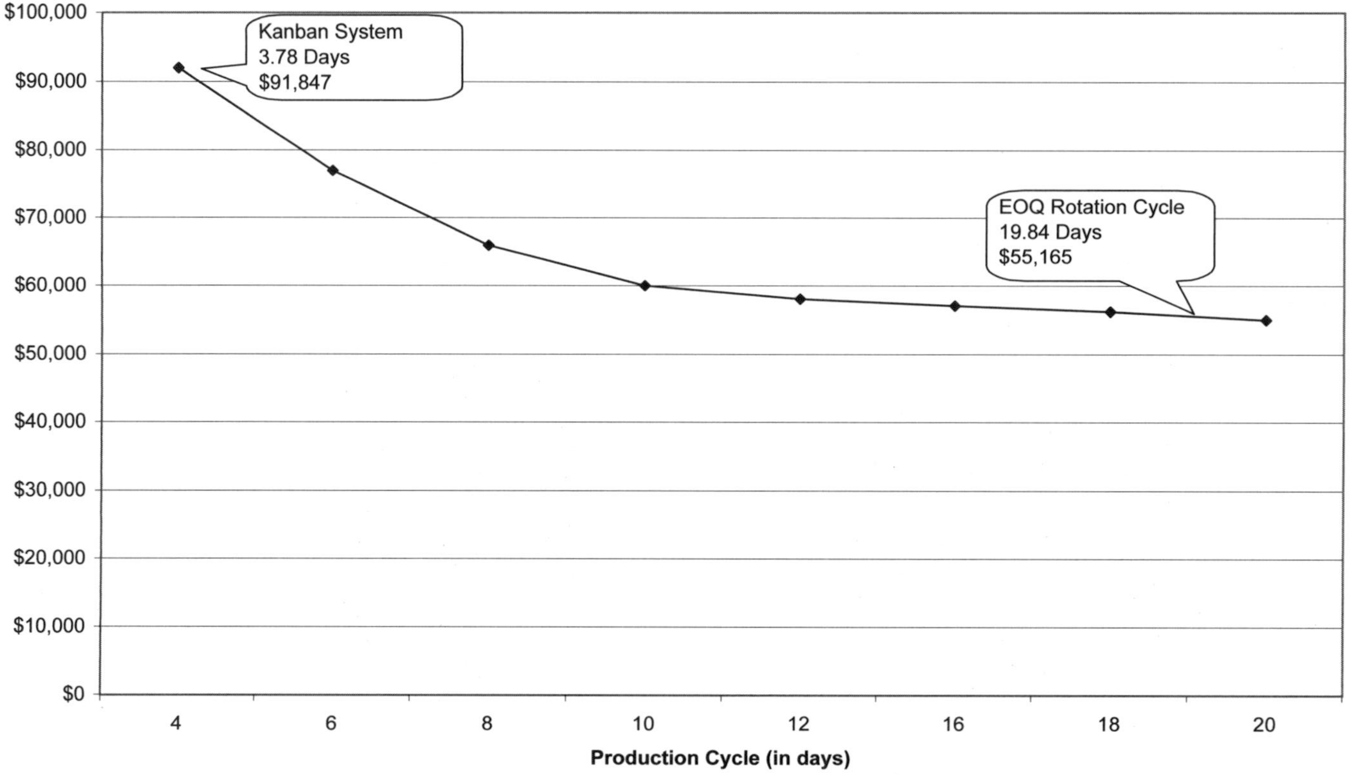

Table E-4.

	Cycle Time (in Days)	Annual Holding Costs	Annual Setup Costs	Total Costs
Current	19.8	$38,709	$16,457	$55,166
After SMED	16.2	$32,093	$13,403	$45,496
After Downtime	19.8	$38,617	$16,499	$55,117
Nirvana	16.1	$32,018	$13,437	$45,455

APPENDIX

F

IMPLEMENTATION IN LARGE PLANTS

Implementing kanban in a large plant can seem like a daunting task. On the surface, it would seem to be extremely difficult to maintain all of the visual signals that would be required to control production in a large plant. In reality, this is not the case. A large plant will be run by a series of small kanbans, all of which are simple to operate. In fact, implementation is the most difficult task in operating a large plant with kanbans, since there are so many different kanbans that need to be installed and so many employees to train. Once the kanbans are implemented, it is simply a matter of auditing the kanbans, keeping people trained, and continuously improving the kanbans.

Figure F-1 demonstrates how these independent kanban loops are linked to control product flow through the entire plant. There are three basic kinds of loops: Finished Goods, WIP, and Raw Materials.

Figure F-1.

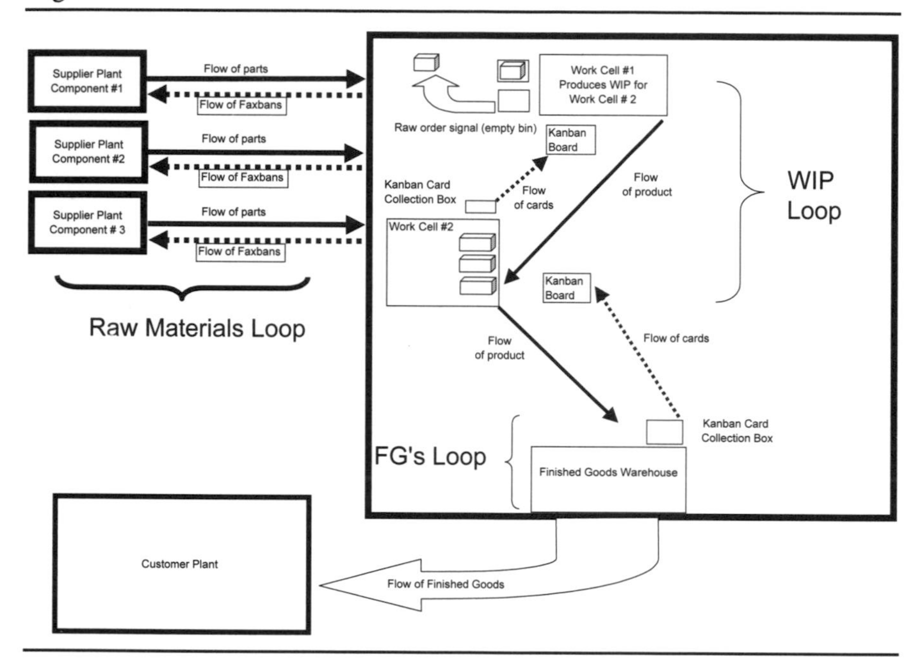

Finished Goods Loops

The finished goods loops control the amount of finished goods (product ready to be shipped to the customer) that you carry. This loop is extremely important, as it protects your customer from disruptions within your process. Having finished goods inventory also allows you to respond quickly to unexpected increases in customer demand. And although disruptions within your plant can cost you money (high scrap or productivity losses), disruptions in shipments to your customer can cost you sales.

WIP Loops

The WIP loops control the plant's WIP inventory. As you continuously improve the kanban by reducing scrap, changeover times, and downtime issues, the size of inventories in this loop should decrease dramatically. While finished goods inventories protect the customer (and thus your sales), WIP loops only protect you from internal failures. Thus, they are a form of waste that needs to be eliminated.

Raw Materials Loops

The raw material loops control the flow of raw materials into your plant. Similar to WIP loops, these loops do not directly protect your customer. These loops, which protect you from downtime due to stock outs, are unique within your plant because they incorporate significant shipping times, supplier-imposed lead times, and freight considerations. The less-than-truckload shipments are costly and therefore can force you to carry significant raw inventories to minimize transportation. The milk runs (discussed in Chapter 9) or consigned inventory can be useful in dealing with these issues.

We can also use Figure F-1 to demonstrate how the different kanban loops in a large plant work together to control production. Let's assume we start in a stable plant with established kanban loops. The production process begins with a customer order.

- ❑ Based on the customer order, product is shipped from the warehouse, the kanban cards are removed from the product and placed in the kanban card collection box.
- ❑ The kanban cards are then collected by a material handler and returned to the kanban board in Work Cell #2. The returning cards authorize the work cell to begin production.
- ❑ When Work Cell #2 begins producing, it consumes WIP inventory produced by Work Cell #1. As the inventory is consumed, the kanban cards (from Work Cell #1) on the WIP containers are placed in the kanban card collection box. A material handler collects the cards and returns them to the kanban board in Work Cell #1.
- ❑ This authorizes Work Cell #1 to begin production to replace the inventory. This uses up raw materials. As the raw material

bins are emptied, the empty bins are returned to the warehouse, authorizing the warehouse to order more materials. The warehouse generates faxbans, which are transmitted to the vendors.

- The vendor receives the faxbans, which authorize them to ship product. Once they ship product, they authorize their work cells to begin production, and the entire loop is repeated.

Thus, even though the plant is large and complex, all of the processes were driven by a customer order whose requirements rippled through the entire plant. Note that the order worked its way through the plant rapidly, and that the amount produced and ordered was linked closely to the amount shipped. Each individual work cell reacted to simple pull signals, yet they were actually part of a large, complex process. That is the power of kanban.

APPENDIX G

INTRA-CELL KANBAN

The main body of this book has been dedicated to how to implement kanbans between processes. We have focused on suppliers producing product based on the demands of the customer. However, as part of Lean manufacturing, we also need to also look at kanbans within cells, or intra-cell kanbans.

For kanbans within cells, there are two cases. The first case is when the process has dedicated equipment. The second situation is when the process shares common equipment within the cell or between cells. Pictorially, Figure G-1 shows these two conditions.

In the first case, strive for single-piece flow between the processes. If process issues or constraints prevent single-piece flow, build strategic buffers to manage the constraint. At the same time, follow the steps proposed by Eli Goldratt (of *Theory of Constraints* fame) to manage and eliminate constraints.

In the second case, you must create a kanban to supply both processes. However, when you create this kanban, you will only use the calculations shown in Chapter 4 if a detailed changeover is required. If no changeovers occur, then you will look at the Takt time

Figure G-1.

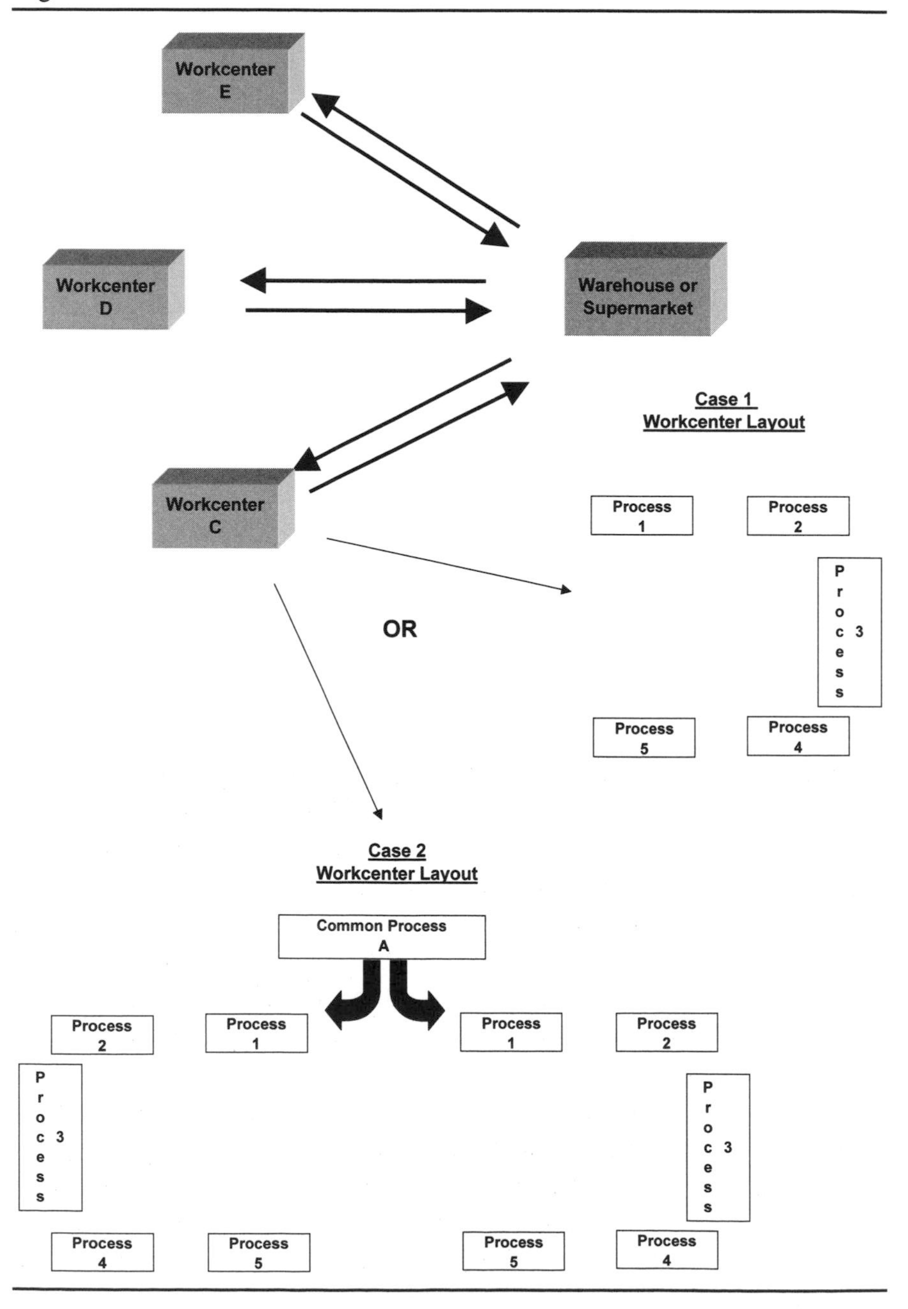
Workcenter E
Workcenter D
Warehouse or Supermarket
Workcenter C
Case 1
Workcenter Layout
Process 1
Process 2
Process 3
Process 5
Process 4
OR
Case 2
Workcenter Layout
Common Process A
Process 2
Process 1
Process 1
Process 2
Process 3
Process 3
Process 4
Process 5
Process 5
Process 4

of each process and the rate of the common process to determine the capacity of the common process and the quantities required to keep the customer processes supplied. In this situation, you will strive to keep the WIP inventory as low as possible while keeping both processes supplied. Try to limit the inventory to under an hour if possible, but definitely keep the inventory quantity between cells to less than a shift.

Additionally, in the second case you can use this situation as an opportunity to help in balancing the cell workloads. The operator of the common process may be able to pick up additional tasks that help the cells. These tasks could include replenishing raw material kanbans, packing parts, etc. To determine whether the operator of the common process can help, factor the cycle time of this operation into your cell load charts and look for opportunities. Figure G-2 shows an example of sizing intra-cell WIP and leveling workload.

Figure G-2.

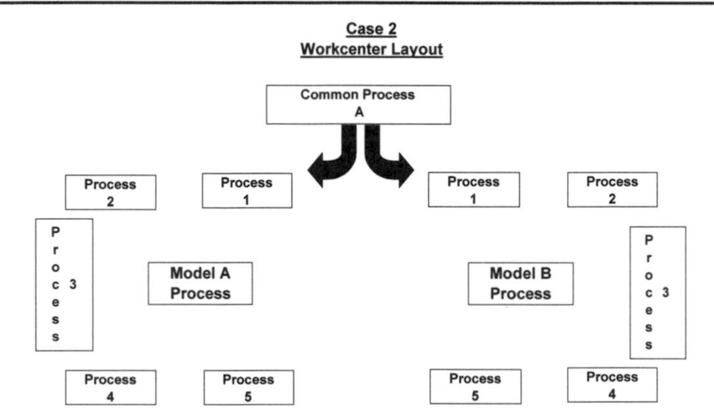

Given:
Common Process A cuts round stock to finished lengths for machining into axles for Model A and Model B Whiz Bang carts.
--Common Process A has a cycle time of 10 seconds per part (or 360 per hour). Special jigs have been installed on the cut table to eliminate changeovers between Model A and Model B shafts.
--Model A process has a 90 second per piece takt time (or 40 shafts per hour).
--Model B process has a 120 second per piece takt time (or 30 shafts per hour).

Proposed Short-term Solution:
-Create a 1 hour inventory for each model:
10 Seconds X (40 shafts + 30 shafts) = 700 seconds
(or 12 minutes per hour)
-Now build load charts of the production process for both models and look for opportunities to utilize the remaining time by integrating this operation with other jobs in the process cells.

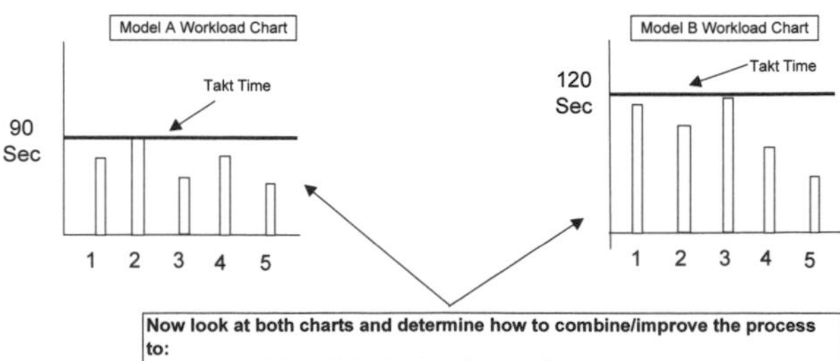

Now look at both charts and determine how to combine/improve the process to:
1. Make use of the available time from Common Process A.
2. Combine operations within each process to further improve productivity.

Proposed Long-term Solution:
Implement single piece flow by installing right sized cutting processes in both cells.

APPENDIX

H

Case Study 1: Motor Plant—Casting Kanban

Setting

This case is set in an electric motor manufacturing plant in the central United States. This plant produces a large variety of small electric motors. The case centers on controlling the inventory of stamped metal castings used in the production of the motors. The castings are made in a supplier plant located in Mexico, and they are shipped weekly in truckload quantities. The large variety of motors produced, combined with large fluctuations in customer demand, caused frequent stock outs, which resulted in missed delivery dates and line downtime. To combat the stock-out problems, the plant carried a large quantity of inventory on these parts.

There were fifty-two unique castings utilized in motor production, thirty-eight of which were used frequently enough to keep stock on hand. Casting demand was forecast using an MRP system and ordered on a three-week lead-time. The timing worked as follows:

- Every Monday, a sales forecast would arrive from the sales office. Every effort was made to "freeze" the first two weeks of the schedule, but customer requirements often made this impossible.
- These requirements were placed into the plant's MRP system, which compared them to the current inventory and forecast casting requirements for the next ten weeks.
- The supplier treated the first three weeks of this schedule as firm orders. Thus, the order placed this week would arrive three weeks from today. Even though there was only a four-day transport time, the orders for the next two weeks were considered firm.

This long lead time, combined with high demand variation, led to both a large inventory and big variations in order quantities. As Table H-1 shows, the average inventory levels on the castings were over eighteen days. These high levels of inventory necessitated the renting of warehouse space at a significant cost.

Solution

Since the variation in demand was based on fluctuations in actual customer orders, there was nothing that could be done to reduce this variation. The plant was committed to reducing inventory and freeing up capital, so increasing finished inventory was ruled out. The approach taken was to implement a pull system and streamline the supply chain.

Table H-1.

	Part family 1					Part family 2						
	1-A	1-B	1-C	1-D	1-E	2-A	2-B	2-C	2-D	2-E		
YTD Weekly Average	863	1170	1562	773	844	1245	750	531	1691	1079		
Standard Container	500	500	500	500	500	500	500	500	500	500		
22-Apr	2011	3384	5235	0	999	1331	750	108	1106	1449		
29-Apr	1665	634	2850	0	330	651	798	434	229	1428		
6-May	507	1610	1148	138	174	1284	579	451	1691	1550		
Container/shipment	2	2	4	2	2	2	2	1	4	2		
Weekly shipment	1000	1000	2000	1000	1000	1000	1000	500	2000	1000		
Std dev	787.69	1394	2053	79.67	438.3	379.8	115.1	193.3	735.8	65.23		
99% confidence	2.3263	2.326	2.326	2.326	2.326	2.326	2.326	2.326	2.326	2.326		
Safety stock	1832.4	3243	4776	185.4	1020	883.4	267.8	449.7	1712	151.7		
In containers	3.7	6.5	9.6	0.4	2.0	1.8	0.5	0.9	3.4	0.3		
Minimum safety stock	2000	3500	5000	500	1500	1000	500	500	2000	500		
Ave daily usage	172.6	234	312.4	154.6	168.8	249	150	106.2	338.2	215.8		
												Total pieces
Beginning inventory	3831	4539	7606	4004	2326	1139	2237	1771	2936	6939		37328
Days on hand	22.196	19.4	24.35	25.9	13.78	4.574	14.91	16.68	8.681	32.15	182.6187	
safety stock	2000	3500	5000	500	1500	1000	500	500	2000	500		
weekly shipment	1000	1000	2000	1000	1000	1000	1000	500	2000	1000		18.26187
On hand	3000	4500	7000	1500	2500	2000	1500	1000	4000	1500		
22 apr usage	2011	3384	5235	0	999	1331	750	108	1106	1449		
Balance	989	1116	1765	1500	1501	669	750	892	2894	51		12127
Days on hand	5.7	4.8	5.6	9.7	8.9	2.7	5.0	8.4	8.6	0.2		
Weekly shipment	1000	1000	2000	1000	1000	1000	1000	500	2000	1000		
on hand	1989	2116	3765	2500	2501	1669	1750	1392	4894	1051		
29 apr usage	1665	634	2850	0	330	651	798	434	229	1428		
Balance	324	1482	915	2500	2171	1018	952	958	4665	-377		14608
Days on hand	1.9	6.3	2.9	16.2	12.9	4.1	6.3	9.0	13.8	-1.7		
weekly shipment	1000	1000	2000	0	0	1000	1000	500	0	1000		
on hand	1324	2482	2915	2500	2171	2018	1952	1458	4665	623		
6 may usage	507	1610	1148	138	174	1284	579	451	1691	1550		
balance	817	872	1767	2362	1997	734	1373	1007	2974	-927		12976
Days on hand	4.7	3.7	5.7	15.3	11.8	2.9	9.2	9.5	8.8	-4.3	67.3	6.7
											Logic:	
Red Zone	4	7	10	1	3	2	1	1	4	1	Safety Stock	
Yellow Zone	7	10	15	4	6	5	4	3	9	4	Safety Stock + Order + 1	
Green Zone	8	11	16	5	7	6	5	4	10	5	Yellow + 1 = cancel order	

In designing a pull system, we had to consider the plant's state of Lean knowledge and commitment. Although the plant was committed to transforming itself into a lean plant, it was still early in the journey. This would be the first kanban implemented in the plant, so its success was crucial to achieving buy-in for future implementations. We also had to involve the supplier (in Mexico), and to streamline the entire process.

Our first step was to classify the castings into three categories (A, B, and C), based on volume.

- ❑ The A category contained the highest runners, with significant production every week.

- ❑ The B volume castings were those that had enough volume to merit keeping a safety stock, but were not run continuously.
- ❑ The C volume parts were those that were ordered infrequently.

In our proposed scenario, we planned to set up the A volume parts on kanban. We also decided to relegate the C volume parts to make-to-order status instead of putting them on kanban. The B volume parts would not be part of the kanban, but they would benefit from its implementation. This benefit would occur because the reduced inventories of the higher running A parts, on kanban, would free up space and inventory dollars to increase our safety stock on the B volume parts. Therefore, the plant would see a large reduction in overall inventory, while reducing the stock outs on the B volume parts. These changes were significant, since a large portion of the stock outs in the plant involved B volume castings.

After reviewing the data, we classified ten parts as A volume. These ten parts made up 48 percent of the production volume. To set up the kanban we used the following methodology:

- ❑ Calculate an average weekly order by calculating an average weekly shipping volume and standard container sizes
- ❑ Calculate the required safety stock
- ❑ Develop a visual system to control the system and trigger the kanban
- ❑ Work with the supplier to reduce order lead-time
- ❑ Develop a procedure to expedite parts through Mexican customs

Calculate Average Weekly Order

This task was made more difficult because the company had recently transferred some production of these motors to a sister plant, so we had limited relevant order history. We decided to size the kanban loop with the history that we had, but made plans to revise this loop once more data became available. Table H-1 shows the results of this averaging. We also contacted the Mexican supplier to establish standard container quantities. Up to this point, the quantity of castings per container was variable. A standard weekly order (in containers) was then developed using these two pieces of information.

Calculate Safety Stock

We utilized a simple method to calculate safety stock. Using historical data, we first calculated the standard deviation of the demand for each product. The next step was to factor in the confidence interval we wished to use. This is where we asked the user to select the confidence he wanted to ensure he did not run out of product. Remember that the higher the confidence desired, the larger the safety stock required. To determine the confidence interval, we discussed the expectation the plant had for stock outs. Based on the plant's assessment of their customer commitments, the plant selected a 99 percent confidence interval.

A simple way to approximate this is to use the "NORMSINV () function" in Excel. You simply place the desired confidence percentage (in decimal format) into this function to generate a multiplier. Multiply this number by the standard deviation and this gives you the required safety stock. This calculation method assumes that demand is normally distributed, which is a fairly safe assumption in most cases. To assist in your use of the confidence intervals, Table H-2 shows the calculated multipliers for 85 to 99 percent.

Table H-2.

Percent confidence	85%	90%	93%	95%
Multiplier	1.04	1.28	1.48	1.64

Percent confidence	96%	97%	98%	99%
Multiplier	1.75	1.88	2.05	2.33

Develop a Visual System

The visual trigger to cancel an order in this kanban was based on maximum inventory targets. The plant set up a standard order to be shipped weekly unless a kanban cancellation card was sent to the vendor. (Figures H-1 and H-2 show the visual sign and cancellation card used by the plant.) A sign was posted over the storage area for each part number, indicating what the kanban cancellation level was. If the inventory exceeded this level on the morning of the order, the cancellation card was faxed to the vendor. If the inventory was below this level, the order was shipped in the standard order quantity. Referencing Figure H-2, the kanban rules work like this:

- ❑ If the inventory on the order date is in the green zone, the

Figure H-1. Cancellation Card

Part 1A
Metal Casting

Vendor: Acme Stamping
Fax # 555-555-5555

Please cancel this week's order for 1A Metal Castings.

If you have any questions, contact Bob at 555-555-5555, ext 123

Thank You.

Bob Smith, Materials Manager
Electric Motor Plant, Inc.

Figure H-2. Kanban cancellation sign

Part 1A **Metal Casting**
Vendor: Acme Stamping
Order time: Noon
Orders placed: Wednesday
Orders due: Friday
If inventory is *more than 9 pallets,* fax cancellation sheet to 555-5555, Attn: John Smith
If inventory falls below 5 pallets, contact Manager at once.
If you have any questions about this product, contact Bob at ext. 123

order is cancelled (fax the cancellation card to the vendor). The green zone is calculated as the quantity in the yellow zone plus one standard container.

- If the inventory on the order date is in the yellow zone, no action is taken and the order ships as planned. The yellow zone is calculated as the safety stock plus the weekly order plus one standard container.
- If the inventory on the order date is in the red zone, a supervisor needs to be notified immediately, as the plant is in imminent danger of a stock out. The red zone is equal to the safety

stock determined by the confidence interval and the standard deviation.

Working with Supplier to Reduce Lead Time

For the kanban system to work effectively, the cooperation of the supplier was critical. After talking to the supplier, two things became obvious.

1. The supplier was not happy with the constant changes in the weekly orders.
2. The supplier was interested in helping to solve the problem.

The solution was to set up a standard order with the supplier that shipped each week. The order would only be changed when the inventory levels exceeded the preset limits or an emergency occurred. If the order were canceled one week, then the parts would be taken the following week.

In exchange for the standard order, the supplier agreed to hold at least one week's worth of inventory in his warehouse. They also agreed to ship on one-day's notice. Thus, the lead time was reduced from three weeks to four days (i.e., the transit time). In addition, there was always a stock of castings waiting in the supplier's warehouse in case of demand spikes that exceeded safety stock.

Develop Expedite Procedures

In order to allow future reductions in inventory levels without increasing the risk of a stock out, a procedure for expediting freight from Mexico was also developed. Instead of an expedited shipment taking seven days, it could be reduced to only three days by utilizing a freight broker and airfreight. This shorter expedite time, along with the supplier commitment to keep inventory on the shelf at all times, gives the plant the flexibility to keep its lines running and its customer supplied (albeit at a cost premium). Figure H-3 shows the proposed rules for the expediting of castings.

Final Results

The results of the kanban implementation are shown in Figure H-4. The total number of castings required to meet demand was reduced from 37,328 to 12,976. In terms of days on hand, the inventory requirement was reduced from over eighteen days to less than seven days.

Figure H-3.

Rules for expediting castings from Mexico:

If on-hand inventories of any castings fall into their preset red zones (see Kanban signs posted over each storage location), the following steps must be taken to expedite parts:

- Contact John Smith of Acme Stampings at 555-555-5555. Inform him of the quantity of parts that we require. Inform him the Billy Bobs International Expediters will pick the parts up in two hours.
- Call Smith International Expediters at 444-444-4444. Inform them of the number of pallets to be picked up, the size and weight of the pallets, and the part number. Let them know that Acme will have the parts ready for pickup in two hours.
- Inform the plant of the expected delivery time for the parts.
- Log this incident into the Stock-out log.
- Form a problem-solving team to determine the root cause of the incident.
- Implement corrective action and close out the incident.

Figure H-4. Before and After Inventory Levels

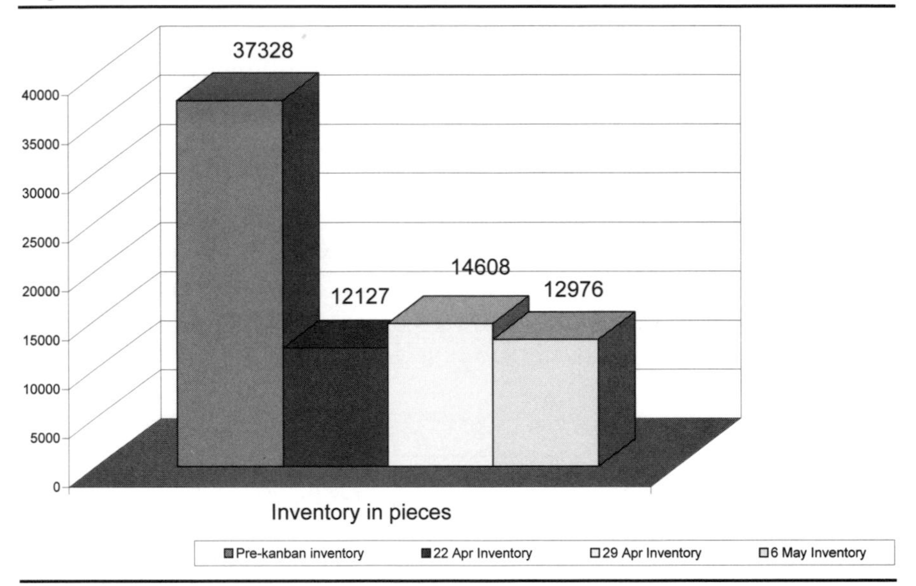

APPENDIX

I

Case Study 2: Rubber Extrusion Plant

Setting

A tier-1 automotive supplier was in the process of expanding one of its manufacturing plants. To support higher levels of production in the expanded plant, four new extrusion lines were going to be added (taking the number of lines from three to seven). Large reductions in work-in-process inventory were required to facilitate this expansion (due to floor space limitations and working capital constraints). Additionally, the ability to mold extruded rubber parts decreases as the parts age, with the secondary molding operations experiencing higher rates of scrap the longer the extrudate ages. The plant also wished to develop a scheduling process that would allow for easy scheduling of the larger department and improved flow between operations. The manual scheduling system used previously was no longer viable, and management did not want to add any more indirect scheduling labor.

Solution

The plant decided to implement a kanban system to schedule production and control WIP inventory levels. They followed the Seven Steps for Implementing Kanban, as described in Chapter 1.

Step 1. Conduct Data Collection

Since data already existed for extrusion line 1, this line was chosen for the first kanban. Scrap, changeover times, line speed, and downtime data for the previous three months were available, as well as production estimates for the next three months.

Step 2. Calculate the Kanban Size

In this step, the production requirements, scrap rates (for both extrusion and the secondary operations), line speed, downtime, and changeover time were used to calculate a replenishment interval. The kanban team followed the same process that was described in Chapter 4. Figure I-1 shows the results of these calculations (note that some of the data has been hidden to protect confidential company information).

Figure I-1.

No. of Working Days per week	5	*Total Set-up Time (hrs)*	6.00
No. of Shifts per day	3	*Total Daily Required Run time (hrs)*	19.09
No. of Available Shifts per week	**15**	*Number of Set-ups Required*	8
Planned Downtime/Shift	**15**	*Total Planned Available Time (hrs)*	20.40
Available Time per shift	**465**	*Total Required time (S/U + Run) (hrs)*	25.09
Unplanned Downtime/Shift (Historic)	57	**Cycles per day**	**0.22**
Adjusted Available Time per shift	**408**	**Days per Cycle**	**4.57**

Step 3. Design the Kanban

In designing the kanban, the plant had several priorities. First, they wanted the kanban to be visual and simple to operate. They also wanted the production workers on the line to schedule their own production. And with fourteen different parts being run on the extrusion line, they did not want to use kanban cards, which they felt would be likely to get lost or destroyed. They decided to design a magnetic kanban board that would be located at the end of the extrusion line (see Figure I-2).

As Figure I-3 shows, line 1 was ideally located for this type of system. The door separating the extrusion department from the secondary operations they supplied was located at the pack-out end of the extrusion line, in plain sight of the extrusion line operators. Additionally, the materials handlers drove their forklifts through this same area in order to take product to the secondary operations.

The team designed a magnetic board with two sections: the bottom portion, which showed completed buggies, and the top portion, which showed buggies left to produce (see Figure I-4). Each part number was given a column with the allowed number of kanban buggies marked on it. On the scheduling half of the board, colored zones were marked (red, yellow, and green). On the top half of the

Figure I-2.

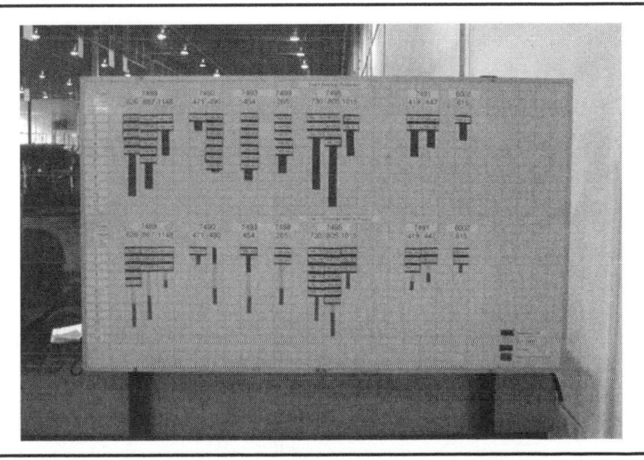

Figure I-3.

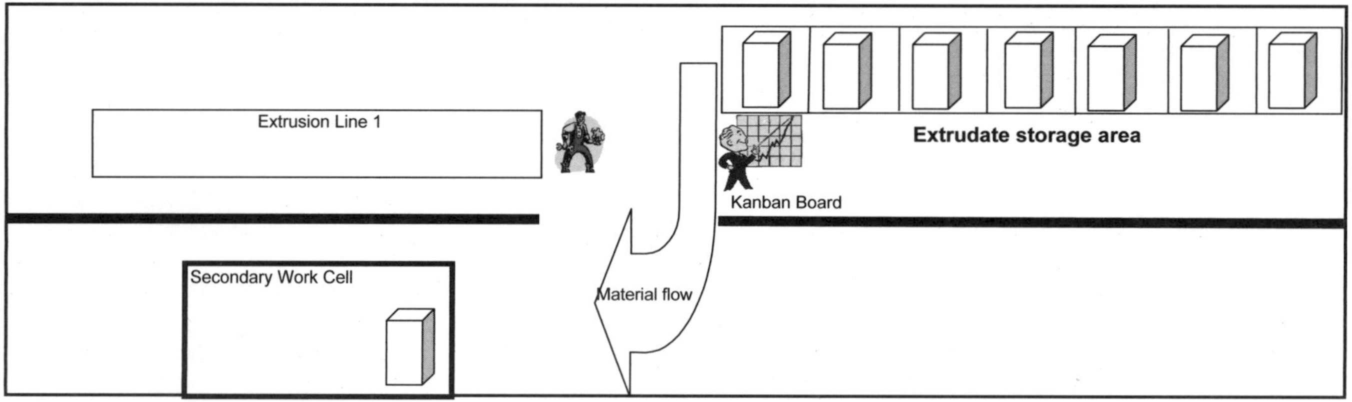

Extrusion Line 1
Extrudate storage area
Kanban Board
Secondary Work Cell
Material flow

Figure I-4.

Awaiting Production

Profile	7489			7490		7493	0058	7488	7495			7491		
Length	626	867	1148	471	490	454	992	265	730	805	1015	299	419	447
Max Buggies	10	9	5	2	7	8	8	7	9	11	5	3	5	4
1														
2														
3														
4														
5														
6														
7														
8														
9														
10														
11														
12														

Completed Work in Process

Profile	7489			7490		7493	0058	7488	7495			7491		
Length	626	867	1148	471	490	454	992	265	730	805	1015	299	419	447
Max Buggies	10	9	5	2	7	8	8	7	9	11	5	3	5	4
1														
2														
3														
4														
5														
6														
7														
8														
9														
10														
11														
12														

board, the area equating to the maximum number of kanbans allowed was marked off to provide a visual check if any magnets are missing. (If all of the production kanbans have been used, and the top portion of the board is not full, some magnets must be missing.)

The team developed a detailed set of rules that explained how the kanban was going to operate. The rules were simple and specific, detailing exactly who was to do what, and when (see Figure I-5 for details). Basically, when a buggy was filled, the line operators moved a magnet from the scheduling portion of the board to the inventory portion of the board. When they ran out of kanban magnets for the parts they were running, they changed over to the next part. The board was designed to run from left-to-right, reflecting the desired operating sequence. The sequence was selected to reduce changeover time and scrap. Thus, for any given part, the part immediately to its right was the most similar in terms of line settings and materials. If you proceeded to the part to the right of the current part, you minimized change over time. Using the rules, the operators were able to schedule their own line and control the WIP inventory without leaving their workstations.

When a material handler removed a buggy of material from the extrusion line and took it to a secondary customer, he simply stopped his forklift in front of the kanban board and moved the appropriate magnet from the top inventory portion of the board to the bottom production-scheduling portion. Thus, the operator received a real-time signal of the production status of all of the parts run on the line (simply by seeing the red-yellow-green status of each part). Additionally, the top inventory portion of the board always displayed the current inventory level for each part.

Step 4. Train Everyone

Once the system was designed, everyone involved was trained. The training involved all of the extrusion line operators, as well as all extrusion supervisors and the materials handlers. The training involved a simple presentation demonstrating the functioning of the board. Special attention was paid to training every individual on his

Figure I-5.

1. **Use magnetic board** to track all buggy moves
   - from extrusion line to WIP
   - from WIP to molding platform

2. **Magnetic board layout:**
   - **Each** magnetic piece represents one buggy of the listed extrudate (profile and length).
   - **Top** half of board has the buggies waiting to be produced.
   - **Bottom** half of board has the full buggies waiting to move to molding.
   - **Colors:**
     - **Yellow**-produce these parts next
     - **Red**-immediately switch to these parts (molding is in danger of running out of parts)

3. **Movement of empty buggies** to extrusion will be done by the secondaries material handler. This person will monitor the empty buggy staging area in GMX 130 Front Door and Rear Door.
   - Whenever the material handler sees an empty buggy in the holding area, they will look for the empty extrudate storage spot, which signals the need to bring another buggy from extrusion.
   - When they remove a buggy from extrusion, they will update the board accordingly.

4. **Moving the magnetic pieces:**
   - When a buggy is **filled** and moved to storage, **move** the appropriate magnetic piece from the **top to the bottom** of the board.
   - When a buggy is **moved to molding, move** the appropriate magnetic piece from the **bottom to the top** of the board.
   - Update responsibilities:
     - Person who moves the full buggy from the line to WIP moves the magnetic piece from the top to the bottom

(*continues*)

Figure I-5. (*continued*)

- Person who moves the full buggy from WIP to molding moves the magnetic piece from the bottom to the top.

5. **Scheduling rules:**
   - Fill all the buggies with the same profile before switching to the next profile unless a red signal occurs.
   - Select the next profile that has pieces in the yellow zone.
   - If more than one profile is in the yellow zone (and no red signal exists), then run profiles (with pieces in the yellow zone) in this sequence:
     - 7489
     - 7490
     - 7493
     - 0058
     - 7488
     - 7495
     - 7491
     - 6002
   - If a red signal occurs, then notify a facilitator or specialist and begin making plans to change over to this profile.
     - The facilitator or specialist should confirm this is a valid red signal before changing over.
   - When no yellow (or run) signals exist, then shut down the line.
     - Notify the facilitator or specialist when this occurs for further instructions.

6. **Monitoring responsibilities:**
   - If person moves the magnetic piece into a red zone, then notify the line 1 packer.
   - If header material is rejected, the person rejecting the material will notify the extrusion facilitator or specialist of the quantity rejected and quantity of buggies left in the control point.
     - The Facilitator or Specialist will make decisions based on this information.

- Line technicians monitor board hourly for schedule signals.
- Facilitators will check each shift.
- Scheduler will inspect board daily

7. All questions should be directed to the Scheduler for clarification.

or her specific role. This is a critical step. Understanding the way the entire system works is important for buy-in, but each individual understanding his or her role is critical to actually making the kanban work. The group was also taken through what-if scenarios that described the kinds of situations they were going to face. This step helped the associates demonstrate their understanding of the system (while not feeling the pressure to say they understood even if they did not).

Step 5. Start the Kanban

Once the training was completed, the kanban was started. All the rules and signs were posted, and the old scheduling system was stopped. The old daily schedules used by the line were not produced, so they had no scheduling information except that given by the board. As a precaution, the inventory level was taken to the maximum allowed by the kanban board before the implementation began. This provided a little cushion in case problems were encountered during the transition.

Step 6. Audit and Maintain the Kanban

The department scheduler was assigned the task of auditing the kanban each week. Figure I-6 shows the actual kanban audit sheet she developed. This sheet forced a reconciliation of actual inventory

Figure I-6.

Date/Time:							Kanban Audit sheet
Profile	Pcs/ Buggy	Total Cards	Control Point	On Board	Differ- ence	Counts in Secondaries	Miscellaneous Comments
7489.626 r/d header 18,19,20,21	1050 Double	10					
7489.867 sed header 04-05	1050 Double	9					
7489.1148 coupe header 06-07	500 Double	5					
7490.471 coupe b-pillar 06-07	1400 Double	2					
7490.490 sed b-pillar 04-05	1400 Double	7					
7493.454 r/d b-pillar 18,19,20,21	1400 Double	8					
0058.992 Z-coupe innerbelt 56-57	525 Double	8					
7488.265 a-pillar 04-07	1400 Single	7					
7495.730 sed innerbelt 88-89	950 Double	9					
7495.805 r/d innerbelt 90-91	900 Double	11					
7495.1015 coupe innerbelt 86-87	475 Double	5					
7491.299 r/d below belt 50-51	4000 Double	3					
7491.419 f/d a-transition 04-07	3000 Double	5					
7491.447 f/d below belt 48-49	3000 Double	4					

with the magnets on the kanban board. When problems were found, they were addressed and retraining was conducted.

Step 7. Improve the Kanban

Once the kanban had been running smoothly for two months, the quantities on the board were reduced. This was accomplished by monitoring how many of the different part numbers were staying in the green zone. This number was determined to be too high, which indicated that there was room to reduce inventories even further. The number of buggies in the loop was decreased by 21 percent, from 136 buggies to 108 (see Figure I-7). Five other parts were marked for possible future inventory reductions. The designers recognized the need to be careful not to reduce inventories too fast, which risked problems developing and people losing confidence in the kanban system.

Figure I-7. Kanban Reductions Made as of 7-11-02

LINE 1 KANBAN REDUCTION				Difference			
	pcs/ buggy	# cards 5/15	# cards 7–15	# buggies	# pcs	$/pc	total $
58.992	525	8	8	0	0	1.33483	0.00
6002.615	2500	4	3	−1	−2500	0.44672	−1,116.80
7488.265	1500	12	10	−2	−3000	0.32939	−988.17
7489.1148	500	8	6	−2	−1000	1.1992	−1,199.20
7489.626	1050	18	16	−2	−2100	0.65377	−1,372.92
7489.867	1050	12	10	−2	−2190	0.90571	−1,901.99
7490.471	1450	4	3	−1	−1450	0.53488	−775.58
7490.490	1450	8	7	−1	−1450	0.55647	−806.88
7491.299	4000	2	3	1	4000	0.22934	917.36
7491.419	3000	6	5	−1	−3000	0.32111	−963.33
7491.447	3000	6	4	−2	−6000	0.3425	−2,055.00
7493.454	1400	14	8	−6	−8400	0.51351	−4,313.48
7495.1015	470	8	5	−3	−1410	1.43276	−2,020.19
7495.730	900	14	9	−5	−4500	1.03046	−4,637.07
7495.805	900	12	11	−1	−900	1.13632	−1,022.69
							−8,161.54

Final Results

Three months after the kanban was implemented, an inventory was taken in order to document the actual, sustained inventory reductions achieved. The results are documented in Figure I-8. The inventory level was $82,604 before kanban implementation, consisting of 106 buggies of product taking up 1,060 square feet of storage space.

After full implementation, the inventory level was $47,518, consisting of 56 buggies of product taking up 560 square feet of floor space. (See Figures I-9 and I-10 for illustrations of a buggy and of the floor space freed up due to kanban-driven inventory reductions.) Thus, in a span of three months, WIP was reduced by 42 percent, $35,086 in working capital was freed up, and 560 square feet of floor space was opened up for alternative uses (such as new business).

Figure I-8.

Part #	Pre-kanban Inventory	Pre-kanban Inventory (days)	Pre-kanban Inventory ($)	Pieces per Cart	Pre-kanban Carts	Weekly Requirements	Post-kanban Inventory	Post-kanban Inventory ($)	Post-kanban Carts
58.992	2241	2.9	$2,991	525	4	3906	922	$1,231	2
6002.615	4800	3.1	$2,144	2,500	2	7700	7500	$3,350	2
7488.265	7877	2.7	$2,555	1,500	5	14522	8890	$2,883	3
7489.1148	4035	7.9	$4,839	500	8	2552	2097	$2,515	6
7489.626	18617	7.4	$12,174	1,050	18	12600	3918	$2,562	4
7489.867	14040	5.6	$12,716	1,050	13	12470	5303	$4,803	4
7490.471	6381	12.5	$3,413	1,450	4	2552	7610	$4,070	5
7490.49	20612	8.3	$11,470	1,450	14	12470	12560	$6,989	5
7491.299	14702	5.4	$3,372	4,000	4	13600	1576	$361	9
7491.419	9148	3.2	$2,937	3,000	3	14122	11109	$3,567	0
7491.447	4945	1.7	$1,694	3,000	2	14140	3000	$1,028	4
7493.454	18848	7.5	$9,678	1,400	13	12600	8302	$4,263	1
7495.1015	2610	4.2	$3,739	470	6	3110	1631	$2,337	6
7495.73	1971	0.8	$2,031	900	2	12200	2339	$2,410	3
7495.805	6029	2.9	$6,851	900	7	10260	4531	$4,149	3
Total	**136856**	**4.6**	**$82,604**		**106**	**148804**	**81288**	**$47,518**	**56**

Figure I-9.

Example of the 50 buggies of inventory eliminated by the kanban.

Figure I-10.

Floor space freed up for new business.

APPENDIX

J

ABBREVIATIONS AND ACRONYMS

Abbreviation or Acronym	Meaning
5W1H	5 Whys and 1 How
CD Rom	Compact Disk Read-only-Memory
EOQ	Economic Order Quantity
FIFO	First In, First Out
ISO	International Standards Organization
JIT	Just In Time
MRP	Material Requirements Planning
PC	Personal Computer
PM	Preventive Maintenance
QCO	Quick Changeover
SMED	Single Minute Exchange of Dies
TPM	Total Productive Maintenance
TPS	Toyota Production System
VSM	Value Stream Mapping
WIP	Work In Process

Index

About the Authors

John Gross attended Washington University of St. Louis on a U.S. Air Force ROTC scholarship. Upon graduation with an electrical engineering degree, he entered the U.S. Air Force as a project manager.

Upon leaving the U.S. Air Force, he entered private industry. In his civilian career, he has been a plant engineer, engineering manager, business unit manager, and corporate engineer in both the food and automotive industries.

In addition to this book, Mr. Gross has also written *The Fundamentals of Preventive Maintenance* (AMACOM 2002), and has been published internationally in various trade magazines on the subject of productivity. He holds a master of administration degree from Central Michigan University. He is a licensed professional engineer, a Six-Sigma Blackbelt, and an ASQ Certified Quality Engineer.

Ken McInnis has held various management positions in the apparel, automotive, and food industries. He has worked in materials and logistics, in production management, and as a business unit manager.

Mr. McInnis has been published internationally in various trade magazines on the subject of productivity. He holds a bachelor of science degree in business from Kansas University, and an MBA in manufacturing and operations from Washington University in St. Louis. He is also a Six-Sigma Greenbelt.